LIBRARY LEGISLATION IN INDIA:
A CRITICAL AND COMPARATIVE STUDY OF STATE LIBRARY ACTS

PROF. K.A ISAAC

Ess Ess Publications

4837/24, Ansari Road, Darya Ganj,
New Delhi-110002
✆ : 23260807
Fax : 23274173
E-mail: info@essessreference.com
url:http://www.essessreference.com

First Published 2004

ISBN: 81-7000-411-X

Price: Rs.995/-

Published by :

Ess Ess Publications

4837/24, Ansari Road, Darya Ganj,
New Delhi - 110 002
Phone : 23260807
Fax : 23274173
E-mail : essess@del3.vsnl.net.in

Printed at :
Print Line

Contents

Preface

Library legislation is widely recognized as a helpful means for the establishment and development of public libraries and the provision of adequate library service to all sections of the people of a country. The Unesco has been laying great emphasis on the development of public libraries as institutions contributing to the progress and advancement of the society and, in its Public Library Manifestos, it has been exhorting its member countries to enact library legislation as a necessary and effective means of placing the development of public libraries on a stable organizational and financial footing. Many countries have responded positively to this appeal and have passed library legislation.

In the federal political set up of India "Library" is a state subject and it is for each state to take initiatives for providing public library service to the people including the passing of legislation for the purpose. Out of 28 states and 7 union territories in India only 12 states have gone in for library legislation so far. These Acts vary in several respects. A comparative and critical evaluation of the main provisions of these Acts is therefore considered useful. This is what has been attempted in this book. The purpose is three fold viz (1) facilitating a proper understanding of the main provisions of the Acts in a comparative perspective, (2) identifying the drawbacks so that they may be avoided in the future Acts that may be passed by other states; and (3) highlighting the desirability of having uniformity as far as the essentials of the Acts are concerned.

One limitation of this study is that it does not cover the Rules framed under each Act as access could not be had to them. However, in so far as the Rules are subsidiary to the Acts and are primarily intended to explain the procedural formalities of implementing the provisions of the Acts, their exclusion does not take away from the importance of this study.

Library legislation is a topic included in Library and

Information Science courses in India and elsewhere. It is hoped that teachers and students of these courses, administrators concerned with library matters in the Central and State governments and members of the library profession in general will find the book useful.

The book "Public Library Acts in India" by S.Kumar, Reader, Vikram University, Ujjain and Dr.Leena Shan, Librarian, Government College, Mehidpur, Ujjain published by ESS ESS Publications, Delhi is a compilation of ten of the twelve Acts. I have drawn on this book for the texts of those Acts that I was not able to procure and I express my thanks to Shri.S.Kumar and Dr.Leena Shan. I am also grateful to Dr.G.Devarajan, professor and Head of the Department of Library and Information Science for extending to me the facilities of the departmental library and for such other help rendered Smt.S.Prasannakumary's help in the preparation of the press copy of the book is also acknowledged with thanks. ESS ESS Publications, Delhi brought out the book in record time in an attractive format. I express my sincere gratitude to them.

The texts of the twelve Acts so far enacted have been added as appendices in the book for ready reference as and when required in the course of the study of the evaluative part of the book.

Prof.K.A.Isaac

Thiruvananthapuram

1

INTRODUCTION

1.1. ROLE OF THE PUBLIC LIBRARY IN SOCIETY

Of all the institutions founded by society for its own progress and development , the public library is one of the most important. By providing people with knowledge, information, values and culture it aims at the moulding of a knowledgeable and responsible citizenry that is capable of exercising its democratic rights and duties in such a manner that the democratic order is preserved and strengthened. This, the library does by stocking appropriate books and other materials and making them available for use by all and also by organizing various programmes and services around the book stock What distinguishes a public library from other types of libraries .. that it serves all members of its community without any distinction whatsoever while the other types of libraries like academic libraries or research libraries are meant for specified groups of people.

The UNESCO considered the public library so important that it felt prompted to bring out a Public Library Manifesto as early as in 1949 defining its purposes and functions and stressing the need for every nation to develop public libraries and provide public library service to its people. The Manifesto was revised by UNESCO in 1972 which was observed as the International Book Year and again in 1994 to reflect the changing perceptions of public library functions and services in accordance with the changing needs of the society.

The Public Library Manifesto, 1974 succinctly defines the role of the public library thus :- "The public library, the local gate way to knowledge, provides a basic condition for life-long learning, independent decision making and cultural development of the individual and social group".

The Manifesto proclaims "UNESCO's belief in the public library as a living force for education, culture and information and an essential agent for the fostering of peace and spiritual welfare through the minds of men and women" . It exhorts the national and local governments of all countries to support and actively engage in the development of public library service.

1.2 WHY LIBRARY LEGISLATION?

Library legislation is concerned with the provision of public library service which, as stated in the UNESCO Public Library Manifesto, is primarily the responsibility of the government of the area sought to be served. It may be the national government or the government of a constituent state or a local government like a Corporation, a Municipality or a Panchayat. . Other types of library service like that of academic libraries, research libraries or libraries of government departments and other institutions do not usually come within the purview of library legislation. The provision of such library service is the responsibility of the institutions concerned.

A question that is sometimes asked is why there should be library legislation for the establishment and development of public library and their services. Cannot this be done through executive action of the government concerned? UNESCO Public Library Manifesto is emphatic that public library development and service must be supported by specific legislation. This view is endorsed by the national professional organizations of librarians of all countries and also by international professional organizations like the International Federation of Library Associations and Institutions

(IFLA), International Federation for Information and Documentation (FID) and others and also by eminent librarians the world over. International and National Conferences of librarians have also repeatedly pleaded for library legislation.

One reason why legislation is thought necessary is that, although public libraries are recognized as important institutions and they constitute a major component of any long term strategy for culture, information provision, literacy and education, the benefits that accrue from them are not immediately visible and pressingly felt unlike, say, medical and other essential services. Therefore no urgency or pressure may be felt to develop the service and if it is solely left to executive action of the government there is the possibility of its being affected by the vagaries of policy changes of the governments in power from time to time. While one government may give it high priority and may be generous in its support for its development another may have a different perspective and may relegate it to a low priority resulting in its virtual neglect and stagnation. Legislation would be helpful in fortifying it from this danger and placing it on a sable basis of development. Another reason is that adequate finance is necessary for public library development, and legislation is a means of ensuring it. Therefore, to place public library development and the availability of the funds required for the purpose on a sound and stable footing, legislation would be helpful. Yet another reason is that legislation can provide the guidelines regarding the structure of the public library system that is suitable for each area and the authorities and machinery that should be set up for the realization of the goals aimed at. It is the recognition of these facts that led to the enactment of library legislation in the UK as early as in 1850.

1.3 PUBLIC LIBRARIES ACT (UK)

The Public Libraries Act of UK (1850) was the first such Act passed by the Parliament of a country. True, an Act relating to libraries was passed in France earlier in 1789, but its scope was limited to the confiscation of church libraries and making them public property and not for the nation-wide development of public libraries. As such it cannot be considered as falling in the category of public library legislation. The importance of the British Act is in the recognition, as early as in 1850, of the statutory obligation of the government of a country to develop and provide public library service to its people. The Act, as such, was a feeble one in that it was only an enabling Act with a tax rate of a paltry half penny in every pound of land tax which could be utilized only for the space or building required to accommodate the library and for its maintenance and not for the purchase of books. However, conceptually and psychologically, it had a powerful universal impact regarding the state's responsibility for the provision of public library service to the people and it served as a persuasive factor for other countries to pass library laws. In that respect the British Public Libraries Act can justifiably be regarded as the mother of all library legislation.

The 1890 Act underwent many revisions over the years on the basis of the reports of several committees on public libraries appointed by the government from time to time and the result of all these is that there is, in Britain, today one of the strongest and most efficient public library systems in the world catering to the needs of all sections of the society and also extending its services globally.

1.4 HISTORY OF LIBRARY LEGISLATION IN INDIA

The British Act exerted its influence on those who were active in the public library field in India and, consequently, library legislation started receiving attention in India from pre-independence days. Dr.S.R.Ranganathan, after completing his training in librarianship in the University College, London in 1925, made an extensive tour of Britain visiting and observing all types of libraries and he was deeply impressed by them especially by the high level of public library service. He attributed this to library legislation and was convinced that library legislation was an essential means for the planned public library development in every country including India.

After returning to India and rejoining the University of Madras as its librarian he involved himself deeply in every aspect of library work – theoretical, practical and organizational. He missed no opportunity to advocate the cause of public libraries and the need for library legislation to put them on a sound and stable footing in India. Thinking perhaps that the most effective way of creating awareness of this need and convincing the authorities of it, was to show them what a library bill would be like, he drafted a model library bill and included it in his book. "Five Laws of Library Science" published in 1930. He presented this bill for discussion at the First All Asia Educational Conference held in Varanasi in December 1930. Although an attempt was made to introduce this bill with some modifications in the Bengal Legislature by Kumar Munindra Deb Rai Mehasaye, it did not succeed.

On the initiative of the Madras Library Association Ranganathan's model bill was introduced in the Madras Legislature thrice. Although the bill was taken up by the Congress Ministry that came to power in 1937 after provincial autonomy was granted, it could not make any progress as the Second World War broke out and the Ministry resigned because it could not, as a matter of policy, cooperate with the war efforts.

In the erstwhile Bombay Presidency a private library bill was introduced in the Legislative Council in 1936 by Rao Bahadur S.K.Bole, a nominated member. A significant feature of the bill was that it empowered the local bodies to levy a library cess and start libraries. But the bill was not taken up for consideration.

One princely state that passed a library bill before independence was Kolhapur, now part of Maharashtra state. This was in 1945. But the Act does not seem to have been implemented with seriousness.

Although there were continuous efforts in the form of lobbying with the powers that be, passing resolutions at library conferences, holding seminars and conferences exclusively on public libraries and library legislation, submitting memoranda to the authorities and publishing articles in professional journals and newspapers, nothing substantial materialised in the matter of library legislation until after independence. The person who spearheaded these efforts was Dr.S.R,Ranganathan. He spared no efforts in corresponding with or personally contacting the authorities of the Provinces of British India and the princely states and driving home to them the importance of public libraries and the need for library legislation for developing them. He drafted library bills for many states and presented them for consideration by their governments. There were others who strived hard to make library legislation a reality and the names of P.N.Kaula, D.R.Kalia, K.M.Ujlamkar and Velga Venkatappiah deserve to be specially mentioned in this connection.

1.5 PUBLIC LIBRARY ACTS IN INDIA

After independence in 1947 and the formation of a Congress Ministry in the then Madras State, Ranganathan took up the question of library legislation with the State Education Minister, Shri.Avinashlingam Chettiar with whom he had good rapport , and presented to him the library bill that he had already drafted, with the request that he should introduce and piolot it in the legislature. The Minister did so with some modifications in the bill and got it passed by the Legislature on the 24th March 1948 as the Madras Public Libraries Act. Later when Madras state was bifurcated and renamed as Tamil Nadu, the Act was renamed as Tamil Nadu Public Libraries Act..

The second state to adopt library law after independence was the princely state of Hyderabad. Apart from Dr,Ranganathan's efforts which had a national impact, the driving force behind the law passed in Hyderabad in 1955, was Shri.K.M.Ujlamkar who was a former student of Ranganathan and was working as librarian of Asfia Library in Hyderabad at the time.

The State of Andhra was formed in 1953 comprising the

Telungu speaking territories of the erstwhile Madras state and later in 1956, when Indian states were reorganized on linguistic basis, the state of Hyderabad was merged with it. Thus the situation in the enlarged Andhra Pradesh in 1956 was that there were two Library Acts in force, viz the Madras Public Libraries Act of 1948 and the Hyderabad Act of 1955. This anomaly was rectified by the enactment in 1960 of a new Act titled the Andhra Pradesh Public Libraries Act which was applicable uniformly to the whole of Andhra Pradesh.

The next state to put library law on its statutes book was Mysore (Karnataka). Public Libraries Act was passed by the State Legislature in 1965. Dr.Renganathan who was based in Bangalore at the time as Head of the Documentation Research and Training Centre was closely associated with the drafting of the bill and many of his ideas were incorporated in it. It was an improvement on the two earlier Acts passed by Tamil Nadu and Andhra Pradesh in several respects especially its financial clauses which were more broad based and consequently ensured substantially higher revenue for public library development.

The other states which have enacted library legislation are Maharashtra (1967), West Bengal (1979), Manipur (1988), Kerala (1989), Hariyana (1989), Goa (1973), Mizoram (1993), Gujarat (2001) and Orissa (2001). Not much was heard of the Kolhapur Public Libraries Act of 1945 and it does not seem to have been given a serious trial. In any case, as Kolhapur was merged in Maharashtra, the Act became extinct with the passing of the Maharashtra Public Libraries Act in 1967.

1.6 MODEL LIBRARY BILLS

In order to give an impetus to the library movement and to give guidelines to the states and union territories in the drafting of library bills for presentation in their respective legislatures, several model library bills were prepared by different agencies and persons. The model library bill drafted by Dr.Ranganthan and included in his book "Five Laws of Library Science" in 1930 was the first such attempt. He revised it in 1957 and again in 1972 to suit the changing perceptions of the functions of public libraries.

There were also two initiatives at the governmental level to prepare model library bills. The Ministry of Education, Government of India appointed an Advisory Committee for Libraries in 1957 under the chairmanship of Shri.K.P.Sinha. One of the major recommendations contained in its report submitted in 1959 was for developing a comprehensive public library system in the country and that for that purpose every state and union territory should enact library legislation. In pursuance of this recommendation the Ministry of Education, Government of India drafted a model Public Library bill in 1963 and circulated it among the states with the request that it may be considered for enactment with such changes as were necessary to suit local conditions.

The second official initiative was taken by the Planning Commission, Government of India whose Working Group on Libraries prepared a Model Public Libraries Bill in 1965 which could be considered for adoption by each state with such suitable modifications as were considered necessary.

Dr.V.Venkatappaiah who is a strong advocate of library legislation drafted two model bills, one in 1989 and the other in 1994 on behalf of the Indian Library Association.

1.7 CONTENT OF LIBRARY LEGISLATION

What should be the content or main provisions of library legislation? Every Library Act has a preamble which is a conscious statement of the objectives sought to be achieved by the Act. The preamble may be very succinct just indicating the targeted goal or it may be a little more detailed and descriptive.

The Act also defines the terms occurring in it in order to make their meaning in the context in which they are used, explicit.

The main clauses of a Library Act pertain to provisions regarding (1) the Library Authorities (State Library Authority and

Local Library Authorities) to be set up for implementing the provisions of the Act (2) Directorate of Libraries as a government department for overseeing the implementation of the Act (3) State Library Service (Personnel) (4) Finance (5) Structure of the public library system to be set up and (6) Miscellaneous matters. In the succeeding chapters an attempt is made to compare and evaluate the clauses relating to these provisions in the twelve Library Acts which have so far been passed in India viz Tamil Nadu (1948), Andhra Pradesh (1960), Karnataka (1965), Maharashtra (1967), West Bengal (1979), Manipur (1988), Kerala (1989) Haryana 91989), Mizoram (1993), Goa (1994), Gurajat (2001) and Orissa (2001). The Acts of Manipur, Haryana, Mizoram and Gujarat have, reportedly, not been implemented or implemented only partially. But it is hoped that whatever hindrances are there to their implementation will be got over and they will also be given full effect to before long to serve the purpose for which they were passed.

2

State Library Authority

2.1 INTRODUCTION

For the implementation of the provisions of a Library Act various bodies have to be set up, the most important of which is a state level body to exercise overall supervision and provide proper direction to the public library movement. Although this body is designated differently in the different Acts, the name "State Library Authority" is used as the heading of this Chapter and it is meant to encompass all state level bodies in all the Acts. This chapter discusses their composition and powers and functions in all the twelve state Acts passed so far.

2.2 TAMIL NADU

The State Library Authority has not been specified in the Act. There is, however, provision in it for a State Library Committee to be constituted by the government for the purpose of advising it on such matters as it may refer to it. The composition, powers and duties of the Committee are to be prescribed in the Rules to be framed under the Act.

The Rules under the Act were framed and approved in 1950. They provide for the constitution of a State Library Committee comprising sixteen members with representation for Government Departments, Universities, Local Library Authorities, etc. The

Director of Public Instruction is the ex-officio Director of Public Libraries and he and the special officer assisting him in the administration of the Act are members of the Committee. (Subsequently provision was made for an independent Director of Public Libraries). Representation for professional librarians is limited to two persons viz "one person with special knowledge of matters relating to libraries" nominated by the Minister and one person nominated by the Madras Library Association (presuming he/she will be a professional librarian which need not always be the case). The Minister in charge of education is the President and the Special Officer in charge of Public Libraries in the office of the Director of Public Instruction is the Secretary of the Committee. The representation for professional librarians on the Committee is inadequate. The Committee is primarily an advisory body advising the government on major mattes with autonomy only in respect of a few minor subjects.

It may be noted in this connection that in the model bill drafted by Ranganathan which formed the basis of this Act, the Minister for Education whose administrative jurisdiction included public library service at the time was named the State Library Authority. It would have been better if, even though the government and specifically the Minister in charge of public libraries is the real library authority, this was explicity mentioned in the Act in order to make him conscious of his responsibility in this matter especially as library development and service is a relatively new responsibility and does not usually enjoy high priority.

2.3 ANDHRA PRADESH (A.P)

The Act provides for the establishment by the government of the Andhra Pradesh Granthalaya Parishad. Although not so specified, on the basis of the objects, powers and functions of the Parishad, as stated in the Act, it can be deemed to be the State Library Authority vested with the overall responsibility of organizing and promoting public library service in the state. From the list of its powers and functions enumerated in the Act, it can be seen that it is an autonomous body in all matters pertaining to library development and service except in respect of (1) the sanctioning of staff and (2) accepting gifts and endowments exceeding Rs.5 lakhs. It is also required to submit to the government the audited statement of accounts and utilization certificates relating to its funds every year, cause the annual report on the working of public libraries under the Act to be placed before the legislature and adhere to the guidelines issued by the government from time to time in preparing programmes of library development. So, for all practical purposes the Parishad is empowered by the Act to function as an Autonomous Library Authority with marginal government control in a few areas. It is also the body to advise the government on all matters under the Act.

The Parishad is a small, compact body of nine members with a Chairman appointed by the government from among persons who have rendered eminent service for the cause of education and library movement, the Director of Public Libraries as the member Secretary and seven other members representing library and related fields. The significant point to be noted about the composition of the Parishad is that all members are either directly involved in or actively associated with public library movement. One of them is an expert having special knowledge about Library Science and another the Chief Librarian of the State Central Library, Hyderabad. These two would undoubtedly be professional librarians and this is good enough representation for librarians on a nine member state library body. The other members are:- (a) two persons from among those who have rendered service for development of library movement and education (b) one person representing the recognized aided libraries (c) one from among the Chairman of Zilla Grandhalaya .Samasthas and (d) one from among the Secretaries of the Zilla Grandhalaya Samasthas. Some among these members and the Director of Libraries may also be professional librarians in which case the representation for librarians would be very good. However, one omission is that there is no representation for M.L.As on the Parishad. It would have been desirable to give them some representation as matters relating to the Act and public libraries in general often come up for consideration of the legislature. Similarly non-representation of educational, literary and cultural bodies is also a lacuna.

2.4 KARNATAKA

The Act provides for a State Library Authority to be set up. This is a more broad based body then the Abdhra Pradesh Granthalaya Parishad. The Minister in charge of Public Libraries is the Chairman and the State Librarian the Secretary of the Authority. There is representation on the State Library Authority for the Legislative Assembly, Legislative Council, Universities in the State, Karnataka Library Association, City Library Authority of Bangalore, Other City Library Authorities (one for each in turn)l, District Library Authorities (one for each in turn), State Education Department and professional librarians. The State Librarian, although named as the ex-officio Secretary of the Authority, has not been named as a member. There are three experts in Library Science nominated by the government as members. In addition the representative of the Karnataka Library Association which is a professional body can also be presumed to be a professional librarian. So there are five professional librarians associated with the State Library Authority of twenty five members and this can be regarded as reasonably good representation.

The functions of the State Library Authority specified in the Act are (1) to advise the state government on all matters connected with the administration of the Act (2) to be the managing authority for the State Central Library and (3) exercise and perform such powers and duties as entrusted to it by the Act and such other powers and duties as may be prescribed (by the Rules to be framed unless the Act) Other than these, there are no powers and duties specified in the Act.

From the functions of the Authority described in the Act it can be seen that it is, in reality, an advisory body and not an autonomous Authority empowered to take its own decisions and implement them. The real authority operating and implementing the provisions of the Act is the government. So it is a misnomer to call it a Library Authority.

2.5 MAHARASHTRA

The apex body at the State level is designated as State Library Council in the Maharashtra Act. The Council, as in the case of the Karnataka Act, is a broad based body with representation for different relevant interests. The Minister for Education is the President, the Deputy Minister for Education the Vice-President and the Director of Libraries the member Secretary. There are, in all, more than twenty members of whom four members are to be persons "who have special knowledge of or interest or practical experience in matters connected with library service" nominated by the government. Presumably the intention is that these four should be professionally qualified librarians although this is not explicitly stated and the relevant clause of the Act can be interpreted to include others also.

The functions of the Council have been stated in just one sentence thus:- "It shall be the function of the Council to advise the State government on all matters connected with the administration of this Act". 'So the Council is a purely advisory body with little administrative authority

2.6 WEST BENGAL

As in the case of Maharashtra, in West Bengal also, the state apex body for public libraries is designated as State Library Council in the Act. The council has twenty seven members with the Minister in charge of Libraries as Chairman and the Director of Libraries as member Secretary. There is representation on the Council for legislators, universities, education departments, professional librarians, library associations, government departments, etc. The

West Bengal Act perhaps stands first among all the Acts in the matter of representation for professional librarians. Excluding the Director of Libraries whose qualifications have not been specified in the Act, there are eleven librarians as members viz (1) two representatives of the Bengal Library Association (2) one representative of the employees of the libraries which come under the purview of the Act (3) one District Library Officer (4) one District Librarian (5) four experts in Library Science nominated by the government (7) the Librarian, Central Library and (8) the Librarian (now Director) of the National Library, Calcutta. Implied in this excellent representation is the recognition by the state government of the important role of professional librarians in guiding the scientific development of public libraries and their services.

The functions of the State Library Council are :- (1) Advising the government on the management of the Central Library, on matters of public library system and on such matters relating to libraries and library service as may be referred to it; and (2) Formulate, in consultation with the Local Library Authorities, the principles governing the eligibility of private libraries to receive recognition or aid under the Act. It is also stated that the Council shall exercise such powers and perform such duties as may be prescribed by the Rules framed under the Act.

In West Bengal also the State library Council is more an advisory body than an autonomous executive body.

2.7 MANIPUR

The state level body for public libraries in the Manipur Act is designated as the State Library Committee. This is a small body of nine members constituted as follows:-

(a) The Minister in charge of Education who shall also be the Chairman of the Committee;

(b) Commissioner/Secretary to the government in the Education Department;

(c) The Director of Public Libraries;

(d) The Chief Librarian of the State Central Library;

(e) One person elected by the Syndicate of Manipur University;

(f) One person nominated by the Manipur Library Association;

(g) Two persons nominated by the State government from among members of the District Library Authorities; and

(h) One person co-opted by the Committee

Assuming that the person nominated by the Manipur Library Association would be a professional librarian, there are two professional librarians on the Committee viz himself and the Chief Librarian of the State Central Library.

The Committee's function is to advise the state government on all matters arising from the Act and exercise and perform such other powers and duties as may be prescribed by the Rules framed under the Act.

2.8 KERALA

2.7.1 Background of the Act

The Kerala Act is titled "Kerala Public Libraries (Kerala Granthasala Sanghom) Act". This title may sound strange to those who are not familiar with the library movement in Kerala because of the appearance in it of the works 'Kerala Granthasala Sanghom' (KGS). This is the name of an Association that was piloting the public library movement in Kerala since 1945. It was a federation of libraries exercising supervisory control in several respects over its affiliated libraries rather than a more library association playing the role normally discharged by associations. It had a strong presence and influence all over Kerala and the large majority of public libraries in the state numbering around five thousand were affiliated to it Government grant was sanctioned to libraries on its recommendation.

Kerala Granthasala Sanghom had set up a three tier hierarchical pattern of organisation with the full participation of library workers.

These were bodies set up for organizational and administrative work, all elected by people who were directly involved in library work. At the lowest Taluk level there is a Taluk Library Union for each taluk, at the district level a District Library Committee for each district and at th state level a Bharana Samithi (Governing Council) with a working Committee elected by it.

Through its concerted work in the public library field for many years ad the support of political parties, it became a powerful organization whose views on public library matters earned respect and support in the state. It lobbyed for a public library law which would, in effect, give statutory recognition to it and to the library set up it had already developed. Although there were several attempts by the government to enact library legislation and a draft bill was prepared by Dr.S.R.Ranganathan in 1959 at the instance of the then government, they did not succeed because of opposition from the Kerala Granthasala Sanghom. The pattern of the present Act passed in 1989 is almost a total concession to the views and demands of the Kerala Granthasala Sanghom.

Over the years elections to the various bodies of KGS came to be contested on political lines and the rivalry and differences among the different political parties began to influence its working especially of the Baharana Samithi and its Working Committee. Matters came to a head when these differences made it almost impossible for the Bharana Samithi and the Working Committee to work with understanding and cohesion which led to a crisis and stalemate in the KGS. This is perhaps an instance of the ill effects of over democratization of educational, cultural and social organizations. The consequence was that the government intervened and took over the administration of KGS through an Ordinance in March 1977. The Ordinance made provision for a Control Board for the KGS with the Education Minister as Chairman and a few nominated members.

This was the position at the time of passing the Public Libraries Act in 1989. The KGS continued to exist although under the control of the government. Therefore the Act had to take cognisance of the KGS and it provides for its merger with all its assets and liabilities in the State Library Council set up by it. Hence it is that the name of Kerala Granthasala Sanghom appears in the title of the Act.

2.7.2 State Library Council (SLC)

State Library Council is the state level apex body under the Act and it consists of (a) one member each from the taluks in each district elected by the District Library Council of that district ; (b) five members of whom one shall be a librarian, another person belonging to the scheduled caste/scheduled tribe and another a women all nominated by the government and (c) five official members of the Executive Committee.

The Act provides for an Executive Committee consisting of twenty five members as stated below:

1) Fifteen members elected by the members of the SLC from among themselves;
2) The five nominated members of the SLC; and
3) Five official members viz the secretaries of the government in the departments of (i) Higher Education (ii) General Education (iii) Finance (iv) Cultural Affairs and (v) Local Administration.

The elected members of the Executive Committee elect a President, a Vice-President, a Secretary and a Joint Secretary as common office bearers of the SLC and the Executive Committee.

The SLC has, in all, seventy three members – sixty three elected members representing sixty three taluks, five nominated members and five official members of the Executive Committee (Government Secretaries). So the SLC is a predominantly elected body, fifteen of the twenty members of the Executive Committee are also elected members. The formation of these bodies and others at the lower levels being primarily through the elective process, the Kerala Act has the aura of being highly democratic as compared to the other state Acts. But a latent danger is that, as elections are fought on political lines, developments of the type that led to the supersession of the Kerala Granthasala Sanghom in 1977 which would be highly detrimental to the public library movement, cannot be ruled out. Also it excludes from the various bodies persons with knowledge of the modern developments in the scientific organization and management of libraries who can make valuable contributions to library development on sound scientific lines."

The representation for librarians is just nominal in the Act. In this respect among the twelve State library Acts, the provision in the Kerala Act is the least satisfactory. The SLC with a total membership of seventy three has only one librarian as a member. He is also one of the twenty five members of the Executive Committee. Although this position has so far been held by a professional librarian, there is no guarantee that it will continue to be so because the word used in the Act in this context is just 'librarian' who can also be an unqualified or semi qualified person working in any of the numerous public libraries and loosely designated as librarian .

The powers and functions of the SLC listed in the Act show that it is basically an advisory body advising the government on all matters pertaining to public library development and it enjoys autonomy in decision making and action only in a few areas. In this respect it is not very different from the other State Library Acts.

2.9 HARYANA

The Act provides for a State library Authority of over twenty members with the Minister in charge of libraries as the Chairman and the Director of Libraries as the Member Secretary. The majority of members are ex-officio, representing various government departments, universities, Legislature and libraries. Not more than four members having special knowledge of libraries are to be nominated by the Chairman of the Authority. In all, there are six professional librarians as members of the Authority.

There is a Standing Advisory Committee of eleven members comprising eight members nominated by the Chairman of the Authority from among members of the Authority, the Secretary to Government, Department of Libraries, the Director of Libraries and the State Librarian. The Chairman of the Authority nominates the Chairman of the Standing Advisory Committee and the Secretary of the Authority shall also be the Secretary of the Standing Advisory Committee.

The function of the Authority is to advise the government on all mattes arising out of the Act and relating to library development in the state. The functions of the Standing Advisory Committee shall be:-

a) to advise the State Library Directorate on all technical matters relating to library development and organization, and

b) to make recommendations to the Authority on matters relating to the promotion and development of library service.

The State Library Authority being a reasonably compact body of around twenty members the need for a Standing Advisory Committee of eleven members with more or less identical functions is not very clear.

2.10 MIZORAM

The state level body under the Act is designated as the State Library Council (SLC). It consists of twelve ex-officio members and six other members either nominated or elected. The Minister for Education and Human Resources shall be the Chairman and the Secretary to the government, Education and Human Resources shall be the Secretary. There is representation on the SLC for all departments of education in the government and departments handling related subjects. Professional librarians have three representatives viz the Librarian, North Eastern Hill University (NEHU), Mizoram Campus, State Librarian and a representative of Mizoram Library

Association. The Director of Public libraries is also a member of the SLC and if he possesses professional qualifications about which nothing is mentioned in the Act, there would be four professional librarians on the SLC.

The duties of the Council are:-

(1) to advise the government on all matters relating to libraries arising out of the provisions of the Act and also in regard to the promotion and development of library services in the state;

(2) to take suitable steps to establish and promote a public library system.

2.11 GOA

The apex body that the Act provides for is the State Library Council composed of twelve members with the Minister in charge of Libraries as the Chairman and the State library Officer as the Secretary. The other members represent government departments, Goa University, Legislature, Library Association, etc.

There are twelve members in all out of whom five are professional librarians viz President State Library Association, State Library Officer, Librarian, Goa University, State Librarian and one expert in Library Science nominated by the Chairman of the Council.

The Council is an advisory body advising the government on the implementation of the provisions of the Act and also in respect of promotion and development of library service in the state.

2.12 GUJARAT

The State level body according to this Act for looking after public library matters is the State library Development Council. It is a fairly large body with the Minister in charge of Libraries as Chairman and the Director of Public Libraries as member Secretary.

There are nineteen other members representing organizations which are capable of playing a significant role in public library development in the state. The representation for professional librarians is limited to three. There is a Vice-President for the Council nominated by the government form among its members.

The powers and functions of the Council are delineated in detail in the Act. It is basically an advisory body to the government but there are certain areas where it can take action on its own.

2.13 ORISSA

Orissa is the latest state in India ro enact library legislation. This Act is different from the other Acts in that it envisages two bodies at the state level – The Orissa Public Library Council and Orissa Public Library Authority. The former is a larger body than the latter and has twenty five members with the Minister in charge of the Department of Tourism and Culture as the Chairman and the Director of Public Libraries as the member secretary and others drawn from relevant departments and organizations. One special feature of this Act is that there is provision for a Member of Parliament from Orissa to be a member of the Council. As far as professional librarians are concerned, there are two representatives viz "an expert in library system and library services" and a teacher in a post graduate department of Library and Information Science of a University in the state. There is provision for the President or Secretary of any library association in the state to be a member and if he is also a professional librarian, the representation would rise to three.

The Council's function are defined as advising the government on matters concerning the management and development of public library system and library services in the state, formulation of training policies and programmes in relation to such system and services and such other matters relating thereto as may be prescribed by the Rules framed under the Act.

The Orissa Public Library Authority is a small three member body consisting of (a) the Minister in charge of the Department of Tourism and Culture (Chairman), (b) the Secretary to Government in the Department of Tourism and Culture (Working Chairperson), and (c) Director of Public Libraries (Member Secretary).

The powers and functions of the Authority have been described in detail. They are an elaboration of the stated functions of the Council. The difference between the Council and the Authority is that while the former is a purely advisory body the latter is an executive body vested with powers to formulate policies and programmes and implement them subject to the availability of funds. However, it is stated that it has to act on the directions of the government. The three members of the Authority are also members of the Council and the Chairman and Secretary of the two bodies are common. The relationship between the two bodies in respect of the performance of the various functions is not specified. According to the Act they are parallel bodies without any mechanism for the coordination of their functions. This may lead to confusion and practical difficulties in their working. Perhaps a better arrangement would have been to designate the present State Library Council as State Library Authority with the same powers and functions as now prescribed for the Council and the Authority and have a small Executive Committee elected or nominated from among the members of the Authority.

2.14 SUMMARY

All the twelve Acts provide for a state level apex body in each state (in Orissa there are two) with the responsibility of helping the government in the implementation of the Act and advising the government in all other respects for promoting and strengthening the public library movement. The body is named differently in the different Acts. In Tamil Nadu and Manipur it is called the State library Committee. In Andhra Pradesh the name preferred is Andhra Pradesh Granthalaya Parishad. In Karnataka and Haryana the body is designated as the State Library Authority. In Orissa there are two national level bodies namely the Orissa Public Library Council and the Orissa Public Library Authority . In Maharashtra, West Bengal, Kerala, Mizoram and Goa the name is the State Library Council. Gujarat has gone in for the designation of State Library Development Council. It may be noted that unlike as in the other states, in Tamil Nadu the constitution and functions of the State Library Committee are prescribed in the Rules framed under the Act and not in the Act itself.

The size of the body ranges from nine members in Andhra Pradesh to as high as seventy three members in Kerala. Kerala's is a special case because it gives representation for each of its sixty three Taluks at the rate of one member per Taluk. The Orissa Public Library Authority is a body of just three members while the Orissa Public Library Council has twenty five members. Excluding Kerala whose State Library Council has an abnormally high number of seventy three members, the average number of the state level bodies of the other eleven states is around eighteen. The composition of the bodies varies from state to state. The Minister whose portfolio includes public libraries is, in most cases, the Chairman and the Director of Public Libraries or the State Librarian as the Head of the Department of Libraries is designated as the Secretary. In some states there is provision for a Vice-Chairman and in some there is an Executive Committee formed from among the members of the State level body and responsible to that body.

Kerala stands apart from the other states in respect of the composition of its State Library Council. The state has sixty three Taluks each of which is represented by an elected member. In addition to these sixty three members there are five members nominated by the government and five Secretaries to the government in various departments as ex-officio members. So the Council is predominantly an elected body. There is an Executive Committee of twenty five members constituted of fifteen elected members, five nominated members and five ex-officio members. The members of the state level body of the other eleven states are predominantly nominated or ex-officio. The representation for professional librarians in all the states except Kerala is satisfactory. In Andhra Pradesh, Karnataka, West Bengal, Goa, Haryana and Mizoram it can be considered as very good.

As regards the functions of the bodies, a key role is envisaged for them in all the Acts in piloting the development of public libraries as per the provisions of the Acts. However, basically they are all advisory bodies advising the government on all major mattes relating to public libraries. Prior government sanction is necessary for their implementation. Their autonomy is limited to just a few subjects. It is the Andhra Pradesh Granthalaya Parishad and the Orissa State Library Authority that enjoy the maximum autonomy in respect of policy formulations and their implementation. All others have only an advisory role and the final decision is of the government. This being the case, the name Library Authority to refer to the body as in the case of the Karnataka and Haryana Acts is a misnomer. It is evidently for this reason that Dr.S.R.Ranganathan preferred the Minister in charge of libraries to be designated as the Library Authority and the state level apex body constituted under the Act as the State library Committee. However, whatever the designation and the powers and functions stated in the Act may be, a Committed and knowledgeable state level body will be able to motivate lower level bodies and even the government regarding sound library development and the provision of adequate public library service to the people and function as the defacto library authority making its presence forcefully felt by all in the field.

3

LOCAL LIBRARY AUTHORITIES

3.1 INTRODUCTION

It is the responsibility of each state level library body to work for the development of a sound public library system in the state and ensure the provision of library service to the entire population of the state. This, it will not be able to do by itself. It needs the help and assistance of various local level bodies for this purpose. Therefore every library Act provides for the constitution of such bodies to concentrate on library development and service at the local level. The Acts also prescribe the composition and powers and functions of such bodies. The term "Local Library Authorities" used as the heading of this chapter is meant to denote such bodies whatever their actual designation may be in the different Acts. This term "Library Authority" gained currency because this was the term used in the first Library Act passed in India viz The Madras Public Libraries Act, 1948 emulating the British Public Libraries Act of 1850. The composition, powers and functions of the Local Library Authorities according to the twelve Acts passed in India so far are examined in this chapter.

3.2 TAMIL NADU

The Act provides for a Local Library Authority for the city of Chennai and one each for the districts of the state. So there are in all, as many Local Library Authorities as the number of districts in the state and one for Chennai.

3.2.1. Composition of Local Library Authority, Chennai

Local Library Authority, Chennai is to have the following members:-

(1) Three members elected by the corporation of Chennai,

(2) Three office bearers of libraries situated in Chennai, two head masters/head mistresses of high schools in Chennai and one Principal of a college in Chennai, all nominated by the government, and

(3) The holder, for the time being, of an office which the government may from time to time specify in this behalf who shall also be the Secretary of the Local Library Authority.

The President is to be elected by the Local Library Authority from among its members

3.2.2. Composition of Local Library Authorities, Districts

The Local Library Authority for each district is constituted as follows:-

(1) Three office bearers of libraries situated in the district and recognized by the government in this behalf and five head masters/ head mistresses of high schools or Principals of colleges in the district nominated by the Director of Libraries;

(2) One member elected by the District Board and where there are two or more District Boards in a district, one member elected by each District Board;

(3) Such number of members as may be elected by the Presidents of the Panchayats in the district, the Presidents of the Panchayat in each taluk electing one member;

(4) Such number of members as may be elected by the Municipal Councils in the district according to the following scale:-

* Municipalities with a population not exceeding one lakh
* One member
* Exceeding one lakh but not exceeding two !akhs
* Two members
* Exceeding two lakhs
* Three members

(5) The holder, for the time being, of an office which the government may from time to time specify in this regard who shall also be the Secretary of the Local Library Authority

The President of the Local Library Authority shall be elected by the members from among themselves.

A Local Library Authority may elect an Executive Committee of not more than seven members and delegate such of its powers to it as deemed necessary. Local Library Authorities may also appoint sub-committees for specific purposes.

3.2.3 Powers and Functions of Local Library Authorities

(1) Preparing schemes for establishing libraries and spreading library service in its area for the approval of the Director and implementing them

(2) Taking all steps like provision of land and buildings for libraries, equipping libraries with books and other reading materials, employing library staff as required, etc. that are necessary to carry out the provisions of the Act.

(3) All properties, movable and immovable, acquired for libraries in an area, shall vest with the Local Library Authority of that area, and

(4) Drawing up regulations in respect of all matters relating to the working of public libraries.

The Local Library Authorities are the bodies which are primarily responsible for the implementation of the provisions of the Act and for the development of libraries and provision of library service in each district and the city of Chennai. They are responsible to the Director of Libraries and the government. There is no linkage between them and the State Library Committee except that four members representing the DLAs are nominated to the Committee by the Minister. Presumably they can function independent of the Committee.

The district Local Library Authorities are large and rather unwieldy bodies However the provision for an Executive Committee for each Local Library Authority to which authority can be delegated reduces the inconvenience of such unwieldiness in decision making and action.

3.3 ANDHRA PRADESH

The designation of the Local Level Library body in the Andhra Pradesh Act is The Zilla Granthalaya Samastha (ZGS). There is provision for a ZGS for the city of Hyderabad one for the district of Hyderabad excluding the city area and one each for the other districts.

3.3.1 Composition of ZGS, Hyderabad

ZGS, Hyderabad city consists of the following members:

(1) Three members who have rendered eminent service in the field of education or public libraries, one member from among the Presidents of the Governing bodies of the aided libraries in the twin cities of Hyderabad and Seconderabad and two members from among the councillors of the Municipal Corporation of Hyderabad and Seconderabad, all nominated by the government;

(2) The District Educational officer, Hyderabad;

(3) The Deputy Director, office of the Directorate of Adult Education, Hyderabad; and

(4) The Librarian, City Central Library, Hyderabad who will be the member secretary.

3.3.2 Composition of ZGS, Districts

The ZGS of each district is composed of the following members:-

(1) Three members from among the residents of the district who have rendered eminent service in the field of education or public libraries, one member from among the presidents of the governing bodies of the aided libraries in the district, one member from among the councillors of every Municipal Corporation or every Municipality in the district, and two members from among the presidents of Mandal Panchayats in the district, all nominated by the government;

(2) The District Educational Officer;

(3) The Deputy Director of Adult Education in the district;

(4) The District Public Relations Officer;

(5) The District Panchayat Officer; and

(6) The Librarian, District Central Library who shall be the Member Secretary.

The President of the ZGS, Hyderabad as well as of the ZGS of each district is nominated by the government from among the non-official members of the ZGS. TheZGSs are compact bodies – the former having ten members and the latter having twelve members. Therefore, the need for the provision in the Act that a Zilla Granthalaya Samastha can elect an Executive Committee and delegate to it such of its powers and functions as deemed necessary is not very obvious.

The number of professional librarians is limited to one in the ZGS – the Librarian City Central library in the case of Hyderabad and the Librarian, District Central Library in the case of a district. Considering the good representation for professional libraries in the Andhra Pradesh Granthalaya Samastha, the state level apex body, the low representation for them at the lower district level where professional expertise is more necessary for work at the grass root level and for the implementation of provisions of the Act, is unfortunate.

3.3.3 Powers and Functions of ZGS

Among the important powers and duties prescribed by the Act for the ZGS are:

(1) Provision of suitable land and buildings for public libraries and equipping them with books and other reading and hindered materials and with furniture fittings and equipments;

(2) Acquiring libraries or closing or shifting existing libraries with the previous sanction of the appropriate authorities;

(3) Distributing grants to public libraries and for social education purposes;

(4) Preparing schemes for establishing libraries and spreading library service in the area of the ZGS, getting them approved by the Parishad and implementing them;

(5) Drawing regulations and rules for the efficient and smooth working of the libraries.

In the Andhra Pradesh Act the ZGSs are subordinate bodies of the Andhra Pradesh Granthalaya Parishad. This is unlike the position in Tamil Nadu where the Act does not envisage any administrative linkage between the Local Library Authorities and the State Library Committee. The ZGS's of Andhra Pradesh are vested with autonomy in a number of areas and can act on their own. But in some they have to take the prior approval of the Andhra Pradesh Granthalaya Parishad and in some others of the government or Director of Libraries. For example while they are required to take the prior approval of the Director to shift or close a public library they have to obtain the approval of the Parishad to acquire a library. Again, for accepting a gift or endowment of an immovable property, the sanction of the government is necessary. The logic of these divergent practices which is somewhat confusing is not clear.

3.4 KARNATAKA

The Karnataka Act provides for (a) a City Library Authority each for the cities of Bangalore, Hubli-Dharwar, Mangalore, Mysore and Belgaum and for such urban areas having a population of more than one lakh as the state government may by notification specify and (b) a District Library Authority for each revenue district

3.4.1 Composition of City Library Authorities

Every City Library Authority consists of:-

(1) The Mayor of the Municipal Corporation or the President of the Municipal Council or other municipal body of the city who shall be the Chairman of the Authority;

(2) (a) Principal of a first grade college of the city who shall be the Vice-Chairman of the Authority; (b) One person from among the members of the governing bodies of aided libraries in the city (c) an officer of the Department of Public Instruction having jurisdiction over the city and (d) two persons from among persons ordinarily resident in the city, all nominated by the state government.

(3) Two persons elected by the Municipal Corporation, Municipal Council or other municipal body of the city; and

(4) One person nominated by the Council of the city branch if any, of the Karnataka Library Association.

The Chief Librarian of the city shall be the Secretary of the City Library Authority and of its committees.

3.4.2 Composition of District Library Authorities

The composition of the District Library Authorities are also more or less on the lines of that of the City Library Authorities. But the District Library Authority is a larger body with over seventeen members representing local bodies, Library Association, libraries, schools, colleges, etc.

The Deputy Commissioner of the district is the Chairman of the Authority and the Chief Librarian of the district is its Secretary. The Vice-Chairman of the Authority is elected by the members from among themselves.

One serious drawback of the constitution of both the CLA and DLA is that there is no representation for professional librarians on either. Of course the chief librarian of the city is the Secretary of the CLA and the Chief Librarian of district the Secretary of the DLA. But they are just secretaries without the status of membership and as such the role they can play in the deliberations of these bodies is limited. This amounts to the denial of authoritative expert advice to LLAs and in formulating sound policies and implementing them.

3.4.3 Powers and Functions of Local Library Athorities

The primary responsibility of every City Library Authority and District Library Authority is to provide library service to the people residing in the area of its jurisdiction and to do every thing that is necessary towards this end like establishing libraries, equipping them with books, journals and other kindered materials, furniture and equipments. It can discharge some of its functions on its own and some with the approval of the government. Every City Library Authority shall establish a City Central Library and branch libraries in the city and every District Library Authority shall establish a District Central Library and branch libraries in the district. The Local Library Authorities are also required to prepare Local Library Development Plans for the development of public libraries in their respective areas of jurisdiction.

3.5 MAHARASHTRA

The designation preferred by the Maharashtra Act for the local level library body is Library Committee. It provides for a District Library Committee for each district and a separate Library Committee for Greater Mumbai

3.5.1 Composition of District Library Committee

(i) The Chairman of the Education Committee of a Zilla Parishad functioning in the district who shall be the President of the Committee;

(ii) The President of the District Library Association of the district;

(iii) One of the Chairmen of the Managing Committees of recognized public libraries functioning in each taluk of the district nominated by the government;

(iv) Five persons nominated by the government, one of whom shall be a librarian possessing the prescribed qualifications and two shall be persons representing libraries in the areas within the limits of a Municipality or Municipal Corporation in the district ;

(v) One of the Presidents of the municipalities in the district nominated by the government; and

(vi) The Education Officer of the Zilla parishad functioning in the district who shall be the Secretary of the Committee.

3.5.2 Composition of Library Committee for Greater Mumbai

(i) The Chairman of the Education Committee of the Municipal Corporation of Greater Mumbai who shall be the President of the Committee;

(ii) Five persons nominated by the government one of whom shall be a librarian possessing the prescribed qualifications and two shall be persons representing libraries in Greater Mumbai;

(iii) Education Officer of the Municipal Corporation of Greater Mumbai; and

(iv) Education Inspector, Greater Mumbai who shall also be the Secretary of the Committee.

The two Committees consist of persons who are either ex-officio or nominated by the government. There is no election involved in the selection of any of the members. There is a professional librarian as a member of each committee. If some of the members representing libraries also happen to be professional librarians there would be more of them on the committees. The recognition by the government of the intimate relationship between libraries and education is reflected in the presidents and secretaries of the committees being drawn from the education sector.

3.5.3 Functions of the Committees

The functions of the committees are succinctly stated in the Act as follows:

(i) To advise the state government on all matters relating to development of library service in the district and Greater Mumbai on proper lines;

(ii) To ensure that the prescribed functions of public libraries are performed by them satisfactorily; and

(iii) To perform such other duties as may be prescribed (by the Rules framed under the Act)

The stated functions show that the committees are basically advisory bodies advising the government on library matters and its executive functions are limited to supervising the working of individual public libraries in their respective jurisdictions.

3.6 WEST BENGAL

The west Bengal Act makes provision for the constitutions of a Local Library Authority for each district of the state.

3.6.1 Composition of Local Library Authority

(i) The District Magistrate of the district who shall be the Chairman

(ii) The District Library Officer who shall be the Secretary

(iii) The District Social Education Officer

(iv) Two representatives of the Association of the employees of the different public libraries, nominated by the government

(v) Two members nominated by the government from among the Commissioners of the Municipalities in the district.

(vi) Two representatives of the district branch of the Bengal Library Association nominated by the Executive Committee of the Association;

(vii) One person nominated by the Sabhadhipati from among the Zilla Parishad in the district;

(viii) Two persons nominated by the government from among the members of the Panchayat Samitis in the district

(ix) Two persons nominated by the government of whom

a) One shall be a member of the governing bodies of recognized libraries in the district and

b) The other from the advisory committees, if any, of the libraries under the District Library

(x) A teacher of a college or polytechnic in the district nominated by the government

(xi) A teacher of a high school or a higher secondary school in the district nominated by the government

(xii) A teacher of a primary school in the district nominated by the government

(xiii) Two M.L.A of the district nominated by the government

(xiv) The librarian of the District Library

This is a broad based body of twenty members consisting of individuals and representatives of institutions and organizations having an interest in libraries and library service and can contribute to their promotion. There are a few ex-officio members, but the large majority are nominated members. There is no member selected by election. There are six professional librarians as members of the LLA assuming that the two representatives mentioned at (vi) above would have professional qualifications.

The LLA has the discretion of appointing an Executive Committee with such number of its members as it may deem fit and delegate to it such of its powers and duties as may be prescribed by the Rules made under the Act.

3.6.2 Powers of LLA's

The powers, functions and duties of the LLA's are (a) provision of land and buildings for the public libraries with furniture, fittings and equipments, (b) stocking libraries with books, periodicals, newspapers and other information sources including the electronic media for information dissemination (c) appointment of the requisite staff to man the libraries, (d) closing existing libraries or shifting them to other sites with the previous sanction of the government and (e) drawing up rules and regulations for the working of libraries to be observed by their users. They enjoy considerable autonomy in their functioning.

3.7 MANIPUR

In the Manipur Act there is a District Library Authority (DLA) for each district of the state

3.7.1 Composition of District Library Authorities

Each District Library Authority shall consist of the following members:-

(i) Four members nominated by the government from among, citizens who have rendered eminent service to the cause of education or public libraries or persons of social eminence;

(ii) Two members elected from among themselves by members of the governing bodies of the public libraries in the district;

(iii) Two members elected from among themselves by the Board of Municipalities or by the Small Town Committees in the district;

(iv) The Librarian, District Library who shall be the Secretary of the Authority; and

(v) The District Education Officer of the district .

The Chairman is elected by the members from among themselves

The LLA is a compact body of ten members representing eminent citizens, libraries, local bodies and education department. Except for four members who are elected by the bodies that they represent, the others are either nominated or ex-officio.

3.7.2 POWERS ANDF FUNCTIONS OF DLAs

The prominent powers and responsibilities of the DLAs include provision of land and buildings for libraries, provision of the requisite furniture, fittings and equipments, equipping the libraries with books, periodicals and news papers and other sources of information including the electronic media, employing staff for manning the libraries with the sanction of the government, distributing grants to public libraries, preparation of schemes for public library development, making bye- laws, etc

There is provision for the appointment of an Executive Committee by the DLA and the delegation of such powers and functions to it as found necessary and also for the appointment of sub-committees as and when found necessary.

3.8 KERALA

As in the case of the state level body colled the State Library Council, Kerala is very unlike the other states in the structuring, constitution and manner of forming the local level bodies. There are two such bodies viz the District Library Council and the Taluk Library Council. Thus Kerala has a three tier hierarchical pattern of bodies constituted under the Act which are involved in the development of public libraries in the state. They are the State Library Council (SLC), District Library Council (DLC) and Taluk Library Council (TLC).

3.8.1 Composition of Taluk Library Councils

Every Taluk library Council shall consist of two representatives of each affiliated library in the Taluk elected by the members of the library. There are around seventy to eighty affiliated libraries on an average in a taluk and two representatives from each of them would make the TLC a large body and so there is also the provision that each Taluk Library Union shall elect an Executive Committee consisting of nine members including a President, a Vice-President, a Secretary and a Joint Secretary.

In the event of the TLC having no woman or a person of SC/ST, then one woman and one person of SC/ST shall be nominated by the Executive Committee

3.8.2 Powers and Functions of Taluk Library Councils

It is the responsibility of the TLC to take all actions that are necessary for the development of public libraries in the taluk and their proper functioning. It has to function as a facilitator for the provision of all facilities required for the purpose such as funds and buildings, furniture, equipments, books and hindered materials, staff, etc.

3.8.3 Composition of District Library Councils (DLCs)

Immediately above the TLC there is another local library body called the District Library Council for each district It is constituted as follows:-

(i) The Presidents and Secretaries of the TLCs in the district

(ii) Seven persons elected by the General Body of each of the Taluk Library Union in the district of whom one should be a woman and one shall be a person belonging to the SC/ST; and

(iii) The President or any other office bearer of any affiliated library in the district nominated by the government

The elected members of every DLC shall elect from among

themselves a District Executive Committee consisting of eleven members including a President, a Vice-President, a Secretary and a Joint Secretary.

3.8.4 Powers and Functions of District Library Councils

The powers and functions of the DLC specified in the Act in respect of the district are more or less similar to those specified for the TLC in respect of the taluk. However there are a few differences. The DLC is empowered to establish new libraries in the district with the prior sanction of the State library Council. The DLC is also empowered to shift, recognize or close or amalgamate any public library maintained or run directly by it. Another major function of the DLC is to prepare a library development plan for the district.

It is the DLC that elects members to the State Library Council at the rate of one member for each Taluk.

The provision for two local level bodies viz the District Library Council and the Taluk Library Council below the state level body viz the State Library Council is a case of unquestioningly copying the pattern that existed under the earlier Kerala Granthasala Sanghom prior to the Act. The DLCs and TLCs have concurrent responsibilities in the seence that the jurisdiction of a TLC falls within the jurisdiction of the DLC under which it functions. The rationale for the provision in the Act for these two bodies is therefore not very clear.

3.9 HARYANA

There are different local level library authorities for which the Act makes provision. They are designated as committees. The committees are (a) District Library Committee (b) City and Town Library Committee (c) Block Library Committee and (d) Panchayat Library Committee

3.9.1 Diastrict Library Committee (DLC)

The composition of the DLC has not been specified in the Act. It is to be constituted in accordance with the regulations framed by the State Library Authority. The functions of the DLC have been enumerated in the Act and the major ones are shown below:-

(i) Frame rules of business and procedure for carrying out the functions of the District Library subject to the approval of the State Library Authority and supervise its work;

(ii) To start branch libraries including library mobiles

(iii) To take all necessary steps to develop public library service in the district;

(iv) To employ staff for the District Library in accordance with the regulations framed by the SLA;

(v) Equip the District Library with books and hindered materials, furniture and equipments;

(vi) Provide land and buildings for libraries and

(vii) Administer the District Library Fund

3.9.2 City and Town Library Committees

There shall be a City Library Committee for each city with a population of over a lakh and a Town Library Committee for every town with a population of not more than one lakh. They are to be constituted in accordance with such rules as may be framed by the DLC concerned. The functions of a City or Town Library Committee shall, as far as may be applicable, be the same as those of the DLC, within its jurisdiction.

3.9.3 Block Library Committee

There shall be a Block Library Committee for each Block and its constitution and functions shall be such as may be laid down in the rules framed by the DLC concerned

3.9.4 Panchayat Library Committee

There shall be a Panchayat Library Committee for each Panchayat (Village) and its constitution and functions shall be such as may be laid down by the DLC concerned.

Like the Kerala Act, the Haryana Act also provides for a hierarchical pattern of several bodies for the implementation of the provisions of the Act. In this pattern, as already mentioned in the context of the Kerala Act, there is the possibility of overlapping jurisdiction for the exercise of functions by the different bodies. Anticipating this problem there is the following stipulation in section 14, sub section 4 of the Act:-

If any question arises whether a particular matter is or is not within the purview or power of the district or any other library committee, the decisions of the State Library Authority shall be final

3.10 MIZORAM

The Mizoram Act does not make provision for any local library authority to function at the local level. This may be because, the state being one of the smallest in India in terms of population (less than one million), it was thought that the State Library Council provided for in the Act would be able to supervise the development of public library service in the whole state by itself unaided by lower level bodies.

3.11 GOA

As in the case of Mizoram there are no local library authorities under the Goa Public Libraries Act also. In the original Act there was provision for committees at the district, taluk and village levels, but this provision was subsequently repealed by an amendment to the Act.

3.12 GUJARAT

The Gujarat Act stipulates a District Library Advisory Committee for each District Library and a Taluk Library Advisory Committee for each Taluk Library. These committees are constituted by the Director of Public Libraries.

3.12.1 District Library Advisory Committee (DLAC)

The composition of the DLAC is as follows:-

(i) The Collector of the district who shall be the Chairman of the Committee

(ii) One representative of the public library association of the district

(iii) One expert in library services or Library and Information Science ;

(iv) One Principal of a college in the district

(v) One Principal or Headmaster of a high school or higher secondary school in the district

(vi) One Headmaster of a primary school in the district

(vii) One representative of the public libraries run by voluntary agencies in the district;

(viii) One lady librarian in the district

(ix) The Assistant Director of Public Libraries in charge of the district;

(x) The librarian of the District Library who shall be the Secretary of the Committee.

3.12.2 Taluka Library Advisory Committee (TLAC)

The TLAC is constituted on the same lines as the DLAC except that the members are drawn from the Taluka concerned. The Mamlatdar of the taluka is the Chairman and the Librarian of the Taluka Library the Secretary of the Committee

3.12.3 Functions of DLAC and TLAC

The functions of the two committees have not been specified in the Act and are to be prescribed by the Rules to be framed under the Act. It is therefore not clear as to whether their functions will be confined to the working of the District Library and the Taluka Library concerned or will extend to the whole district or taluka. It may be mentioned in this connection that in the Haryana Act, although the District Library Committee is stated to be for the District Library, the statement of its functions shows that its jurisdiction extends to the whole district. The same is the case with the City and Town Library Committee, Block Library Committee and Panchayat Library Committee in Haryana. Similarly it can perhaps be presumed that each DLAC and TLAC in Gujarat will have the responsibility for library development in the whole district or taluka concerned.

The good representation given for professional librarians in DLAC and TLAC is a welcome feature of the Act.

3.13 ORISSA

What may be deemed as a Local Library Authority in the Orissa Act is a District Library Committee for each district. The relevant provision of the Act reads thus: (1)" The government may, by notification, constitute in the prescribed manner, a committee in each district to be called the District Library Committee to look after the management of library services in the district.

(2) The term of office of, the procedure to be followed in the discharge of its functions by, and the manner of filling casual vacancies among, members of the District Library Committee shall be such as may be prescribed"

So the constitution, powers and functions of the District Library Committee are left to be prescribed by the Rules to be framed under the Act.

3.14 SUMMARY

All the library Acts except those of Mizoram and Goa have made provision for the setting up of local level bodies vested with the responsibility of the development and provision of public library service in their respective areas. Mizoram and Goa, in excluding them from the Act, were perhaps influenced by their small size and population.

The local level bodies are named differently in the different Acts as shown below:-

Tamil Nadu:- Local Library Authority, one for the city of Chennai and one for each district.

Andhra Pradesh:- Zilla Granthalaya Samastha, one for the city of Hyderabad and one for each district

Karnataka:- Local Library Authority, one for each city having more than one lakh population (called City Library Authority) and one for each district (called District Library Authority)

Maharashtra:- District Library Committee for each district and a committee for Greater Mumbai.

West Bengal:- Local Library Authority for each district

Manipur:- District Library Authority for each district

Kerala:-District Library Council for each district and taluk Library Council for each taluk

Haryana:- District Library Committee for each district, City and Town Library Committee, Block Library Committee and Panchayat Library Committee

Mizoram:- No provision

Goa:- No provision

Gujarat:- District Library Advisory Committee for each district and Taluk Library Advisory Committee for each Taluk

Orissa:- District Library Committee

It may be seen from the above that some of the states have more than one local level body, some on a parallel pattern like one LLA for the city of Chennai and one for each district in Tamil Nadu and some on a hierarchical pattern like one DLC for each district and one TLC for each Taluk one BLC for each Block, etc. In the latter case overlapping jurisdiction for the performance of functions may arise causing confusion.

All local level library bodies except those of Kerala are

predominantly formed of members who are both nominated and ex-officio by virtue of their holding certain offices. The nomination is by the government or the Director of Libraries concerned. A few members of the bodies in some states are elected by the organizations they represent like the Legislature, the Municiapl Councils, etc.

In Kerala, however, the constitution of the District Library Council and Taluk Library Council is almost entirely by election. While the aura of the democratic process is claimed for election it is a prolonged and delaying process and has the inherent danger of political rivalry effecting its functions.

The Presidents of the authorities are ex-officio, nominated or elected and the Secretaries are ex-officio.

The representation for professional librarians are just nominal except in a few cases. This is unfortunate in view of the fact that professional expertise is an essential input for the formulation of informed and sound public library development policies and programmes and their implementation especially in the context of the impact of information technology on libraries.

4

DEPARTMENT OF PUBLIC LIBRARIES

4.1 INTRODUCTION

All State Library Acts with the exception of the Kerala Act make provision for a Department/Directorate of Public Libraries or some other unit in the government to attend to matters relating to the development of public libraries and the provision of library service to the people as envisaged in the Act. This is essential to ensure the focussed attention of the government on the effective implementation of the Act. Without it there is the possibility of library matters being relegated to a low priority and not receiving adequate and prompt attention and support at the governmental level. The department is headed by an officer designated as director in most cases.

4.2 TAMIL NADU

The Tamil Nadu Public Libraries Act, 1948, the first Act to be passed in India, lists the following powers and functions for the Director of Public Libraries:-

(a) Manage the Central library being a library constituted by the government as the Central Library or an existing government library recognized by them as the Central Library, together with the branches of such library;

(b) Superintendent and direct all matters relating to public libraries;

(c) Declare, in accordance with the rules made under the Act what libraries are eligible for aid from the government and superintendent and direct all matters relating to such libraries;

(d) Superintendent and control the work of all Local Library Authorities under the Act;

(e) Submit to the government every year a report on the working of libraries; and

(f) Perform such other duties and exercise such other powers as are imposed or conferred by the Act or the rules made there under.

4.3 ANDHRA PRADESH

All the functions listed in the Tamil Nadu Act for the director are mentioned in the Andhra Pradesh Act also and, in addition, there are the following two functions:

(i) Publish annually a bibliography of all the books published in the state in languages other than English and Sanskrit;

(ii) Arrange for centralized classification, cataloguing, inter-library loan, coordination of book selection and maintenance of copyright registry.

4.4 KARNATAKA

In the Karnataka Act the functions of the Department of Public Libraries and of the State Librarian who is its Head are listed separately.

The following functions have been listed for the department:-

a) Superintend and direct all matters relating to all public libraries;

b) Promote the establishment of public library service so as to achieve the purposes of this Act;

c) Supervise and direct all matters relating to libraries receiving aid from the state government;

d) Maintain State Registers of Libraries and of Librarians;

e) Superintend, direct and deal with the exercise of powers and the performance of duties of Local Library Authorities under this Act;

f) Ensure the proper utilization of the library funds and the library manpower of the state;

g) Perform such other functions as may be entrusted to the department by or under the provisions of this Act.

The following are the functions mentioned for the State Librarian:-

a) Function as the librarian of the State Central library;

b) Superintend, direct and deal with all matters relating to the Press and Registration of Books Act, 1867 and to the maintenance and service of the books sent under the said Act;

c) Control the appointments, postings and transfer of officers and servants in the State Library Service;

d) Generally assist the State Library Authority in performing its functions;

e) exercise such other powers and perform such other duties a may be conferred on him under the Act.

The reason and logic for the separate listing of the functions of the department and of the State Librarian who, as the Head of the Department, is responsible for carrying out the functions of the department are not clear.

4.5 MAHARASHTRA

The following are the new major functions prescribed for the Director of Libraries in the Maharashtra Act other than those included in the Acts of Tamil Nadu, Andhra Pradesh and Karnataka:-

(i) Collect and preserve old and rare books, periodicals, manuscripts and other documents of educative value in public libraries;

(ii) Organise programmes for training candidates in Library Science and conduct examinations for the candidates of recognized training courses

4.6 WEST BENGAL

The inspection of libraries and the steps to be taken to rectify defects found including the prosecution of persons responsible for any loss or injury to libraries are spelt out in the list of functions to be performed by the Director in addition to the functions of the Directior according to the earlier Acts.

4.7 MANIPUR

There are no new functions for the Director listed under this Act other than those already mentioned in the earlier Acts.

4.8 KERALA

As already pointed out there is no provision for a Department of Public Libraries and a Director in the Kerala Act. The fear that such a provision would dilute the authority of the State Library Council seems to be the main reason for this omission. This is unfortunate. The SLC is not a fully autonomous body and in many matters, it has to take the sanction of the government. A separate Department of Libraries in the government would have been helpful to ensure the prompt attention of the government to library matters and in ensuring prompt disposal of mattes referred to the government by the SLC and other bodies. The fear of any threat to the authority of the SLC if a Department of Libraries is instituted by the Act is misplaced. It is relevant to point out in this context that local bodies like Corporations, Municipalities and Panchayats which, despite being self governing and autonomous, have Directorates in the government to offer them governmental support in the effective discharge of their duties and responsibilities. The non-provision in the Kerala Act for a Department of Libraries is a serious lacuna in the Act. Libraries are at present under the large and busy

Department of Education and there is the danger of library matters being treated as relatively unimportant and not receiving prompt and adequate attention and support of the government.

4.9 HARYANA

One important new function highlighted in the Haryana Act for the Directorate of libraries is "to prepare the annual as well as short or long term plans for libraries in the State in Cooperation with the Development Department and other concerned departments"

4.10 MIZORAM

Except that on the commencement of the Act the Department of Public Libraries shall be constituted with a Director as its Head and that the Director shall be assisted by a Joint Director, a Deputy Director and other supporting staff, nothing has been mentioned in the Act regarding the functions of the Director. Obviously the functions are left to be specified by the Rules to be framed under the Act.

4.11 GOA

Goe, does not have a Department of Public Libraries. Instead it has a State Library Development Cell in the Directorate of School Education headed by a State Library Officer. The functions of the cell and the State library Officer are separately listed as in the case of the Karnataka Act. No new functions other than those already included in the other Acts are seen in the list of the functions of the cell. The list of functions allotted to the State library Officer is shown below:-

a) He shall participate in all meetings of the Council and the Committees which may be set up by the Council;
b) He shall be responsible for carrying out such of the recommendations of the Council as have been approved by the government;

c) He shall perform such other duties as may be prescribed in the regulations made by the Council;

d) Subject to any rules made by the government and State Library Development Cell, he shall

   (i) be responsible for implementing the programme of work for the year as approved by the Council;

   (ii) administer the grant-in-aid scheme for aided libraries;

   (iii) decide where district and other libraries in the state are to be set up and approve the constitution and bye-laws of a public library;

   (iv) absorb; if necessary, an aided library into the public library system of the state.

These functions clearly indicate the relationship between the State Library Officer and the State library Council. The role envisaged by the Act for the State Library Officer is primarily that of carrying out the decisions of the Council.

4.12 GUJARAT

Even before the adoption of the Act there was a Director of Libraries in Gujarat. The Act states in Chapter III – Director of Public Libraries, that for the purpose if this Act the existing Director of Libraries shall be the Director of Public Libraries".

Apart from the functions as in the other Acts, the Director of Public Libraries is empowered to constitute for each District Library and each Taluka Library a District Library Advisory Committee and a Taluka Library Advisory Committee respectively. This is mentioned not in the list of the functions of the Director, but in the context of the establishment of District Central Library and Taluka Central Library.

4.13 ORISSA

Although the Orissa Act provides for the constitution of a separate Directorate of Libraries headed by a Director, it is stated that the Director of Culture shall be the Director of Libraries. The statutory merging of the two posts will create problems later on when a separation of the two posts is found necessary as it will call for an amendment of the Act. If for any administrative or other reasons the merging of the posts was considered necessary, it could have been accomplished by an executive order. It must also be mentioned that a combined Director of Culture and public Libraries will find it difficult to do justice to both and it would have been better if the Department of Public Libraries had its own separate and full time Director from the beginning of the operation of the Act.

The functions of the Director are concisely stated as follows:-

a) Be responsible to implement the plans, policies, schemes and programmes of the Library Authority; and

b) Subject to the provisions of this Act, exercise such powers and perform such functions as may be prescribed (by the rules framed under the Act)

4.14 SUMMARY

Tamil Nadu, Andhra Pradesh, Karnataka, Maharashtra, West Bengal, Manipur, Haryana, Mizoram, Gujarat and Orissa have full fledged departments each with a Head and other officers and staff. Goa has a State Library Development Cell in the Directorate of School Education of the government. As already stated Kerala does not have provision in its Act for a Department of Public Libraries.

The Heads of Departments of Public Libraries are designated as directors except in Karnataka. In Karnataka the designation preferred is State Librarian. This designation is more apt and precise for the Head of a department dealing with libraries and helps to enhance the prestige and image of librarians as a professional group.

Qualifications have not been prescribed in the various Acts for the directors of libraries except in the Karnataka and Maharashtra Acts with the result that most of the directors do not possess professional qualifications. If a professional librarian happens to occupy the office it is by chance. However, in the Karnataka and Maharashtra Acts, the requisite qualifications are indicated. The Karnataka Act stipulates that the State Librarian who heads the department should possess prescribed qualifications to practice the library profession or, in other words, that he should be a professionally qualified librarian. This is a highly welcome acceptance of the fact that librarianship, being a field calling for the application of specialized knowledge and skills, the Department of Public Libraries should be headed by a person who has acquired such knowledge and skills in order to be able to direct the development of a public library system on scientific lines and streamline its services for the maximum benefit of the society it seeks to serve.

The corresponding clause of the Maharashtra Act states that the state government shall appoint a whole time officer having the prescribed qualifications to be the Director of Libraries. Although the intention of this clause obviously is that the Director should be a professional librarian, its wording, unlike as in the Karnataka Act, does not make this intention explicit and is liable to be interpreted to include non-librarians also to be considered for the office. However, the directors appointed so far in Maharashtra under the Act are known to be professional librarians.

The powers and functions of the Director/ Department of public libraries delineated in the different Acts are more or less similar with only some marginal differences.

5

STATE LIBRARY SERVICE (PERSONNEL)

5.1 INTRODUCTION

The successful implementation of a Public Libraries Act and the development of a sound public library system that is capable of providing adequate library service to the people would, to a very great extent, depend on the availability of competent and motivated personnel to work in the public library field and in individual libraries. The question of manpower to operate the public library system envisaged by an Act should therefore receive proper attention in the Act. But this has not been dealt with in a satisfactory manner in the Acts passed so far in India except in a few of them, viz those of Andhra Pradesh, Karnataka, Maharshtra and Haryana. In the other Acts the treatment of this important matter is rather casual. An attempt is made below to examine the provision relating to this in the different Acts.

5.2 TAMIL NADU

The only mention regarding staff made in the Act is under clause (9) "Powers of Local library Authorities where in it is stated that a Local Library Authority can employ from time to time such staff as it considers necessary for libraries.

5.3 ANDHRA PRADESH

Section 19A of the Andhra Pradesh Act pertaining to library service states thus:- "notwithstanding anything in this Act, the Government may, by notification, constitute a Library Service for the Zilla Granthalaya Samasthas in the state and appoint to that service such categories of librarians as may be prescribed (by the rules passed under the Act).

In section (25) of the Act which enumerates the subjects to be covered by the rules to be prescribed, the following clauses relating to staff are included as (e) and (f)

(e)The employment of necessary staff for the public libraries maintained by a Zilla Granthalaya Samastha and for regulating the classification, methods of recruitment, pay and allowances, discipline and conduct and other conditions of service of the staff employed in such libraries;

(f) The classification, methods of recruitment, pay and allowances, discipline and conduct and other conditions of service of the members of the Library Service constituted under section 19-A.

It would appear from the above clauses that there are two categories of staff in the libraries functioning under a Zilla Granthalaya Samastha – members of the Library Service constituted under section 19-A of the Act and others. The reason for this differentiation are not available and so no detailed comments on it are possible. However on the face it, it seems to be an unnecessary differentiation unless it is that the posts in the State Library Service are meant to comprise professional staff and the other category is meant for semi or non-professional staff.

Presumably the salary of the library staff will be paid by the government from the state exchequer. If so it will rid the State Library Fund of the liability of paying staff salary and free the Fund entirely for utilization for meeting expenditure on items like library buildings, purchase of books, furniture and equipments and modernizing library organization and services with the help of information technology.

5.4 KARNATAKA

Like the Andhra Pradesh Act, the Karnataka Act also makes provision for the creation of a State Library Service, but in a more explicit manner Section 15 of the Act relating to this is reproduced below:-

Section 15

(1) Notwithstanding anything contained in any other law, all posts in the Department of Public Libraries, the State Central library and every Local Library Authority shall be filled by appointment of persons who belong to the State Library Service;

(2) The Karnataka State Library Service shall consist of the State Librarian, Chief Librarians of cities and districts and such other classes and categories of posts as the state government may, from time to time, determine. All members of the said service shall be government servants, and their recruitment and conditions of service shall, subject to the provisions of Article 309 of the constitution, be regulated by such rules as may be prescribed.

(3) The salary, allowances, gratuity, pension and other benefits of the members of the Karnataka State library Service shall be met from the Consolidated Fund of the State.

These provisions in the Karnataka Act are more comprehensive and precise than the corresponding provisions in the Andhra Pradesh Act.

5.5 MAHARASHTRA

An exactly similar provisions as in the Karnataka Act has been made in the Maharashtra Act also for the State library Service (Section 10 of the Act)

5.6 WEST BENGAL

There is no provision in the West Bengal Act for the establishment of a Stat Library Service. Among the duties assigned to the Director of Libraries who is appointed by the government is the management of the Central library together with its branches. It can therefore be presumed that personnel of the Central Library and its branch libraries working under the Director would also be government appointees and hence government servants (Sections 3 and 6 (b) of the Act). Also section 16 of the Act provides for the appointment by the government of a District Library officer and a District Librarian Presumably they are also government servants with their salary paid by the government.

5.7 MANIPUR

There is no State Library Service in Manipur according to the Act

5.8 KERALA

The Kerala Act has deliberately kept professional librarians at a distance for inexplicable reasons. This is evident from the fact that it makes no provision for a Directorate of Libraries and for representation for professional librarians on the various authorities set up by it except for one nominated librarian on the State library Council. He need not necessarily be a professional librarian although the person so far nominated under this provision has been a professional librarian. But insofar as all persons working in the thousands of public libraries in the state are called librarians the possibility of a non-professional being nominated to the SLC cannot be ruled out. In this situation the institution of a State Library Service was a totally incomprehensible or unpalatable proposition for the framers of the Act and so it causes no surprise that there is no provision for it in the Act. The only references to library personnel made in the Act are in Section 17 and 25 pertaining to the Powers and functions of the District Library Council and Taluka Library

Council respectively. Sub-section (b) of both sections states thus; "To appoint and control such officers and servants as may be necessary for the efficient performance of its duties and functions under the Act and the rules made there under".

5.9 HARYANA

There is provision in the Haryana Act for the state government to create cadres for public library employees similar to those of employees of government departments and lay down the qualifications and other terms and conditions of service for those cadres (section 18(1), Section 18(2) states that within a year of its first constitution, the State Library Authority shall frame service rules for the various categories of library employees.

5.10 MIZORAM

Section 10 and 11 of the Act deal with staff. Section 10 says that the appointment of officers and the supporting staff shall be made by the government in accordance with the provisions of the rules made under the Act. According to section 11 the existing library staff, for the purpose of absorption (into the government cadre) shall have to obtain necessary qualifications within a time limit as may be prescribed.

5.11 GOA

In the original Act there was provision for the creation of cadres of public library employees as per section 16, but this section along with some other sections were subsequently deleted through an amendment. So as it is, there is no provision for a State Library Service

5.12 GUJARAT

There is no provision for a State library Service in this Act. Nothing has been mentioned in the Act regarding the personnel to be employed for running the libraries and payment of their salary.

5.13 ORISSA

In the Orissa Act also provision for State Library Service is absent.

5.14 SUMMARY

Library legislation is not an end in itself. It is only a means for establishing a sound public library system for providing comprehensive library service to one and all. To achieve this objective of library legislation certain essential pre requisites have to be satisfied. The availability of qualified, competent and motivated staff is one such pre-requisite. Therefore a library Act should keep in view this important requirement and make provision for it. The position in this respect is not uniform in the different Acts. While the Acts of Andhra Pradesh, Karnataka, Maharashtra and Haryana stipulate the institution of a State Library Service comprising different categories of staff, the others authorize one or another of the authorities constituted under the Act to appoint the requisite staff. The advantages of the former provision are (1) that members of a statutorily established State library Service would be government servants with status and salary on a par with their counterparts in other departments and (2) that, freed from the responsibility of meeting expenditure on staff salary which would be a substantial amount, the entire State Library Fund raised under the provisions of the Act would be available for the development of libraries and their services. In the latter case the State library Fund would be substantially depleted because of the salary commitment and what is left after payment of salary would be hardly adequate for public library development and services on desirable lines.

6

LIBRARY FINANCE

6.1 INTRODUCTION

A major objective of library legislation is to put the public library movement on a stable financial footing. This is often cited as one of the reasons in favour of library legislation. Financial bottleneck is very often the most serious constraint hindering sound library development. It is therefore incumbent on a library Act to make provision for the raising of adequate funds to be utilized for library purposes. The Indian Acts do not adopt a uniform method for raising funds. While some of the Acts have stuck to the traditional method of levying cess supplemented by other sources of funds, some have totally depended on sources other than cess, primarily government grants. The practices in this regard adopted by the twelve Acts so far passed in India will be examined in this chapter.

6.2 TAMIL NADU

In the Tamil Nadu Act there is provision for the levy of a cess by the Local library Authority concerned at the rate of six paise for every whole rupee in the property tax or house tax levied by the local body of the area concerned. The Local library Authority may, with the previous sanction of the government and shall, if so directed by them, increase the rate of cess. The cess is to be collected by the local body or local bodies concerned (Corporation,

Municipality or Panchayat) within whose jurisdiction the LLA's area falls, and credited to the Library Fund of the LLA.

The LLA Fund shall consist of the following

(a) The cess collected by the local bodies

(b) Contributions, gifts and income from endowments, if any made for the benefit of public libraries

(c) Special grant which the government may make for any specific purpose connected with libraries.

(d) Fees, fines and other amounts collected by the LLA under any rules or regulations made under the Act; and

(e) The mandatory contribution of the government to the Library Fund of every LLA other than the LLA for the city of Chennai of a sum not less than the cess collected from the area of the LLA

The rationale of empowering the LLA to levy the cess and increase it with the prior sanction of the government is not clear. If one LLA increases the cess it will become necessary for the other LLAs also to increase it, whether they want it or not, for the sake of a uniform cess throughout the state. From this point of view, it would have been better if the government was the authority to fix the rate of cess for the whole state and alter it when necessary.

6.3 ANDHRA PRADESH

The provision for library finance in the Andhra Pradesh Act is exactly similar to that in the Tamil Nadu Act. There is a library cess levied by the Zilla Grandthalaya Samastha the counter part in A.P of the Local Library Authority in Tamil Nadu. But the rate of cess in A.P is 4 paise per rupee of the property/house tax instead of 6 paise as in Tamil Nadu. Also no quantum has been fixed for the statutory contribution by the government to the Library Fund of the ZGS. What is stated in the relevant section is "Grants released from time to time". This is different from the provision in the Tamil

Nadu Act where the government contribution is fixed as not less than the total cess collected.

The comments made regarding the rationale of authorizing the LLAs in the Tamil Nadu Act to levy or increase the cess hold good in this case also

6.4 KARNATAKA

Different patterns of cess are proscribed in the Karnataka Act for City Library Authorities and District Library Authorities. Section 30 of the Act relating to Library cess is quoted below:-

"(30)(1) With effect from the date of commencement of the Act:-

(a) A library cess in the form of a surcharge on –

(i) Tax on lands and buildings;

(ii) Tax on entry of goods into the area for consumption, use or sale therein!

(iii) Tax on vehicles;

(iv) Tax on professions, trades, callings and employment shall be levied in the area within the jurisdiction of every City Library Authority at the rate of three paise 2 for every rupee of the taxes so levied.

(b) A library cess in the form of a surcharge on tax on lands and buildings shall be levied in the area within the jurisdiction of every District Library Authority at the rate of three paise 3 of every rupee of the tax so levied.

As in the case of the Tamil Nadu and Andhra Pradesh Acts, the Local library Authorities of Karnataka also have been empowered by the Act to increase the cess with the previous sanction of the government, but a ceiling of 6 paise has been fixed for the increase. The comments offered in respect of the Tamil Nadu and Andhra Pradesh provisions in this regard are valid in this case also.

The cess is to be collected by the Local bodies concerned,

but they can retain ten percent of the amount collected as collection charges

1.The tax on entry of goods has now been abolished by the government and it is learnt that in lieu of the cess on this tax, the government is paying a compensation to the City Library Authority.

2 & 3 The cess has reportedly been raised now from 3 paise to 5 paise

The cess base for the City Library Authorities in Karnataka is much wider than in Tamil Nadu and Andhra Pradesh and this would make them financially more resourceful. However, the cess for the District Library Authorities is confined to land and building tax alone. But, perhaps as a compensation, each DLA is eligible for a government grant of an amount equal to three percent of the land revenue collected from the district. It is not mentioned that the CLAs are eligible for this grant.

Each CLA and DLA has a City Library Fund or a District Library Fund comprising the following:-

(a) Ninety percent of the cess collected by the Local Body;

(b) Government grant (only in the case of DLA)

(c) Contributions, gifts and income from endowments made to the Library Authority for the benefit of public libraries;

(d) Grants which the central government or state government may make (for specific purposes);

(e) Funds and other amounts collected by the LLA under rules or bye-laws made under the Act.

The Act also makes provision in section 33 for a State Library Fund to which the following shall be credited:-

(a) The grants made by the state government to the State Library Authority to perform the duties entrusted to it;

(b) grants which the Central Government may make;

(c) contributions and gifts made to the State Library Authority;

and

(d) funds and other amounts collected by the SLA under the rules and bye-laws made under the Act

The financial provisions of the Karnataka Act are quite liberal and are sure to yield substantial resources to promote the objectives of the Act. The happy combination of the provisions for library cess, government grant and payment of salaries to the staff of the public library system from the consolidated fund of the state government is a unique and healthy feature of this Act.

6.5 MAHARASHTRA

Maharashtra was the fourth state to pass library legislation and the first one to deviate from the practice of levying library cess. The relevant section 18 of the Act states as follows:-

(1) The state government shall constitute a Fund called the State library Fund.

(2) The Library Fund shall consist of :-

 (a) contribution made by the state government under section 20 (According to section 20, state government shall contribute to the Library Fund a sum not less than twenty five lakhs of rupees);

 (b) any special grants given by the state government under section 21 (According to section 21, the state government may make special grants to the Library Fund);

 (c) any grants given by the Government of India to the state government for the development of public libraries; and

 (d) any contributions or gifts made by the public for the development of public libraries.

The library finance that would be made available according to these provisions would appear to be very paltry and totally inadequate for public library development. The firm commitment of the government is only rupees twenty five lakhs per annum. It can be more, but that is at the discretion of the government. The sanctioning of special grants according to section 21 is an enabling provision. But in real practice the government is reported to have been very generous in the matter of sanctioning grants and, reportedly there have been no serious financial constraints experienced so far for library development. It should be remembered in this context that the Act provides for the establishment of s State library Service and the employees belonging to this service are directly paid by the government. However , it would have been better if the Act had made certain the firm availability of adequate funds without leaving it to the changing perceptions of the governments in power from time to time. As it is library matters being relegated to a low priority if the government so chooses resulting in the slashing of funds cannot be ruled out.

6.6 WEST BENGAL

In the West Bengal Act also there is no provision for a library cess and public libraries are almost totally dependent on government grants for their development. The quantum of government grant has not been indicated. The relevant section 17 is reproduced below:-

"(1) Every Local library Authority shall maintain a Library Fund out of which payments under this Act shall be met;

(2) There shall be credited to the Fund the following sums:-

(a) contributions, gifts and income from endowments made to the Local library Authority for the benefit of public libraries;

(b) grants which the government may make for the general maintenance or for any specific purpose connected with libraries or social education.

(c) any amount collected by the Local Library Authority under any rules or regulations made under this Act".

This section, like the corresponding section in the Maharashtra Act has the inherent weakness that it does not guarantee the availability of a specified quantum of funds for public library development. But experience so far has been that like the Maharashata government the West Bengal government also has a generous policy in this regard and has not given room for any serious complaints of dearth of funds

6.7 MANIPUR

The Manipur Act has identical provisions as in the West Bengal Act regarding library finance.

6.8 KERALA

The Kerala Act although passed after the passing of the Act of Maharashtra, West Bengal and Manipur, which made no provision for library cess, has opted for library cess. Sections 30,31 and 48 of the Act relate to Finance. The relevant clauses of these sections are given below:-

30(1) The government may make every year a grant to the State Library Council of a sum which shall not be more than one percent of the amount allotted for education in the state budget for the year, taking into account the progammes and projects of the State Library council for that year.

31 State Library Fund

The following sums shall be credited to the State Library Fund:-

(a) grant that the state government or the central government may make to the State library Council;

(b) contributions and gifts made to the State library Council by any other person, body or authority

(c) * * *

(d) cess collected under section 48

Section 48 pertains to the levy of a Library Cess by the SLC in the form of a surcharge on the building/property tax levied by the local bodies (Panchayats, Municipalities and Corporations), at the rate of 5 paise in the whole rupee in the building/property tax, so levied. The cess levied is to be collected by the local body concerned in its area and paid to the State library Council.

The main components of the State Library Fund are annual state government grant and the cess. The stipulation that the government grant should not exceed one percent of the annual educational budget of the state is a curious and retrograde measure. It should have been "not less than" instead of "not more than" as was suggested in an earlier bill introduced in the Assembly. Nevertheless, the linking of government grant to the education budget is a recognition of the educational role of the library and is to be welcomed.

6.9 HARYANA

In the Haryana Act also there is s section on Library cess (section 20) which states that every Local Body in a district may levy in its area library cess in the form of a surcharge on property tax and house tax at such rate as the government may decide from time to time.

There are three types of library fund viz (a) The State Library Fund (b) The District Library Fund and (c) The City or Town or Block or Village Library Fund.

Each of these funds is made up of the following:-

State library Fund

(a) Amount provided by the state government for development, improvement and maintenance of library service in the state;

(b) Contribution received from the Central government;

(c) Any special grant that the Central or State Government may make for any special purposes;

(d) the amount received under the Library Rules of the State Central Library;

(e) any amount received as gift, contribution or endowment for the development of public libraries in the state

District Library Fund

(a) The amount transferred to it from the State Library Fund, the state contribution to the District Library Fund being in no case less than the total amount of cess collected in the district (what is meant by this clause seems to be that the state should make an annual grants of an amount not less than the amount collected from the cess to the District Library Fund and that the cess amount as such is not credited to it)
(b) any special grant that the State library Authority may make to the District Library Committee for any specific purpose;
(c) the amount collected under the rules of the District library;
(d) any amount received as gift, contribution or endowment for the development of the libraries in the district;
(e) any loan that the District Library Committee may raise.

City, Town, Block or Village Library Fund

(a) The amount raised as library cess in the City, town, block or village;
(b) any special grant that the District Library Committee may make for any purpose;
(c) the amount collected under the town or block library rules.;
(d) any amount received as gift, contribution or endowment for the development of the library in the city, town, block or village;
(e) any loan that a City Library Committee may raise.

The establishment of four different library funds is a special feature of the Haryana Act. The amount of cess collected from the area of each City, Town, Block or Village is directly credited to the City, Town, Block or Village library Fund concerned and is available for exclusive utilisation for the development of public libraries in that area. The cess amount has not been specified in the Act; but is to be determined by the government from time to time. This gives freedom to the government to fix and also alter it as found necessary without having to go in for an amendment of the Act.

6.10 MIZORAM

There is no cess proposed in the Mizoram Act; nor is any other source of finance indicated. Presumably the entire expenditure on the public library system comprising the State Library, District Libraries and Sub-divisional libraries is to be directly met by the government. There is also provision for the payment of grant-in-aid by the government to recognized village libraries.

6.11 GOA

The Goa Act makes provision for library cess. The relevant section 18 of the Act reads thus:-

(1) The government shall levy a cess in the form of a surcharge on the excise duty payable under Goa Excise Duty Act, 1964 at the rate of fifty paise per proof litre of the Indian Made Foreign Liquor and at the rate of fifty paise per bulk litre of beer;

(2) the cess levied shall be collected to be utilized for the purpose of implementation of this Act by the government.

Section 19 of the Act is titled "Public Library Finance" and it states as follows:-

"The government shall frame the annual budget of Public Libraries in the state within the broad frame work of the plan and shall provide one percent of the education budget for promoting the service of public libraries in the state".

There is yet another section relating to finance captioned as Library Fund (section 17) and it is quoted below:-

"(1) The government shall institute a fund called library Fund

(2) The Library Fund shall consist of:-

(a) contribution made by the government;

(b) any grants given by the Government of India to the state government for the development of public libraries;

(c) any special grant given by the government

(d) any contribution of gifts made by the public for the development of public libraries

There are some ambiguities in these sections relating to finance such as the following:-

(1) It is not stated as to who will operate the Library Fund;

(2) The Cess is not shown as a component of the Library Fund;

(3) Whether the government contribution of an amount of grant equal to one percent of the state education budget shown in section 19 is inclusive or exclusive or the amount of library cess.

The intention seems to be

1) the cess to be collected by the government and credited to government account;

2) the government contribution to the Library Fund to be inclusive of the amount of cess

3) the annual budget of Public libraries mentioned in section 19 to be on the basis of the Library Fund as per section 17.

The cess proposed as a surcharge on the excise duty on IMFL is a novel idea and is likely to yield a sizable amount ensuring adequate financial resources for public library development if the whole amount is made available to be utilized for the purpose by way of regular or special government grants.

6.12 GUJARAT

There is no library cess prescribed Section 17 and 18 of the

Act deal with finance for public libraries. The following are the sub-sections of section 17:-

(1) The Director of Public Libraries shall prepare, every year the annual budget proposed for the Directorate of Public Libraries for plan and non-plan expenditure and submit it to the government

(2) The Director shall utilize the grant so sanctioned to defray expenditure for the following purposes only:-

(a) to carry out the purpose of this Act and rules;

(b) to establish new public libraries in the state;

(c) maintenance and development of public libraries in the state;

(d) payment of grant-in-aid and other financial aids to the public libraries, public library associations and recognized institutions conducting training courses in Library and Information Science; and

(e) such other purposes as may be prescribed for Section 18 has the following sub-sections:-

(1) There shall be a fund to be called the State Library Development Fund for modernisation and development of public libraries in the state

(2) The State Library Development Fund shall consist of:-

(a) grant received from the state government other than the grant specified in sub-section (2) of section 17 above;

(b) any contribution or special grants from central government for modernization and development of public libraries;

(c) all money received by way of contributions or gifts made by the public or any other agency for modernization and development of public libraries.

(3) The money in the State library Development Fund shall be utilized by the Director in consultation with the State Library Council to defray expenditure for the following purposes:-

(a) modernization and development of public libraries in the state;

(b) payment of allowances to the members of the Council

(c) such other purposes as may be prescribed.

The quantum of finance available has not been indicated and there is no assurance of a stable provision of finance from year to year. There is special stress in this Act on the modernization of public libraries as in no other Act.

6.12 ORISSA

In Orissa also, as in Gujarat there is no cess and the main source of finance is government grant. Section 12 of the Act relating to Orissa Public Library Fund indicates the following sources of finance:-

(1) The Library Authority shall have a fund called the Orissa Public Library Fund to which shall be credited:-

(a) grants made by government, Raja Ram Mohan Roy Library Foundation (channel for Central Government grant) and other sources for the purpose of library services in the state;

(b) contributions donations and gifts made by any person;

(c) endowments, donations and bequests as may be made by any non-resident Indian or any Corporate house;

(d) interest from fixed deposits and receipts from any other source.

The whole of the fund is earmarked for utilization for carrying out the purposes of the Act.

The absence of a library cess and the non-specification of the quantum of government grants are factors that might deprive the Public Library Fund of a steady and stable source of income as in the case of Gujarat. The other sources of income indicated in the Act like endowments. donations, etc are not dependable in the Indian situation.

6.13 SUMMARY

Six out of the twelve states which have so far passed library legislation have prescribed a library cess as a main source of revenue for public library development. They are Tamil Nadu, Andhra Pradesh, Karnataka, Kerala, Haryana and Goa. The other six states viz Maharashtra, West Bengal, Manipur, Mizoram, Gujarat and Orissa have opted not to levy a cess.

The cess levied is in the form of a surcharge on building and property tax in the case of Tamil Nadu, Andhra Pradesh, Haryana and Kerala.

In Karnataka, the levy of library cess goes beyond buildings and property tax and includes taxes on vehicles, professions, trades callings and employments. In Goa the cess is on the excise duty payable on Indian made foreign liquor and beer and excludes building and property tax.

The main advantage of levying a cess is that it yields a sizable amount which steadily increases from year to year and combined with the other sources of income indicated in the various Acts, assures reasonably adequate financial resources for public library development.

As regards the non- cess levying states, their main financial stay is the state government grants. However, the quantum of the government grant has not been specified in some cases and this stands in the way of any long term public library development plan being formulated and implemented. In Kerala and Goa the annual government grant is linked to the state education budget. This is a welcome measure because, implied in it is the recognition by the authorities, of the educational role of public libraries. In Kerala it is not more than one percent of the state education budget and in Goa it is one percent of the education budget and this is bound to go up from year to year corresponding to the increase in the education budget. In some of the cess levying states it is a matching grant, ie a grant equal to the amount of cess collected.

Among the list of sources of finance given in the various Acts, contribution by the central government and donations and endowments are also included. There is provision for a central government library grant to all states channelled through the Raja Rammohan Roy Library Foundation. This is, usually, not a very substantial amount. In the Indian situation donations and endowments will also be scarce. So public libraries are by and large dependent on state government support whether it is by way of cess, grant or both.

7

LIBRARY STRUCTURE

7.1 INTRODUCTION

One of the objectives of Library Legislation is to provide guidelines for the establishment of a public library system or structure, The structure will consist of different libraries each functioning as an organic part of the structure and not in isolation as an independent unit. In the prevailing context of the inadequacy of the book resources of individual libraries due to a variety of reasons, especially the escalating cost of books, journals and other sources of information, a mutually dependent structure of libraries is essential. The holdings of all the libraries forming part of the structure will constitute a common pool of books that can be shared in common by all. A member of one library should have access to this common pool if the material he needs is not available in the library to which he has immediate access. In modern library parlance this is called resource sharing. The revolutionary developments in information technology have made the inter-linking of libraries of comparable nature and functions possible for the benefit of the people whom they seek to serve. If a person has access only to his library and is solely dependent on it for his library needs, a good percentage of his needs will remain unmet. Public library legislation should take into account this fact and make provision for the establishment of a library system rather than of just individual libraries functioning in isolation from each other. The position in this regard in the twelve Library Acts in India is proposed to be examined in this chapter.

7.2 TAMIL NADU

Nothing has been mentioned in the Act about the public library structure intended to be set up under the Act. But piecing together the provisions in the Act at various places, some idea can be formed of the intended structure.

Section 2 of the Act on Definitions defines Aided Library and Public Library. Aided Library is defined as a library declared by the Director of Libraries to be eligible for aid from the government. The definition of a Public Library is that it is a library established or maintained by a Local library Authority, and includes the branches and delivery stations of such library. It can be inferred from this that the Act envisages two types of libraries – grant-in-aid libraries established and run by private agencies and public libraries with their branches run by Local Library Authorities

Among the duties of the Director of Public Libraries in Section4, the first item mentioned is management of "the Central library, being a library constituted by the government as the Central Library or an existing government library recognized by them as the Central Library, together with the branches of such library". Obviously the library meant here is the State Central library. So a State Central Library with branches directly under the control of the Director is also envisaged by the Act.

From section 9, sub-section (a), (b) and (c), it can be seen that the LLAs (City Library Authority for Chennai and District Library Authority for each district) are empowered to provide land and buildings for libraries, employ staff for running them and equip them with books and other information sources, fittings and furniture.

From the above it can be concluded that the intention is to set up the following types of public libraries within the ambit of the Act:-

(1) A State Central Library with branch libraries under the direct management of the Director of Public Libraries;

(2) A City Central Library for the City of Chennai with branch libraries under the control of the City Library Authority for Chennai;

(3) A District Central Library with branches in each district under the control of the District Library Authority concerned;

(4) Grant-in-aid libraries established and run by private agencies which are recognized to be eligible for grant by the Director of Libraries.

There is obviously linkage between the State Central library and its branches, the City Central library and its branches and each District Central library and its branches. Each of these can be regarded as a library system. But the relationship between these three systems and also that between them and the grant-in-aid libraries has not been specified.

In this connection section 8 of the Act relating to the schemes to be submitted by Local Library Authorities is perhaps relevant. According to this section each Local Library Authority is to prepare a scheme for establishing libraries and spreading library service within in its area and submit it to the Director. The Director can accept or alter it or substitute it by a new scheme.

The linkage between the State Central Library and its branches, the City Central library and its branches, each District Central Library and its branches and the grant-in-aid libraries and all of them constituting a State Library System can be indicated in the schemes which the Director of Libraries has been given the authority to coordinate.

7.3 ANDHRA PRADESH

There are four types of libraries mentioned and defined in section 2 of the Act on Definitions. They are (i) aided library (ii) Public library (iii) State Central Library and (iv) State Regional Library.

Aided library is a library declared by the Director of Libraries to be eligible for aid either from the government or from the Library Fund in accordance with the Rules made under the Act.

Public Library means

(a) A library established or maintained by a Zilla Granthalaya Samastha including the branches and delivery stations of such a library;

(b) a library established and maintained by the government and declared open to the public;

(c) a library established and maintained by any local body or co-operative society and thrown open to the public; and

(d) an aided library.

State Central Library is defined as a library established by the government as the State Central Library.

State Regional Library is also defined as a library established by the government as a State Regional Library.

One of the stated objectives of the Andhra Pradesh Granthalaya Samastha, the state level apex body created for the development of Public Libraries in the state listed under section 4 of the Act, is "To establish, equip, maintain and develop an integrated, comprehensive and efficient library service in the state. This means that the intention of the Act is to develop a well integrated public library system for the state. There is no explicit mention of such a system and a description of its components in the Act. But it is, evidently, keeping this in view that among the duties of the Department of Public libraries "arrangement for centralized classification, cataloguing, inter-library loan and coordination of book selection" is included (section 8(h).

The responsibility for the establishment and development of libraries in each district is vested in the Zilla Granthalaya Samastha concerned and in the city of Hyderabad it is vested in the Hyderabad City Granthalaya Samastha. There is no mention of a City Central library for Hyderabad or a District Central library for each district, but there is an oblique reference to them in section 8A (1) where it is stated that the government may, at any time, create such number of posts of librarians for the City Central Library, Hyderabad and for the District Central libraries, as they may consider necessary, for carrying out the purposes of this Act.

The following are the types of libraries envisaged by the Act

1. State Central library and its branches functioning directly under the government (Section 2 Definitions, item 11 and section 8(a)
2. State Regional Library directly under the government (Definitions, item 11)

   It is not made clear in the Act how many such libraries will be established and where they will be located.
3. City Central library, Hyderabad and District Central libraries in the districts including branches and delivery stations (section 8A).
4. Libraries established and maintained by the government and declared open to the public (Item 9(b) of Definitions)
5. Libraries established and maintained by local bodies and declared open to the public (Item 9(c) of Definitions)
6. Aided libraries (Item 1 of definitions and section 8(e)

Apart from the obvious linkage of the State Central Library with their branch libraries and the linkage of the City Central library, Hyderabad and each District Central library with their respective branch libraries and delivery stations, no integrating connection between the major libraries to constitute a well formed public library structure has been presented by the Act.

As in the Tamil Nadu Act there is provision in this Act also for every Zilla Granthalaya Samastha to prepare a scheme for establishing libraries and spreading library service in its area. Perhaps this scheme is expected to spell out the details of a public library structure for each district and based on the schemes submitted by all Samasthas the Andhra Pradesh Granthalaya Parishad is expected to give shape to an integrated public library structure for the whole state.

7.4 KARNATAKA

The Karnataka Act is more clear than the Tamil Nadu and Andhra Pradesh Library Acts about the public library structure to be developed in the area of jurisdiction of each Local Library Authority. Section 27 of the Act relates to Library Development Plan and spells out the details of the procedure to finalize and implement it. Each Local library Authority is authorized to prepare a Local library Development Plan. The relevant features of the Plan will be given wide publicity and it will be forwarded to the State Librarian who, along with his comments, will send it to the Government and the government, in consultation with the State Library Authority, if necessary, is to finalize it. So, in the preparation of the Local Library Development Plan and its finalization, the LLA, the State Librarian, the State Library Authority and the state government are involved. Once the plan is given final shape by the government, the State Librarian shall issue an order called the Local Library Order specifying the Central library and the branch libraries including branches to be located in educational institutions, prisons and hospitals and the service stations which shall be established and maintained by the LLA.

This gives a picture of the library structure to be developed in the area of each LLA which will be as shown below:-

1. A District Central Library in each district and a City Central Library in each city where there is a City Library Authority.
2. Branch libraries of the above libraries including branches to be located in educational institutions, prisons and hospitals as found necessary

3. Service stations of the district central libraries and the branch libraries intended to make library service within the easy reach of the people.

Branches of the Central Library in educational institutions, prisons and hospitals is a novel feature of this Act and is reflective of the responsibility of a public library to serve all people of its community.

The state government being the authority to approve and give final shape to each Local Library Development Plan, they can ensure a certain degree of uniformity of all such plans so that the state, as a whole, will have a uniform pattern of public library structure which can facilitate the mutual linkage of the different libraries and their integrated functioning.

Section 36 of the Act describes the Karnataka State Central library and its various sections and functions in detail. It is headed by the State Librarian who is also the Head of the Department of Pubic Libraries. It is a government library having the following sections vested with the responsibility for the functions indicated by the name of each section:-

(i) A State Bureau of copy right collections;

(ii) A State Library for the Blind;

(iii) A State Bureau of Inter-Library Loan;

(iv) A State Bibliographical Bureau;

(v) A State Bureau of Technical Service; and

(vi) Such other sections as may be prescribed (by the Rules framed under the Act)

No organizational or administrative link has been indicated in the Act between the Central Library and other libraries, but the role of implementing schemes of inter-library loan between the libraries in the state and centralized classification and cataloguing work for all the libraries is assigned to it. So it is expected to perform a leadership role vis a vis the other libraries of the state.

7.5 MAHARASHTRA

In section 2 of the Act on Definitions, Public Library is defined as

a) A library established and maintained by the state government for the use of the public;

b) A library recognized by the Director for the purpose of grant-in-aid from the Library Fund; and

c) Any other library which the state government, by notification in the official gazette declare to be a public library for the purpose of this Act.

Section 11 of the Act relating to the establishment and maintenance of public libraries states that the government may establish a State Central library for the whole state and a Divisional library for every division and also establish public libraries at places where a genuine need is felt for them and no suitable agencies can be found to start them.

All libraries so established shall be maintained, organized and developed by the state government through the Department of Libraries.

In addition, the Director of Libraries is empowered in Section 9 of the Act to recognize libraries for the purpose of grant-in-aid from the Library Fund and sanction and disburse grants to them. Such libraries also belong to the category of public libraries. So the libraries that come within the ambit of the Act are:-

1) The State Central library;
2) Divisional libraries, one for each Division;
3) Other libraries that the government may establish at other places; and
4) Grant-in-aid libraries

It is not mentioned whether they constitute a library system in the sense of the libraries being linked to each other

7.6 WEST BENGAL

Section 5 of the Act refers to a Central library (Presumably the State Central library) which shall, in addition to running a library and a reading room, perform such other functions as may be entrusted to it from time to time by the government or any other officer authorized by the government in that behalf. According to section 6(b), it is the responsibility of the Director of Libraries to "manage the Central Library together with the branches of such library and shall superintend and direct all matters relating to the Central Library"

It is seen from this that the Central Library may have branch libraries functioning under it.

It is the responsibility of the Local Library Authority constituted for each district, to do all that is necessary to establish and run libraries in that district and ensure provision of library service to the people of the district. The LLA is also the body authorized to prepare a scheme for establishing libraries and spreading library service in each district and get it approved by the Director.

The Act contemplates district libraries, but the provision for them is not direct and has to be inferred from section 16 (2) (ii) where it is stated that the District Librarian shall, subject to the control of the Local Library Authority, manage the affairs of a District Library.

Apart from the libraries discussed above, the Definitions section of the Act includes three more types of libraries viz Aided Library, Private Library and Recognized Library the services of which are also available to the people of the state.

Aided library, as usual, is defined as a recognized library receiving aid from the government or from a Local Library Authority. Recognized library is a library recognized by the Director and declared as such for the purposes of the Act. Private library means a library other than an aided, recognized or a public library.

So the different libraries that function under the Act are:-

1. The Central library and its branches
2. The District Library
3. Other libraries in the district set up by the LLA
4. Aided libraries
5. Private libraries
6. Recognized libraries

7.7 MANIPUR

The Act mentions no type of library other than the State Central library and its branch libraries except in section 2 on Definitions. The mention of the State Central library and its branches is in section 9 (a) and is an oblique one in that it is mentioned among the duties of the Director of Libraries. The caption of the section is "Constitution of the Department of Public Libraries and appointment of the Director of Libraries and His duties". The first duty listed is "Supervise the State Central Library and the branches of such library". There is no other mention of the State Central library or any other type of libraries and their functions in the body of the Act.

In section 2 Definitions, the following types of libraries are defined:

(a) Aided Library (b) Public Library (c) State Central Library and (d) District Library. Public Library includes the following libraries according to the definition:-

(i) A library established or maintained by a District Library Authority including the branches and delivery stations of such library;

(ii) A library established or maintained by the state government and declared open to the public;

(iii) A library established or maintained by any local body or co-operative society and declared open to the public;

(iv) An aided library or any other library notified by the state government as a public library for the purposes of the Act.

As in the case of the other Acts, in the Manipur Act also it is the District Library Authority that is made responsible for the establishment of libraries and the provision of library service in the district. The libraries visualized for the state by the Act as far as can be ascertained from the section on definitions and other sections are (a) the State Central library (b) the District Library (c) Libraries established and maintained by the District Library Authority in each district including their branches and delivery stations (d) Libraries established and maintained by the state government and declared open to the public (e) Libraries established or maintained by local bodies and declared open to the public and (f) aided libraries. No indication regarding the interlinking of these libraries or mechanism for their cooperation has been given in the Act.

7.8 KERALA

The Kerala Act, as already mentioned earlier, provides for a three tier set up of bodies to be responsible for the development and provision of public library service in the state. They are (i) the State Library Council (ii) District Library Council and (iii) Taluk Library Council., Each of these bodies has been assigned one or more specific responsibilities in this regard.

In the list of powers and functions of the State Library Council given under section 8, the items mentioned at (e), (f), (h)(vii) and (h)(ix) are relevant to the understanding of the library structure envisaged by the Act. They are stated below:-

8(e) Reorganize in a phased manner the library service in the state into an integrated library system with close linkages between the several libraries as also to comprise book banks and mutual loaning;

8(f) With the prior concurrence of the government establish one or more State Libraries at such place or places in the state as may be considered necessary provided that the Trivandrum Public

Library shall be deemed to be a State Library established by the SLC under the clause; provided further that the Trivandrum Public Library shall continue to be a Department of the state.

8(h)(vii) Provide in the Trivandrum Public Library or in such other state libraries books, periodicals, newspapers, maps etc.

8(h)(ix) Provide mobile libraries to District Library Councils which can give book services to each Panchayat.

Each District Library Council is vested with the responsibility of establishing libraries and spreading library service in the district and/or supervising and coordinating their service. Similarly each Taluk Library Council also is entrusted with similar responsibility as far as the Taluk is concerned.

Section 29 of the Act is on Library Development Plan and according to it the plan is to be drawn up by each District Library Council for establishing, coordinating and spreading library service within the entire district or part thereof, in such form and manner and containing such particulars as may be prescribed (by the Rules framed under the Act). The plan is to be forwarded to the President, State Library Council and finally approved by the government before implementation by the District Library Council.

The Rules framed under the Act in 1991 prescribe the guidelines for the preparation of the Development Plan. Although the types of libraries to be established in each district have been mentioned in the Rules, it is not made clear how any linkage will be established between them and how they will constitute a district library system. The libraries envisaged for the whole state by the Rules are:-

a) One state library in each city which has a population of five lakhs and above;
b) One district library for each revenue district;
c) One taluk library for each taluk;
d) One village library in a locality with a population between 5000 and 25000.

These libraries are to function under the SLC, DLC or TLC as the case may be according to the jurisdiction of their service. In addition there are over four thousand affiliated libraries spread over the whole state.

Although it is well over a decade now since the Act came into force no District Library Development Plan, as contemplated in the Act , is known to have been prepared and reached the final stage of approval by the government as yet.

7.9 HARYANA

The Haryana Act is unique in its definition of a public library as a library which permit members of the public to use it for reference or borrowing without charging fee or subscription. This is in conformity to Unesco's stipulation that public library service should be free of charges. None of the other Acts in India has made this aspect explicit in their definition of a public library. The following are the libraries sought to be established under the Act:

a) State Central Library headed by the State Librarian;

b) District Library for each district;

c) Municipal/city/town library;

d) Block library,

e) Village library, and Book Deposit Centres,

f) Subscription libraries

There is nothing in the Act to show that that an integrated inter dependent library system is envisaged by the Act. As the provisions of the Act stand at present the different types of libraries would function as independent isolated units.

7.10 MIZORAM

Section 12 of the Act lists the categories of public libraries to be set up. They are:-

(i) State Library

(ii) District Library in each district

(iii) Sub-Divisional library in each sub-division

(iv) Village library

It is stated that the State Library shall function as a library and as a reservoir of books. This means that it has also the responsibility to function as a feeder library for the other libraries by lending or donating books to them to enrich their book collection. Apart from this linkage of the state library with other libraries no other relationship has been indicated.

7.11 GOA

The Act vests the primary responsibility for the development and provision of public library service in the state government. The Sate library Council and other agencies like the State Library Development Cell and the State library are to help and advise the government in the discharge of this responsibility. The categories of public libraries are as shown below:-

(a) State library;

(b) A district library in each district;

(c) Municipal library;

(d) Taluk library;

(e) Panchayat library;

Among the duties of the State Library are mentioned

(i) to act as a centre for book exchange and inter-library lending within and outside the state;

(ii) to replenish from time to time the book stocks of district libraries.

These clauses indicate some responsibility to be discharged by the State Library in respect of other libraries. Apart from this, there is no linkage indicated between the different libraries.

7.12 GUJARAT

Among all the twelve Acts, it is only the Gujarat and Orissa Acts that have used the term "Public Library System". In section 2 of the Gujarat Act on Definitions, Public Library System is defined as follows;

"Public Library System means a set up of public libraries in the state with the State Central Library at the apex and village libraries at the bottom"

Chapter IV of the Act is on Public Library System and it is stated therein that the state government may designate one or more libraries as State Central Libraries and establish a District Library for each district and a Taluka Libarary for each Taluka at the district head quarters and taluka head quarters respectively. It is also stated that every District Library and Taluka Library shall be managed, orgaised and developed by the Director. As mentioned in the definition of Public Library System, there may be village libraries also either as independent units or as branches of District Libraries or Taluka Libraries. But nothing has been stated anywhere in the Act indicating any linkage between the libraries to justify the use of the term Public Library System in the Act. The Act also envisages two other units mentioned in the section on definitions as part of the public library structure of the state. They are "Book Deposit Centre" and "Book Service Centre". "Book Deposit Centre" is defined as "a Centre where books are deposited from where members of the public can borrow books". "Book Service Centre" means a centre from where members of the public can borrow books through a mobile library".

7.13 ORISSA

Public Library System is defined in the Orissa Act as "an organic inter linking of all Public Libraries in the state into a net-work to facilitate library service in a systematic and organized manner".

It is perhaps in pursuance of the realization of such a public Library System that the first item in the list of Powers and Functions of the Orissa State Library Authority is stated as "to evolve and subject to the approval of the government, finalise perspective plans for the development of a public library system in the state which shall be executed by it through the Director (of Public Libraries) and to co-ordinate and determine the standard of library services from village level to state level".

The types of libraries provided for in the Act are (a) the State Library (b) a District Library in each district)c) a City Library in each city with a population of two lakhs or more. In addition, as per section 2 on Definitions, it can be seen that, "Gandhi Pathagars"(libraries established by government at the block level) and aided libraries are also contemplated by the Act.

7.14 SUMMARY

Each one of the twelve states has made an earnest effort to make provisions in its Library Act for the establishment of public libraries and the spreading of library service throughout the state. In each state there was some kind of a library set up in existence prior to the passing of the Act and that seems to have influenced the provisions in the Act relating to the structure of public libraries. The attempt in the Acts has been more to expand the existing libraries in the form of establishing more of them and diversifying their types than to develop a public library system that has the built in efficiency to ensure the maximum service output from the available financial input. So the picture of public libraries projected by most of the Acts is one of increased number and types of public libraries with better financial and book resources, but by and large, existing and functioning in isolation from each other as earlier. But there are some exceptions where some kind of a linkage between the central libraries and their branch libraries has been brought about. The situation, as a while, has improved, but not to the extent that would have been possible if a proper organizational set up of public libraries that is more conducive to their growth had been conceived and implemented through the instrumentality of the Acts. What should have been attempted was a well integrated and inter-linked public library system encompassing the public libraries at all levels and of all types in each state the book resources of which would be accessible to all people of the state wherever they are based. In fact only two of the Acts, namely those of Gujarat and Orissa have mentioned and defined the term "Public Library System" although they have not spelt out the details of how it should be established. The Kerala Act in a different context has referred to "an integrated library system with close linkages between the different libraries".

The Acts of Tamil Nadu, Andhra Pradesh, Karnataka, West Bengal, Manipur and Kerala have empowered the Local Library Authorities to draw up schemes or plans for the development of libraries in their respective areas according to the guidelines prescribed by the Rules framed under the Acts and get them approved by the government. The agencies authorized by the Goa and Orissa Acts to do likewise are the State Library Development Cells and the Orissa Public Library Authority respectively. These plans or schemes may contain the details and modus operandi of setting up State Public Library Systems. Although the Acts of Maharashtra, Haryana, Mizoram and Gujarat do not refer to any development plans or schemes it can be presumed that the Rules framed under them would have paid attention to this matter.

Each of the twelve Acts has provided for the establishment of some or all of the libraries listed below:-

State Central Library, Regional or Divisional Libraries, District Central Libraries and their branches including delivery or service stations, Taluka, Block and Village libraries, City and Town Libraries and mobile libraries with a view to spreading library service to the maximum extent in each state.

8

MISCELLANEOUS PROVISIONS

There are certain provisions in the different Acts which do not fall under the headings of the earlier Chapters and hence not discussed in them. They are, nevertheless, important and are intended to be examined in this chapter. The scope of this chapter is not confined to the matters listed under the chapter/section labelled as "Miscellaneous" in some of the Acts, but goes beyond them and includes matters contained in other sections also.

8.1 PREAMBLE

Every Act opens with a preamble which is a concise statement of the purpose of the Act. In most of the Acts the preamble is substantially alike with some minor variations in content and wording . But in some it is more detailed with substantive variations. The relevant portions of the preambles as given in the different Acts are reproduced below:-

8.1.1 Tamil Nadu

An Act to provide for the establishment of public libraries in the state of Tamil Nadu and the organization of comprehensive rural and urban library service therein".

8.1.2 Andhra Pradesh

"An Act to consolidate and amend the laws relating to the

establishment and maintenance of Public Libraries in the state of Andhra Pradesh and matters connected there with".

When this Act was passed in 1960, there were two library Acts in force in parts of Andhra Pradesh, One was the Madras Public Libraries Act of 1948 which was in force in the erstwhile Andhra which, until October 1953, was part the then Madras Province and the other was the Hyderabad Public Libraries Act, 1955 passed when Hyderabad was a princely state.. The enlarged Andhra Pradesh formed in 1956 included Andhra formed in 1953 and the Hyderabad state. Therefore the Act passed by the new Andhra Pradesh had to provide for the merging of the Madras Public Libraries Act and the Hyderabad Public Libraries Act with amendments. Hence the words "to consolidate and amend the laws" in the preamble. Section28 clauses (1) and (2) of the Andhra Pradesh Act relate to this.

8.1.3 Karnataka

"An Act to provide for the establishment and maintenance of public libraries and the organization of a comprehensive rural and urban library service in the state of Kernataka".

8.1.4 Maharashtra

"To provide for the establishment , maintenance organization and development of public libraries in the state of Maharashtra".

8.1.5 West Bengal

An act to provide for the establishment of public libraries in the state of West Bengal and to regulate, guide, control, supervise and to grant recognition to the existing libraries in the state as also to provide for a comprehensive, rural and urban library service in the state of West Bengal ".

There is a verbal and marginally substantive variation in this Act from the Acts of Tamil Nadu, Karnataka and Maharashtra. The variation is in respect of the role of the Act with regard to the emphasis on the supervision and recognition of existing libraries..

8.1.6 Manipur

"An Act to provide for the establishment and maintenance of public libraries in the state of Manipur and matters connected therewith"

8.1.7 Kerala

"An Act to consolidate and unify the library laws in the state and to provide for the reorganization of the entire library system in the state of Kerala with a view to the development and maintenance of rural and urban library service and for matters connected therewith or incidental thereto".

The Kerala Act was passed in a context different form that of the other states. There was the Kerala Granthasala Sanghom with defact quasi government status represented by a Board of Control appointed by the government as explained in section 2.7.1 of this book. Also the Malabar area of Kerala which was earlier part of the erstwhile Madras Presidency was governed by the Madras (Tamil Nadu) Public Libraries Act of 1948. These had to be consolidated in the new Act and that is why the words "to consolidate and unify the library laws in the state" occur in the preamble. "Section 38 of the Act pertains to the merger of Kerala Grandhasala Sanghom with the State Library Council set up by the Act and section 46 pertains to transfer of public libraries established or maintained by any Local Library Authority in the state set up under the Madras (Tamil Nadu) Public Libraries Act, 1948.

8.1.8 Haryana

An Act to provide for the establishment, maintenance and development of public libraries in the state of Haryana and for matters ancillary thereto".

8.1.9 Mizoram

"An Act to provide for the establishment, maintenance and development of comprehensive public libraries system in the state of Mizoram".

Mizoram is the only state that has used the term ?ublic Library System in its preamble. However theAct does not spell out the details of the establishment of such a system. Therefore the purpose indicated by the use of the term remains unsubstantiated by the text of the Act.

5.1.10 Goa

"An Act for the establishment, maintenance and development of Public Libraries in the State of Goa and for matters ancillary thereto:

5.1.11 Gujarat

"An Act to provide for the promotion and development of public libraries in the state of Gujarat and for that purpose to constitute a State Library Development Council and for the matters connected there with or incidental thereto".

It is only in the Gujarat Act that the constitution of a State Library Development Council as a purpose of the Act is mentioned. The establishment of the various bodies at the state and local levels is incidental to the basic purpose of the Act which, as rightly stated in the former part of the preamble, is "to provide for the promotion and development of public library service in the state of Gujarat". It may be noted that the Act provides for the constitution of District Library Advisory Committees and Taluka Library Advisory Committees by the Director of Public Libraries. To name, any body meant to implement the provisions of the Act in the preamble as a purpose to be achieved smacks of the lack of a proper perspective of the Act.

8.1.12 Orissa

"An Act to provide for the establishment of a network of public libraries in the state of Orissa and to maintain, regulate, guide, control, supervise, integrate and consolidate the libraries in the state as also to provide for a comprehensive rural and urban library service in the state and for matters connected therewith or incidental thereto".

The intention of the Act, as clearly explained in the preamble, is the establishment of a well integrated public library system with all the libraries linked to each other so that the resources of all the public libraries will constitute a common pool of resources which can be shared by all people of the state according to need. This intention is followed up in the body of the Act under section 5 relating to the powers and functions of the Orissa Public Library Authority.

8.2 STATE CENTRAL LIBRARY

All the twelve Acts provide for the establishment of a State Central library or the recognition of an existing library as the State Central library. Some Acts use the designation of Central Library, some of State Library and some of State Central Library, but here all are taken to stand for State Central Library and treated as such. A few states provide for more than one such library. The provision in this regard in each of the Acts may now be examined.

8.2.1 Tamil Nadu

There is only a brief reference to the Central Library in this Act. It occurs as the first item under section 4 relating to appointment and duties of the Director of Public Libraries and reads thus. "Manage the Central Library constituted by the government as the Central Library or an existing government library recognized by them as the Central Library together with the branches of such library". Nothing has been mentioned about the functions of the Central Library.

8.2.2 Andhra Pradesh

The State Central Library has been defined in the Act as a library established by the government as the State Central Library. Here again it figures rather insignificantly under the section (section 8) describing the duties of the Director of Public Libraries. The relevant clause says "Supervise the State Central library and the branches of such library". No details regarding its functions have been given.

8.2.3 Karnataka

The treatment of State Central Library is elaborate and detailed. The entire chapter VI of the Act is devoted, to it. Section 35 of the Act vests the management of the Bangalore Public Library in the State Library Authority and section 36(1) provides for its designation as Karnataka State Central Library. Section 36(2)(a) and (2)(b) and section 37 describe the functions of the library in detail. In addition to functioning as a general library the State Central Library shall consist of the following sections:-

(i) A State Bureau of copyright collection;

(ii) A State Library for the Blind;

(iii) A State Bureau of Inter-Library loan;

(iv) A State Bibliographical Bureau;

(v) A State Bureau of Technical Services, and

(vi) Such other sections as may be prescribed.

The functions of each of these sections have been elaborated in section 37 of the Act.

8.2.4 Maharashtra

As in the case of the Tamil Nadu and Andhra Pradesh Acts, in the Maharashtra Act also the State Central Library figures rather unobtrusively in section 11 of the first item under which is stated thus: "The State Government may establish a State Central library for the whole of the state". There is no other mention about the State Central library in the Act.

8.2.5 West Bengal

There are two references to the Central Library in the Act. One is in section 5 where it is stated that the Central Library shall, in addition to running a library and a reading room, perform such other functions as may be entrusted to it from time to time by the government or any other officer authorized by the government in that behalf. The second reference is in section 6 on the functions of the Director of Public Libraries. The second function listed under this section is "Manage the Central library together with the branches of such library and superintend and direct all matters relating to the Central library".

8.2.6 Manipur

The State Central Library is defined in the Act as a library established by the state government as the State Central Library. It also occurs in section 9 where one of the duties of the Director of Public Libraries is stated as "Supervise the State Central Library and the branches of such library".

8.2.7 Kerala

The Kerala Act authorizes the State Library Council to establish one or more State Libraries at such places or places as may be considered necessary with the prior concurrence of the government (section 8f). The following provisos of this clause causes confusion regarding the administrative status of the Trivandrum Public Library:-

"Provided that the Trivandrum Public Library shall be deemed to be a State Library establishment by the State Library Council under this clause.

Provided further that the Trivandrum Public Library shall continue to be a department of the government".

The two provisos would appear to be contradictory to each

other. If the Trivandrum Public Library is to be deemed as a library established by the State Library Council, then it should be under the administrative control of the SLC. Then how can it continue to be a government department as it was before the Act came into force. This confusion in the Act needs to be set right.

8.2.8 Haryana

The State Central Library is given prominent treatment in this Act. There are four sections of the Act dealing with it viz sections 7,8,9 and 10. Section 7 states that the state government shall, by an order, establish a State Central Library located in the state. Section 8 describes the types of books to be acquired and stocked in the library and section 9 is on the mode of book acquisition. Section 10 states that the library shall have two sections – the State Reference Library and the State Lending Library . The functions of these two sections are then described in detail.

8.2.9 Mizoram

Section 13 of the Act is on State Library and the relevant clauses of the section are reproduced below:-

(1) There shall be a State Central Library located in the Capital of the State

(2) The State Library shall consist of the following sections:-

(i) Bureau of copy right;

(ii) State Library for the Blind;

(iii) Inter-library loan;

(iv) State Bibliographical Bureau;

(v) Technical services; and

(vi) Mobile services.

It is also stated in section 14 that the state library shall function as a library and as a reservoir of books.

8.2.10 Goa

The Goa Act also gives prominence to the State Library.

The relevant clauses of sections 6 and 7 are quoted below:-

6. State Library

"The government shall, by an order, establish a State Library located in the state".

7. Book stock of the State Library

(1) "The stock of books of the State Library shall consist of books obtained through any legislation for the time being in force providing for compulsory acquisition of two copies of books of every author published in the state, books acquired otherwise by purchase, exchange, gifts and bequests and its own publications"

(2) Materials in the State Library may also include films, film strips, slides, tapes and gramophone records, maps, ...bulletins, photos, pictures, compact disc, etc".

Section 9 is also on the State Library and describes its departments and functions

The provision relating to the State Library in this Act are identical to those of the Haryana Act.

8.2.11 Gujarat

The State Central library figures in the definition of Public Library System in the Act The definition is "Public Library System means a set up of Public Libraries in the state with the State Central Library at the apex and village libraries at the bottom".

Chapter IV of the Act is on Public Library System and section 13 under this chapter reads thus, "subject to such rules as may be prescribed, the state government may, by order, designate one or more libraries as State Central Libraries and establish a District Library for each district and a Taluka Library for such Taluka".

8.2.12 Orissa

Section 9 of the Act pertains to the State Library and it is reproduced below:-

9(1) "The State Library shall be headed by the Director of Public Libraries who shall be not below the rank of a class I officer:

(2) "The State Library shall function as a Reference Library and not as a lending library in respect of the books therein, except in the case of inter-library loan".

In the Definitions Section of the Act the State Library is defined as a library established by government at the state capital which has been named as Harekrishna Mahatab State library.

8.3 AIDED LIBRARIES

Public libraries had been functioning in India from early times. They were initially started by private agencies as a concomitant of the spread of education. The people who were educated and developed interest in reading while in their educational institutions were anxious to have reading facilities even outside the portals of the educational institutions. Also the freedom movement encouraged the establishment of public libraries and reading as it needed a knowledgeable citizenry for its sustenance and success. Governmental interest in public libraries came later. It was initially in the form of promoting library movement by encouraging private agencies to take the initiative of starting libraries and offering grants for library buildings and purchase of books. Later the governments began to involve themselves directly in the establishment and maintenance of libraries. Almost all the state libraries in the different states came up as a consequence of such direct government involvement. They were established either afresh or by the government taking over an existing library and elevating it as the state library. But, apart from the state libraries, there were few other libraries started and run by the government. Except in the states where legislation was passed, the majority of public libraries were in the private sector and many of them were eligible for grant. There is specific provision in the various Acts to continue the practice of providing grants to libraries. Such libraries are called aided libraries and it is intended to examine in this section the provision in the various Acts relating to these aided libraries.

The term 'aided library' occurs both in the section on definitions and in the section listing the powers and duties of the Director of Public Libraries in the Acts of Tamil Nadu, Andhra Pradesh, Karnataka and Manipur. In the Goa Act also it is defined, but it is the State library Development Cell that administrates the grant-in-aid scheme for aided libraries in the absence of a Directorate of Libraries In the Maharashtra Act, it does not occur in the Section on Definitions, but the recognition of libraries eligible for grant and the sanctioning of the grant is listed as a duty of the Director. In the West Bengal Act it occurs only in the Section on Definitions. The definition is "Aided library means a recognized library receiving aid from the government or a Local Library Authority". In Kerala, for historical reasons already explained, the term used is "affiliated library", ie affiliated to the State Library Council. For affiliation a library has to submit an application to the Taluk Library Council and, on being satisfied of its eligibility, it will recommend the application to the State Library Council through the District Library Council and the SLC takes the final decision regarding its eligibility for affiliation and grant. Haryana has only 'subscription libraries' outside the stream of public libraries and it is defined thus: 'subscription library means a library run on the subscription of its members". The Act does not say anything about the eligibility of subscription libraries for government grant' In the Act of Mizoram there is no definition of 'aided library'. But section 18 is on Grant-in-aid to Recognized Village Libraries and it states thus:- "The government may sanction grant-in-aid to recognized village libraries in accordance with the rules made under this Act". "Aided library" is not defined in the Gujarat Act. But section 20 of the Act empowers the Director of Public Libraries to recognize a library open for public use as a public library eligible for the purpose of grant-in-aid or other financial assistance. In the Orissa Act ' aided library' is defined as a library open to the public and declared by the Director to be eligible for grant-in-aid from the Library Fund in accordance with rules made under this Act and includes a library which is receiving grant-in-aid from the government'. There is no reference to 'aided libraries' in any of the other sections of the Act.

8.4 RULES

Every Act passed by a legislature provides for the framing of Rules within the ambit of the Act. They are for the purpose of elucidating or supplementing or indicating the method of executing the provisions of the Act and should not, in any way, be inconsistent with or contradictory to them. They are in the nature of subsidiary legislation, that is, subsidiary to the main legislation which is the Act itself. It is the Act and the Rules framed under it that constitute the total law pertaining to a subject. The Act is generally concise and is a broad frame work of the major topics falling under the subject legislated upon. Some topics may be inadvertently left out in the Act and they can be provided for in the Rules. The Rules can also spell out the details and procedure for implementing the provisions of the Act, The word "prescribed" occurs at various places in an Act. It means "prescribed by the rules framed under the Act".

It is the responsibility of the concerned department of the government to draft the Rules after an Act is passed. The draft, as approved by the government has to be placed before the legislature and got passed.

The twelve Library Acts discussed here conform to the patterns of legislations described above. The word 'prescribed' is defined in all the Acts except those of Haryana and Goa. But all the Acts have a section on Rules. As an example section 18 of the Tamil Nadu Public Libraries Act relating to Rules is reproduced below:-

"(18) Powers to make Rules

(1) The government may, by notification, make rules consistent with this Act to carry out the purposes thereof.

(2) In particular and without prejudice to the generality of the foregoing provisions such rules may provide for:-

(a) All matters required or allowed to be prescribed under the Act;

(b) The method of conducting the election of members to Local library Authorities and all matters connected therewith;

(c) The matters to be included in the scheme referred to in section (8) (scheme for establishing libraries);

(d) The maintenance of the minutes of the proceedings of Local library Authorities;

(e) The publication of audited statement of accounts of such authorities and of the reports of the auditors; and

(f) A Library Grant-in-aid code regulating the government aid to and the declaration, inspection and coordination by the Director, of aided libraries and the standards to be maintained by such libraries'.

The other Acts also make provisions for the framing of rules on similar lines but with such variations as required by the nature of the Acts and by local conditions.

It may be noted that while in eleven of the twelve states the constitution, powers and duties of the state level apex body ie the State library Authority have been specified in the Acts themselves, in Tamil Nadu where the body is designated as the State Library Committee, this responsibility has been kept within the domain of the Rules. This may be because the basic function of the State Library Committee is stated as "to advise the state government on such matters relating to libraries as they may refer to it" and there are few executive functions envisaged for it.

8.5 ACCOUNTS AND AUDITING

Accounts should be maintained of the monetary transactions involved in the establishment and maintenance of public libraries according to the provisions of every Library Act and there should be proper auditing of the accounts. The Library Act of Tamil Nadu, Andhra Pradesh, Karnataka, Maharashtra, West Bengal, Manipur, Kerala and Orissa have specific sections relating to this. However in the Acts of Haryana, Mizoram, Goa and Gujarat there is no mention of this. Presumably, in these states the Rules framed under the Acts are expected to deal with it.

8.6 PRESS AND REGISTRATION OF BOOKS ACT, 1867

This is a central Act section 9 of which stipulates the free supply of a copy of every book published to an officer named by the state government in the official gazette from time to time. The Library Acts of Tamil Nadu, Karnartaka and West Bengal have provisions in their Acts amending the above provision increasing the number of free copies supplied to 5 in Tamil Nadu and 3 in Karnataka and West Bengal.

9

LOOKING AHEAD

9.1 PRESENT PUBLIC LIBRARY SCENARIO

Out of 28 states and 7 Union territories in India only 12 states have passed library legislation so far. Even among these 12 states not all have implemented it fully. The majority of the states and all union territories have not thought it necessary yet to enact library legislation. This does not mean that there is no public library service in these states. No recent national survey of the situation regarding public libraries has been made, but it seems safe to presume that public library service is better organized and made available to the people in the states having legislation than in those not having it. But the general situation is that public libraries are yet to receive the recognition that their importance in society warrants and they enjoy only a low priority in the scheme of things. The overall position is such that it does not reflect the faith of the powers that be and the society at large in the library as a powerful instrument for progress and advancement. The cause of public library movement receives only lip service and not the kind of treatment that is necessary to enable it to perform the roles envisaged for it in the Unesco Public Library Manifesto. It has to be continuously born in mind that the library is a centre for the storage and dissemination of information and that information is an essential input in all human endeavours - material, intellectual and cultural - to ensure their maximum productivity.

9.2 PUBLIC LIBRARIES AND DISTANCE EDUCATION

Apart from the traditional role of contributing to the all round development of the individual and the society a new role that has emerged for the public library in the latter half of the twentieth century is to support distance education which has now established itself as a mode of education catering to those who have not had the privilege of completing their education in formal institutions like schools, colleges and universities. Initially started in subjects which did not involve laboratory work it has now been extended to almost all subjects, thanks to the facilities offered by developments in information technology. India has not lagged behind in introducing and popularizing this stream of education. We have distance education programmes offered by open universities specially started for the purpose and also by traditional universities through their distance education wings. In distance education the emphasis is on self study which means heavy dependence of those who are enrolled in the stream, on libraries. Of course there are printed lessons distributed to the students, lessons that can be accessed through electronic channels, small book collections kept in the study centres and occasional contact classes, but the main prop of distance education is the library especially the public library which is open for use by all without any distinction whatsoever. The reading needs of the students of distance education are, therefore, to be primarily met by public libraries. It may be pointed out here that when the first Open University was started in the UK in 1969 there was a strong public library system there and it has been further strengthened over the years. In India the greatest weakness of the distance education programmes is that our public library facilities are far from adequate to lend support to them. To start distance education without the assurance of the support of a sound public library system is to put the cart before the horse with the inevitable consequence of educational standards sliding down. This is a new factor that should make the authorities aware of the urgency to devote serious attention to the development of a strong public library system in each state and union territory and the spread of public library service throughout the country.

9.3 ROLE OF STATE AND CENTRAL GOVERNMENTS

Constitutionally, "library" is a state subject and it is the responsibility of the states to take steps for the development of public libraries and the provision of their services to the people. The states have been doing this in varying measures, some of them, as we have seen, taking recourse to library legislation. But the financial resources that the states can command for organizing and providing adequate public library service are limited. This is true, to some extent, also in the case of the states which have enacted library legislation although in these states the level of public library development and service is reportedly, better than in the other states.

As in several other sectors, in the library sector also the central government has been supplementing the efforts of the state governments. This has been in the form of offering financial support to the states and also in some other ways. A brief account of the involvement of the central government in this respect is given below:-

9.3.1 Central Acts

The Union government passed certain Acts relating to libraries of national importance and to certain library related matters of national relevance since independence. The first such Act to be passed was The Imperial Library (Change of Name) Act, 1948. The Imperial Library established in 1902 by Lord Curzon, Viceroy of India, was functioning in Calcutta at the time of independence. The Union Government felt the need for establishing a national library. The easiest way of doing it was to convert this library into the National Library and hence the Act. This library located at Belvedere, Calcutta, the former Viceregal Seat, is now the largest library in India. Another

Act titled "The National Library of India Act" was passed in 1976 defining the scope and functions of the library as a national library and modifying its administrative set up.

Another Central Act is "The Delivery of Books and Newspapers Act, 1954" (amended in 1956) which stipulates that every publisher in the country should deposit a copy each of his publication to four designated libraries. The libraries are the National Library, Calcutta, Connemara Public Library, Chennai, Central library (Asiatic Society), Mumbai and Delhi Public Library, Delhi. This Act has enabled the Central Reference Library established in the premises of the National Library, Calcutta to take up the responsibility of compiling and publishing the Indian National Bibliography from 1958 on the basis of the copies of publications received in the National Library under the Act.

Indian Copy Right Act intended to protect the rights of authors, musicians and artists was passed in 1957.

Three other Acts passed by the Union Government were:-

(i) Khudabaksh Oriental Public Library Act, 1969;

(ii) Rampur Raza Library Act, 1975, and

(iii) Asiatic Society Act, 1984

Khudabaksh Oriental public Library was started by Khan Bahadur Khuda Baksh in Patna. In view of the rarity and richness of its collection the government passed the Act and took over the library declaring it as an institution of national importance.

The Rampar Raza Library started by Nawab Faizullah Khan in Rampur State which is now part of Uttar Pradesh is equally rich in its Oriental Collection and the Act was intended for the better management of the library and the up keep of its collection.

The Asiatic society started in 1784 in Calcutta had also built up a rare and valuable collection of books and manuscripts on oriental subjects, and the government, in passing the Act, was motivated by the same considerations as in the case the Khudabaksh library and Rampur Raza Library Acts.

9.3.2 Five Year Plans

Library development received the attention of the Planning Commission right from the First Five Year Plan started in 1951. In the context of the formulation of each Plan a Working Grouop on Libraries to formulate proposals for library development and indicate the financial outlay was formed. This exercise gained special prominence when, in connection with the Seventh Five Year Plan, a Working Group for the Modernization of Library Services and Information was appointed by the Planning Commission and this Group brought out a report making an extensive survey of the existing situation and containing specific proposals for implementation during the Seventh Plan period. The scope of the report was not confined to public libraries alone but extended to all types of libraries and the financial implications for the implementation of the recommendations in respect of each type of library and information centre was indicated. Working Groups continue to be appointed for the Five Year Plans. However, the Five Year Plans have not made any significant national impact on the public library arena

9.3.3. The Delhi Public Library

A welcome initiative that was taken by the government jointly with Unesco was the establishment of the Delhi Public Library in 1951 as a piolot project to function with all modern techniques and amenities and to serve as a model public library for Asia. This was a landmark in the history of library movement in India. The project has been developed into a modern public library system with a central library, branch libraries, sub-branch libraries, deposit stations and mobile units, all providing free and efficient library service to the people in and around Delhi. It has a children's section also.

9.3.4 Advisory Committee on Libraries

The government of India appointed a Library Advisory

Committee in 1957 under the Chairmanship of K.P.Sinha, the then Director of Public Instruction Bihar to study the public library situation in India and suggest steps for strengthening it. The Committee which made an extensive survey of libraries all over the country found their condition everywhere far from satisfactory. In its report submitted in 1959 it made several recommendations for establishing a strong network of public libraries all over the country over a period of time on the basis of a uniform library legislation to be adopted and implemented by all states and union territories. In pursuance of this recommendation a committee appointed by the government drafted a Model Library. In pursuance of this recommendation a committee constituted by the government prepared a Model Public Libraries Act and circulated it to all the states, but with no result. The recommendations of the Committee made after careful study and a lot of efforts remained practically unimplemented.

9.3.5. Raja Ram Mohan Roy Library Foundation

One of the most significant developments in the public library field in India that has occurred on the initiative of the central government was the establishment of Raja Rammohan Roy Library Foundation in 1972 on the occasion of the be-centenary of the birth of Raja Rammohan Roy, the great social reformer. This is an autonomous body fully financed by the Department of Culture, Ministry of Human Resources Development, Government of India. During the period of its existence of over 30 years it has made its impact on the public library scene in India. Among its important and on-going programmes are (i) providing financial assistance to selected libraries in each state on the basis of a system of matching grant from the state (ii) strengthening the book collections of State Central libraries, District Central Libraries and other prominent libraries in each state by extending to them books assistance directly and (iii) sanctioning grants including building grants to libraries run by voluntary agencies. It has also strived for the enunciation of a library policy and working towards its adoption by the central and state government. The Foundation, on the basis of its activities so far, and the programmes envisaged for the future, promises to develop into a strong instrument for the accelerated progress of public library movement in the country.

9.3.6 National Policy On Library And Information Systems

The formulation and adoption of a National Policy on library and Information system was a long cherished desire of the library profession in Indian. Dr.S.R.Ranganathan and others had been strongly advocating it. To work for such a policy and its adoption by the central and state government was one of the stated objectives of the Raja Rammohan Roy Library Foundation. In 1985, the Department of Culture, Ministry of Human Resources Development, Government of India finally took the decision to appoint a committee under the chairmanship of Professor D.P.Chattopadhyaya who was the then chairman of Raja Rammohan Roy Library Foundation to draw up a National Policy on library and Information System. The Committee lost no time in embarking on the work of drafting a National policy. In this endeavour it had the benefit of two earlier documents on the theme, one drafted by RRRLF and the other drafted by the Indian Library Association. It also held wide consultation with members of the library profession, academics and others all over the country before finalizing the document. "National Policy on Library and Information system. A presentation" The document was submitted to the Ministry of Human Resources Development, Government of India in 1986. The document is a comprehensive blueprint dealing with all types of libraries and information centres and showing the directions for developing them, development of manpower required for the purpose and their status, bibliographical services and modernization of library and information systems. It also spells out the details of the agencies and machinery for implementing the policy. The Policy Document, was reportedly, referred by the government to an empowered committee and is known to be under active consideration of the Committee.

9.3.7 Future Library Legislation

One of the objectives set for the Raja Rammohan Roy Library Foundation was to work for the enactment of library legislation in each state and Union territory in India. But in pursuance of this objective the Foundation has not been able to do and achieve much. As already seen, only 12 states out of 28 states and 7 union territories have library legislation in their Statutes Books so far. Although library legislation has been under consideration in some more of the states it is yet to become a reality. Although according to the constitution, "library" is a state subject and its development is a responsibility of the states, the Union Government having the responsibility of the overall development and progress of the country in all fields, should play a crucial role in this regard. It has already expressed its conviction of the need for library legislation as a necessary means for public library development as evidenced by the fact that it has included "the working for the adoption of legislation" in the objectives of Raja Rammohan Roy Library Foundation, an institution founded by it. What, therefore, is needed is a vigorous pursuit of this objective with a determination of realizing it within a specified time frame. But before such a drive is initiated some preparatory work has to be done.

9.3.8 Survey of Public Libraries

A thorough and comprehensive survey of public libraries in the country should be made. The survey should cover the twelve states having library legislation and others including the union territories. The survey should aim at a proper evaluation of the adequacy or otherwise of the present organizational structure of public libraries and their services. This should be done with reference to a model public library development plan. There is a role model for preparing such a plan in Dr.S.R.Ranganathan's book "Library Development Plan: A Thirty Year Programme for India" published in 1950 by the University of Delhi. It delineates the responsibilities of the Union and State governments and defines the shape of a national library system with the National Library at the apex and state central libraries, District Central libraries and other libraries including branch libraries, mobile libraries and delivery stations at the lower levels all of which together will be able to spread library service to the far corners of the country. The book gives the outline of a national library system and describes the functions of the National Library, State Central Libraries and other component libraries of the system. What is require to draw up a new library development plan is to adopt this outline with such variations as are necessitated by new changes and developments and with the data and statistics updated. The financial lay out will also have to be worked out afresh.

Keeping such a model plan as the basis, the proposed public library survey can be conducted and the present deficiencies in the public library field identified. All important proposals and recommendations of various professional associations and conferences and eminent professionals and others associated with the library field should be considered in connection with the survey. The survey will give a clear picture of the deficiencies and inadequacies of the present library set up in the country and of what need to be done to remove them and develop a sound public library system that will be capable of providing adequate library service to one and all. With the help of these findings two Model Public Library Bills, one for the state and Union Territory governments to be uniformly adopted and implemented by them and one for the Union government should be drawn up. The model state Act will replace the existing state Acts in addition to being adopted by all the other state/Union Territories. The Union Act is intended to define the structure and role of the National Library System. The Union government's role in the national library system will be one of coordination and facilitation.

The most essential pre-requisite for the success of the programme proposed here is the identification of an existing agency or the constitution of a new agency that is capable of translating the programme into action and realizing the intended goals. The programme in a nutshell is (a) to prepare a public library development plan (2) to conduct an evaluative survey of the present set up of public libraries in the country and their services and (c) to draft a model state library bill and a Union library bill (d) get the bills adopted and implemented and (e) coordinate the public library programmes and activities of the states and the centre in accordance with the Acts and (f) oversee the establishment of a national public library system. It is difficult to identify an existing organization or body for that purpose. The central government should therefore constitute a body which may be designated as National Board of Public Libraries on a permanent basis. The Board should consist of eminent persons representing the library profession, educationalists and persons who have distinguished themselves in the field of social work. The Minister in charge of Culture in the central government should preferably be the Chairperson of the Board. In that case it is desirable to have a full time Vice-Chairperson who should be a renowned librarian or educationist. There should be a full time Secretary for the Board who should be a librarian of national standing. The criteria in constituting the Board are that it should have representation from the different regions of India (North, Centre, South, East and West) and will be able to function with proper knowledge of and insight into its mission and with a full sense of commitment to it.

The idea behind the proposal suggested here is that the whole nation should become aware of the important role of public libraries in contributing to national progress and be fully involved in the efforts of developing them in such a manner that they will be able to lend effective support to all nation building programmes and activities.

APPENDIX I

1. TAMIL NADU (MADRAS) PUBLIC LIBRARIES ACT (1948)
(came into force w.e.f. 1 April 1950)
(As amended from time to tome)

An act to provide for the establishment of public libraries in the province of (Madras) Tamil Nadu and the organization of comprehensive rural and urban Library Service therein.

Whereas it is expedient to provide for the establishment of public libraries, and the organization of a comprehensive rural and urban library service, in the Province of (madras) Tamil Nadu. It is hereby enacted as follows:

PRELIMINARIES

(1) Short title, extent and commencement

(1) This Act may be called Tamil Nadu (Madras) Public Libraries Act, 1948.

(2) It extends to the whole of the (state) of (Madras) Tamil Nadu.

(3) This section shall come into force at once; and the rest of this Act shall come into force on such date as the Government may; by notification, appoint.

(2) Definitions

In this Act, unless there is anything repugnant in the subject or context:

(1) 'Aided Library' means a library declared by the Director to be eligible for aid from the Government.

(2) 'Director' means the Director of Public Libraries appointed under section 4.

(3) 'District; means a revenue district

(4) 'Government' means the (state) Government;

(5) 'Notification' means a notification published in the Fort St.George Gazatte:

(6) 'Prescribed' means prescribed by rules made under this Act.

(7) 'State' means the (state) of (Madras) Tamil Nadu.

(8) 'Public Library' means a library established or maintained by a local library Authority, and includes the branches and delivery stations of such library; and

(9) 'Year' means the financial year.

STATE LIBRARY COMMITTEE

(3) State Library Committee and its functions

(1) A state Library Committee shall be constituted by the Government for the purpose of advising them on such matters relating to libraries as they may refer to it.

(2) The Committee shall be constituted in such manner, and shall exercise and perform such other powers and duties as may be prescribed.

DIRECTOR & HIS DUTIES

(4) Appointment and Duties of Director

The Government shall appointment a Director of Public Libraries for the State and he shall subject to their control

(a) Manage the central library, being a library constituted by the Government as the central library or an existing Government library recognized by them as the central library, together with the branches of such library:

(b) Superintend and direct all matters relating to public libraries:

(c) Declare in accordance with the rules made under this Act what libraries are eligible for aid from the Government and superintend and direct all matters relating to such libraries;

(d) Superintend and control the work of all Local library Authorities under this Act;

(e) Submit to the Government every year a report on the work of libraries or other duties conferred by this Act or the rules made thereunder.

(f) Perform such other duties and exercise such other powers as are imposed or conferred by this Act or the rules made thereunder.

LOCAL LIBRARY AUTHORITIES

(5) Constitution of Local library Authorities

(1) For the purpose of organizing and administering public libraries in the State there shall be constituted Local Library Authorities one for the City of (Madras) Chennai and one for each district.

(2) The Local Library Authority for the City of Chennai (Madras) shall consist of-

(a) Three members elected by the Corporation of Chennai (Madras):

(b) Eight members nominated by the Government of whom:

(i) Three shall be office bearers of Libraries situated in the City of Chennai (Madras) and recognized in this behalf by the Government,

(ii) Two shall be headmasters of headmistresses of high

schools in the City of Chennai (Madras) and

(iii) One shall be the Principal of a College in the City of (Madras) Chennai.

(c) The Holder for the time being of an office which the Government may from time to time specify in this behalf.

(3) The Local Library Authority for each district shall consist of-

(a) The members nominated by the Director, of whom -

(i) Three shall be office bearers of Libraries situated in the district and recognized in this behalf by the Government; and

(ii) Five shall be headmasters or headmistresses of high schools or principals of colleges in the district;

(b) One member elected by the district board, and where there are two or more district boards in the district one member elected by each district board;

(c) Such number of members as may be elected by the presidents of the Panchayats in the district, the presidents of the Panchayats in each taluk electing one member; and

(d) Such number of members as may be elected by the municipal councils in the district, such municipal council electing one or more members in accordance with the following scale:

NUMBER OF MEMBERS

Municipalities with a population not exceeding one lakh : 1 Exceeding one lakh but not exceeding two lakhs : 2 Exceeding two lakhs : 3

e. The holder for the time being of an office which the Government may from time to time specify in this behalf

(4) The member referred to in clause (c) of sub-section (2) or in

clause (e) of sub-section (3) as the case may be shall be, the Secretary of the Local Library Authority concerned.

(5) Every Local Library Authority shall elect one of its members to be its Chairman

(6) Subject to the provisions of sub-section (8), the term of office of a nominated or elected member of Local Library Authority shall be three years from the date of his nomination or election as the case may be.

(7) A vacancy to the office of a nominated or elected member of a local Library Authority occurring otherwise than by efflux of time shall be filled by nomination or election in accordance with the provisions of sub-section (2) or sub-section (8) and he should hold office only for the remainder of the term for which the member whose place he takes was nominated or elected.

(8) A member nominated in his capacity as the holder of a particular office shall, if he ceases to be the holder of that office, cease to be a member of the Local Library Authority.

(9) No act of a Local Library Authority shall be deemed to be invalid by reason only of the existence of any vacancy in or any defect in the constitution of that Authority.

(10) Members of Local Library Authorities shall be eligible for renomination or re-election

(6) Incorporation of Library Authorities

Every local Library Authority shall be a body corporate, by the name of the area for which it is constituted, shall have perpetual succession and a common seal and shall be vested with the capacity of suing or being sued in its corporate name, of acquiring holding or transferring property, movable or immovable, of entering into contracts and of doing all things necessary, proper of expedient for the purposes for which it is constituted.

(7) Executive Committees and Sub-committees of Local Library Authorities

(1) A Local Library Authority may appoint an executive Committee consisting of such number of its members, not exceeding seven, as it may deem fit, and delegate to such committee all or any of its powers or duties under this Act.

(2) A Local Library Authority may also, from time to time appoint sub-committees to enquire into and report or advise on any matters which it may refer to them.

(8) Schemes to be Submitted by Local Library Authority

(1) As soon as possible, after a Local Library Authority is constituted and thereafter, as often as may be required by the Director, every Local Library Authority shall be and whenever it considers it necessary so to do, a Local Library Authority may prepare a scheme for establishing libraries and for spreading library service within its area and submit it to the Director for sanction. The Director may sanction it with such modifications and additions, if any, as he may think fit and the Local Library Authority shall give effect to the scheme as so sanctioned by him.

(2) The Director may suo motu or on application by the Local Library Authority concerned modify any scheme sanctioned under sub-section (1) or replace it by a new scheme.

(9) Powers of Local Library Authorities

A Local Library Authority may –

(a) Provide suitable lands and buildings for public libraries and also the furniture, fittings, materials and conveniences requisite therefore;

(b) Stock such libraries with books, periodicals, newspapers, maps, works and specimens of art and science, lantern slides, cinema reels and any other things suitable for their purpose;

(c) Employ from time to time such staff as it considers necessary for such libraries;

(d) With the previous sanction of the Government, close or discontinue any public library or change the site thereof;

(e) Accept with the previous sanction of the Director or the Government, any gift of books or with previous sanction of the Government, any other gift or endowment for any purpose connected with its activities.

(f) Provide for lecturers and the holding of classes; and

(g) In general do everything necessary to carry out the provision of this Act.

(10) Vesting of Properties in Local Library Authorities

All property, movable and immovable, acquired or held for the purpose of any public library in any area shall vest in the Local Library Authority of that area.

(11) Regulations by Local Library Authorities

(1) Subject to the provisions of this Act and the rules made there under a Local Library Authority may make regulations generally to earry out the purposes of this Act and without prejudice to the generally of this power such regulations may provide for-

(a) The Admission of the public to public libraries in its area on such conditions and on payment of such fees as it may specify;

(b) Requiring from persons desiring to use such libraries any guarantee or security against injury to or misuse, destruction or loss of the property of such libraries;

(c) The manner in which the property of such libraries may be used and the protection of such property from injury, misuse, destruction or loss; and

(d) Authorizing its officers and servants to exclude or remove from any such library any person who contravenes or fails to comply with the provisions of this Act or the rules or regulation made thereunder.

(2) The Government may in their discretion, modify or cancel any regulation made by a Local Library Authority under sub-section (1)

Provided that before modifying or canceling any regulation, the Government shall give the Local Library Authority concerned a reasonable opportunity to make its representations in the matter.

FINANCE AND ACCOUNTS

(12) Library Cess

(1) (a) Every Local Library Authority shall levy in the area a library cess in the form of a surcharge on the property tax or house tax levied in such area under the (Madras) Tamilnadu City Municipalities Act, 1919, the (Madras) Tamilnadu Disstrict, Municipalities Act 1920, or the (Madras) Tamilnadu Local Boards Act, 1920, as the case may be at the rate of six pies for every whole rupee in the property tax or house tax so levied.

(b) A Local Library Authority may, with the previous sanction of the Government and shall, if so directed to them, increase the rate specified in clause(c),

(2) The cess levied under sub –section(1) shall be collected—

(a) In the City of Chennai (Madras), by the Corporation of (Madras) Chennai;

(b) In an area within the jurisdiction of a Municipal Council, by the municipal council;

(c) In an area within the jurisdiction of a panchayat, by the panchayat; and

(d) In an area in a district not included within the jurisdiction of a municipal council or a panchayat, by the District Board;

as if the cess were a property tax or house tax payable under the (Madras) Tamilnadu City Municipal Act, 1919 or the (Madras) Tamilnadu. District Municipalities Act, 1920 or the (Madras) Tamil Nadu Local Boards Act, 1920, as the case may be, and all the relevant provisions of the said Acts shall apply accordingly:

Provided that the Government may, by notification, direct that for the purposes of the collection of the cess aforesaid, the provisions of the (Madras) Tamilnadu City Municipal Act, 1919, or the (Madras) Tamil Nadu District Municipalities Act, 1920, or the (Madras) Tamil Nadu Local Boards Act, 1920, as the case may be, shall apply subject to such modifications as may be specified in the notification.

(3) The cess collected under the sub-section (2) shall be paid to the Local Library Authority concerned by the Corporation of Chennai (Madras), the Municipal Council, the Panchayat or the District Board, as the case may be.

(13) Library Fund

(1) Every Local Library Authority shall maintain a fund called the Library Fund from which all its expenses under this Act shall be met.

(2) There shall be credited to the Library Fund the following sums, namely:-

(a) The cess collected under section 12, sub-section(2)

(b) Contributions, gifts and income from endowments made for the benefit of public libraries

(c) Special grant which the Government may make for any specific purpose connected with libraries;

(d) Fees, fines and other amounts collected by the Local Library Authority under any rules or regulations made under this Act.

(3) The Government shall contribute to the Library Fund maintained by every Local Library Authority, other than the Local Library Authority for the City of (Madras), Chennai a sum not less than the cess collected under section 12, sub-section (2).

(14) Maintenance of Accounts

(1) An account shall be kept of the receipts and expenses of each Local Library Authority.

(2) The account shall be cpen to such inspection, shall be subject to such audit, disallowance and surcharge and shall be dealt with in all other respects in such manner, as may be prescribed.

(15) Supersession or Reconstitution of Library Authorities

Notwithstanding any provision in the Act, the Government may, in cases where they think it necessary to do so, supersede or reconstitute any Library Authorities constituted under the Act:

Provided, however, the Government shall give notices to the Authority concerned together with the grounds on which they propose to supersede or reconstitute and shall consider any explanations that may be offered by such authority.

REPORTS, RETURNS AND INSPECTION

(16) Reports and Returns

Every Local Library Authority and every person in charge of a public or aided library shall submit such reports and returns and furnish such information to the Director or any person authorized by him as the Director or the person authorized may from time to time require.

(17) Inspection of Libraries

The Director or any person authorized by him may inspect any public or aided library or any institution attached thereto for the purpose of satisfying himself that the provisions of this Act and the rules and regulations thereunder are duly carried out.

RULES

(18) Power to make Rules

(1) The Government may, by notification, make rules consistent with this Act to carry out the purposes thereof.

(2) In particular and without prejudice to the generality of the foregoing power such rules may provide for—

(a) All matters required or allowed to be prescribed under the Act;

(b) The method of conducting the election of members to Local Library Authorities and all maters connected therewith;

(c) The matters to be included in the scheme referred to in section 8;

(d) The maintenance of the minutes of the proceedings of Local Library Authorities

(e) The Publication of audited statements of the accounts of such Authorities and of the reports of the auditors; and

(f) A Library Grant-in-aid code regulating the Government's aid to and the declaration, inspection and co-ordination by the Director of aided libraries and the standards to be maintained by such libraries.

MISCELLANEOUS

(19) Amendment of the Press and Registration of Books Act, 1867, in its application to the (State)

The Press and Registration of Books Act, 1867 shall in its application to the State he amended as follows:

(i) In section 9, first paragraph, clause (a) which relates to the delivery to the Government (of copies of books by the printer of a press) for the words 'one such copy', the words 'five such copies' shall be substituted

(ii) In the same section in the last paragraph, clause (i), for the words 'a copy of the first or some preceding edition of which book has been delivered', the words 'five copies of the first or some preceding editions of which books have been delivered' shall be substituted.

APPENDIX II

ANDHRA PRADESH PUBLIC LIBRARY ACT (1960) (AMENDED)

(Received the assent of the Governor on the 18th February 1960 and first published in the Andhra Pradesh Gazette, dated the 25th February, 1960).

An Act to consolidate and amend the laws relating to the establishment and maintenance of Public Libraries in the State of Andhra Pradesh and matters connected therewith.

Be it enacted by the Legislature of the State of Andhra Pradesh in the Eleventh Year of the Republic of India as follows:

CHAPTER I

Preliminary

(1) This Act may be called the Andhra Pradesh Public Libraries Act, 1960

(2) It extends to the whole of the State of Andhra Pradesh

(3) It shall come into force on such date that the Government may, by notification, appoint

(2) In this Act, unless the context otherwise required -

(1) 'Aided Library' means a library declared by the Director to be eligible for aid either from the Government or from the Library Fund in accordance with the rules made under this Act.

(2) 'Committee' means the state library committee constituted under section 3;

(3) 'Director' means the Director of Public Libraries appointed under section 8:

(4) 'District; means a revenue district;

(5) 'Government' means the State Government;

(6) 'Library cess' means the cess levied under sub-section (1) of section 20;

(7) 'Notification' means a notification published in the Andhra Pradesh Gazette;

(7a) Parishad means the Andhra Pradesh Granthalaya Parishad established under section 3;

(8) 'Prescribed' means prescribed by rules made under this Act

(9) 'Public Library' means:-

(a) A library established or maintained by a Zilla Grandhalaya Samstha, including the branches and delivery stations of such a library.

(b) A library established or maintained by the Government and declared open to the public,

(c) A library established or maintained by any local body, or co-operative society and declared open to the public;

(d) A library declared to be eligible for aid and receiving aid from the Government or from the Library Fund; and includes, any other library notified by the Government as a public library for the purposes of this Act,

(10) 'State' means the State of Andhra Pradesh;

(11) 'State Central Library' means a library established by the Government as the State Central Library;

(12) State Regional Library' means a library established by the Government as a State Regional Library;

(13) 'Year' means the financial year.

CHAPTER II

The Andhra Pradesh Grandhalaya Parishad

(3) (1) There shall be established by the Government by

notification for the State of Andhra Pradesh, a Parishad by the name of 'The Andhra Pradesh Grandhalaya Parishad'

(2) The headquarters of the Parishad shall be at Hyderabad

(3) The Parishad shall be a body corporate, having perpetual succession and a common seal with power subject to the provisions of this Act and the rules made thereunder, to acquire, hold and dispose of property and to enter into contracts and shall by the said name sue and be sued.

(4) The Parishad shall consist of the following members, namely:-

(a) a Chairman to be appointed by the Government from among the persons who have rendered eminent service for the cause of education and library movement;

(b) The Director of Public Libraries, who shall be the Member Secretary; and

(c) Seven members to be nominated by the Government of whom:-

(i) One shall be an expert having special knowledge of library science;

(ii) Two shall be from among those who have rendered service for the development of library movement and education;

(iii) One shall be a person representing the recognized aided libraries;

(iv) One shall be from among the Charimen of the Zilla Grandhalaya Samsthas;

(v) One shall be from among the Secretaries of the Zilla Grandhalaya Samsthas;

(vi) The Chief Librarian , State Central Library, Hyderabad shall be member, ex-officio.

(4) The Objects of the Parishad shall be :-

(i) To organize and promote library service in the State:

(ii) To establish, equip, maintain and develop and integrated, comprehensive and efficient library service in the State;

(iii) To augment the supply of books and periodicals to all the libraries in the State;

(iv) To develop infrastrucutral facilities such as buildings, furniture, equipment to all public libraries and Zilla Grandhalaya Samsthas in the State;

(v) To raise finances and regulate their usage for the promotion of library service;

(vi) To undertake other related activities;

(vii) To augment the income of the Parishad and Zilla Grandhalaya Samsthas and suggest ways and means for raising additional resources; and

(viii) To prepare long term and short term plans for improving the library service in the State and also to supervise the implementation of approved plans,

(5) (1) The Parishad shall be the principal policy formulating body and shall exercise the following powers and perform the following functions, namely:-

(a) To evolve perspective plans for the development of library services and to co-ordinate and determine the standard of library service in Zilla Grandhalaya Samsthas;

(b) To prepare consolidated programmes in accordance with the guidelines issued by the Government and the Raja Ram Mohan Roy Library Foundation and also to implement the developmental programmes;

(c) To approve the budget estimates of the parishad and Zilla Grandhalaya Samthas;

(d) To sanction the opening of Library branches, village libraries and book deposit centers. subject to the availability of funds and creation of full time posts with the approval of the Government;

(e) To accord administrative and financial sanction for the construction of buildings for the purpose of public libraries;

(f) To accord administrative and financial sanction for additional staff with the approval of the Government;

(g) To approve the shifting of regional and mobile libraries;

(h) To accept gifts or endowments for any purpose connected with the library activities of a value upto rupees five lakhs and with the permission of the Government of a value exceeding five lakhs;

(i) To approve and submit to Government every year the audited statements of accounts and utilization certificates of its funds;

(j) To approve the annual audited statements of accccounts of the Zilla Grandhalaya Samsthas ;

(k) To approve the annual report on the working of public libraries under the Act and cause to be placed before the Legislature;

(l) To decide the policy for the selection and purchase of books required by the public libraries in the state and for this purpose to constitute sub-committees, which shall include one expert in the subject of language concerned besides other eminent persons in the faculties concerned.

(m) To organize and conduct library seminars, meetings and conferences;

(n) To set up sub-committees, as may be necessary from time to time to regulate the work;

(o) To co-ordinate all the activities concerned with the library service and also to supervise the proper utilization of funds allotted to such activities including the cess collected by the Zilla Grandhalaya Samsthas, and

(p) To prepare consolidated programme in accordance with the guidelines issued by the Government from time to time.

(2) The Parishad shall advise the Government on all matters arising under this Act and shall exercise such other powers and perform such other functions as may be prescribed.

(3) The Parishad shall meet at least once in two months. The number of members necessary to constitute a quorum at the meetings and the procedure to be followed in the meeting shall be such as may be prescribed.

(6) The Chairman shall be Head of the Parishad and shall preside over all its meetings. He shall supervise the implementation of the policies and programmes of the Parishad and exercise such other powers and perform such other functions as may be prescribed.

(7) (1) The Chairman of the Parishad shall be entitled in such salary and allowances and shall be subject to such conditions of service as may from time to time be prescribed.

(2) The Chairman and every member of the Parishad, other than the ex-officio members, shall hold office for a period of three years from the date of his nomination,

(3) The other members of the Parishad shall receive such allowances as may be prescribed.

(7A) The Member Secretary shall be the Chief Executive of the Parishad and shall exercise the following powers and perform the following functions, namely:-

(1) Implement all the policies and programmes of the Parishad;

(2) Exercise general supervision and control over the Parishad office staff, field staff of libraries or any other employees of the Parishad and all the libraries under Zilla Grandhalaya Samsthas:

(3) To deal with all the administrative matters pertaining to appointments, postings, transfers, promotions and disciplinary action of the staff of Prishad and Zilla Grandhalaya Samsthas;

(4) Run the day-to-day administration of the Parishad and conduct all its financial and administrative transactions;

(5) Be the custodian of the finances of the Parishad;

(6) Prepare and present the audited statements of accounts and utilization certificates to the Parishad for its approval;

(7) Obtain audited statements of accounts of all the Zilla Grandhalaya Samsthas and place them before the Parishad for its approval alongwith utilization certificates; and

(8) Recommend administrative and financial sanctions for the creation of the posts of Officers and the other employees for the performance of functions of the Parishad.

(7B) Any Vacancy occurring in the office of the Chairman or as the case may be of the member of the Parishad before the expiration of the term shall be filled up by nomination of another person in the manner provided in section 3 and the persons so nominated, shall hold office for the residue of the term of his predecessor.

(7C) (1) The Parishad shall have its own funds, consisting of :-

(a) The grants made by the State Government;

(b) All moneys received by or on its behalf under the provisions of this Act or any other law for the time being in force or under any other contract;

(c) All proceeds of the disposal of the property by or on behalf of the Parishad;

(d) All moneys received by or on behalf of the Parishad from Public bodies, private bodies or private individuals by way of grants, donations or deposits;

(e) All interests and profits arising from any investment or from any transactions in connection with any money belonging to the Parishad; and

(f) Such other sums from the Zilla Grandhalaya Samsthas

as may be required for specific purposes as provided under the Act or as per the instructions of the Government, from time to time.

(2) All moneys belonging to the Parishad shall be deposited in such banks or invested in such manner as may be prescribed.

(3) The Parishad may spend such sums as it may deem fit for performing its functions under this Act and such expenditure shall be created as expenditure payable out of this fund.

(7D) The Government may, at any time after the constitution of the Parishad transfer to it, any properties of the public libraries along with the staff on such terms and conditions as it may deem proper.

(7E) The Parishad shall function under the general supervision and control of the power to give such directions as it may deem fir from time to time and may review the actions of the Parishad.

CHAPTER III

Department of Public Libraries

(8) For the purpose of this Act, the Government shall constitute a separate Department of Public Libraries and appoint a Director for that Department. The Director so appointed shall subject to the control of the Government:-

(a) Supervise the State Central Library and the branches of such library;

(b) Superintend and direct all matters relating to public libraries;

(c) Declare, in accordance with the rules made under this Act, what libraries are eligible for aid from the Government and supervise and direct all matters relating to such libraries;

(d) Direct and control the work of all Zilla Granthalaya Samsthas under this Act in the manner prescribed;

(e) Submit reports to the Committee on the working of libraries, whenever necessary;

(f) Publish annually a bibliography of all the books published in the State in any language other than English or Sanskrit;

(g) Perform such other duties and exercise such other powers as are imposed or conferred on him by this Act or the rules made thereunder;

(h) Arrange for centralized classification, cataloguing, interlibrary loan, co-ordination of book selection and maintenance of copyright registry;

(8A) (1) The Government may, at any time, create such number of posts of Librarians for City Central Library, Hyderabad and for the District Central Libraries, as they may consider necessary, for carrying out the purposes of this Act;

(2) All appointments to the posts of Librarians created under sub-section (1) and transfers of the holders of such posts shall be subject to the provisions of the Andhra Pradesh Public Employment (Regulation of Age of Superannuation) Act, 1984 as amended from time to time and also such other rules as may be made under the provision to article 309 of the Constitution of India;

(3) The Government shall pay out of the Consolidated Fund of the State. the salaries, allowances, leave allowances, pension and contributions, if any, towards the Provident Fund or Pension cum Provident Fund of the Librarians referred to in sub-section (1).

(4) The Classification and methods of recruitment, conditions of service, pay and allowances and discipline and conduct

of the Librarians referred to in sub-section (1) shall be regulated to accordance with the pensions of the Andhra Pradesh Public Employment (Regulation of Age of Superannuation) Act, 1984 as amended from time to time and to such other rules as may be made under the proviso to article 309 of the Constitution of India.

(5) Every holder of the post of Librarian, who is appointed under this Act, immediately before the commencement of the Andhra Pradesh Public Libraries (Amendment) Act, 1986 shall, notwithstanding anything in this Act, continue to hold such post, subject to the provisions of the Andhra Pradesh Employment (Regulation of Age of Superannuation) Act, 1984, as amended from time to time and to such other rules as may be made under the proviso to article 309 of the Constitution and until provision in that behalf is so made, the rules for the time being in force regulating the recruitment and conditions of service applicable to such holder immediately before such commencement, except the provision relating to age of superannuationm, shall continue to apply to such holder.

(6) The Government may, from time to time, by order give such directions to any Zilla Granthalaya Samsthas or Director, as may appear to them to be necessary for the purpose of giving effect to the provisions of this section: and Zilla Granthalaya Samsthas or Director as the case may be, shall comply with all such directions.

CHAPTER IV

The Zilla Granthalaya Samsthas

(9) (1) For the purposes of organizing and administering public libraries in the State, there shall be constituted Zilla Granthalaya Samsthas, one for the City of Hyderabad City Granthalaya Samsthas, one for the district of Hyderabad excluding the said City by the name of the Hyderabad Zilla Granthalaya Samsthas and one for each of the other districts by the name of the district concerned;

(2) Every Zilla Granthalaya Samsthas shall, by the name of the area for which it is constituted, be a body corporate having perpetual succession and a common seal with power to acquire, hold and dispose of property and to enter into contracts and may by the said name sue and he sued.

(3) It shall be the duty of every Zilla Granthalaya Samstha to provide library service in the area of its jurisdiction.

(10) (1) The Zilla Granthalaya Samsthas for the twin cities of Hyderabad and Secunderabad shall consist of the following members; namely:-

(a) Three members nominated by the government from among the residents of the twin cities of Hyderabad and Secunderabad who have rendered eminent service in the field of education or public libraries;

(b) One member nominated by the Government, from among the Presidents of the Governing bodies of the aided libraries in the cities of Hyderabad and Secunderabad;

(c) Two members nominated by the Government, from among the Councillors of the Municipal Corporation of Hyderabad;

(d) The District Educational officer, Hyderabad, Ex-Officio.

(e) The Deputy Director, Office of the Directorate of Adult Education, Hyderabad, Ex-Of-Officio.

(f) The District Public Relations officer, Hyderabad, Ex-Officio.

(g) The Librarian, City Central library, Hyderabad, Ex-Officio, who shall be the Member-Secretary.

(2) The Zilla Granthalaya Samsthas for each District shall consist of the following members, namely:-

(a) Three members nominated by the government from among the residents of the District, who have rendered eminent service in the field of education or public libraries;

(b) One member nominated by the Government from among the Presidents of the Governing bodies of the aided libraries in the District;

(c) One member nominated by the Government from among the Councillors of every Municipal Corporation or of every Municipality as the case may be of the District;

(d) Two members nominated by the Government from among the Presidents of Mandal panchayats in the District concerned;

(e) The District Educational officer of the District concerned, ex-officio;

(f) The Deputy Director of Adult Education In charge of the District concerned, ex-officio;

(g) The District Public Relations officer of the district concerned, ex-officio;

(h) The Librarian, District Central library, ex-officio, who shall be the Member Secretary;

(i) The District Panchayat Officer of the district concerned ex-Officio.

(3) The Government shall nominate one of the non-official members as "the Chairman of the Zilla Granthalaya Samsthas".

(11) (1)Every member of a Zilla Granthalaya Samstha not being an ex-officio member shall hold office for a period of three years from the date of his nomination.

(2) A member nominated to the Zilla Granthalaya Samstha in his capacity as a holder of particular office shall, if he

ceases to be the holder of that office, cease to be a member of the Zilla Granthalaya Samstha.

(3) Save as otherwise provided in this Act, the term of office of the Chairman of a Zilla Granthalaya Samstha shall be three years from the date of his nomination as Chairman. The Chairman shall however cease to hold office before the expiration of such term on his ceasing to be a member of the Zilla Granthalaya Samstha.

(11a) (1)A person shall be disqualified for being a member of the Zilla Granthalaya Samstha, if he -

(a) Is or has been sentenced by a criminal court to imprisonment for a period of more than six months for any offence involving moral delinquency, such sentence not having been reversed or the offence pardoned, and a period of five years has not elapsed from the date of the expiration of such sentence;

Provided that the Government may direct that such sentence shall not operate as a disqualification;

(b) Is of unsound mind and stands so declared by a competent court;

(c) Is a deaf-mute or is suffering from leprosy;

(d) Applies to be adjudicated as an insolvent or is an undischarged insolvent;

(e) Absent himself from three consecutive meetings without excuse sufficient in the opinion of the Zilla Granthalaya Samstha to exonerate the absence.

(f) Where a person ceases to be a member under clause (e) of sub-section (1), the Secretary hall at once intimate the fact in writing to such person and report the same to the Zilla Granthalaya Samstha at its next meeting. Where such person applies for restoration of membership to the Zilla Granthalaya Samstha on or before the date of its next meeting or within fifteen days of the receipt by him of such intimation, the Zilla Granthalaya Samstha may at the meeting next after the receipt of the application, suo motu; restore him as member thereof:

Provided that a member shall not be so restored more than twice during his term of office.

(12) A Vacancy occurring in the office of a nominated member of a Zilla Granthalaya Samstha before the expiration of his term shall be filled by nomination of another person in the manner provided in section 10, and the person so nominated shall hold office for the residue of the term of his predecessor.

(12A) (1) Where, for any reason, there is a delay in the constitution of the Committee in accordance with the provisions of section 3 or the constitution of the Zilla Granthalaya Samstha for the twin cities of Hyderabad and Secunderabad under subsection (1) of section 10 or the Zilla Granthalaya Samstha for the District under sub-section (2) of section 10 or the nomination of the Chairman of the Zilla Granthalaya Samstha under sub-section (3) of section 10, the Government may appoint a person or persons to manage, the affairs of the Committee or of the Zilla Granthalaya Samstha or to perform the functions of the Chairman, as the case may be, for a period not exceeding six months and they may in the manner from time to time extend such period beyond six months so however, that the aggregate period including the extended period, if any, shall not exceed two years.

(2) The person or persons so appointed shall, subject to the control of the Government and to such instructions or directions as they may issue from time to time exercise the powers, discharge the duties and perform the functions of the Committee or of the Zilla Granthalaya Samstha and its Chairman, as the case may be, and take all such section as may be required in the interest of the Zilla Granthalaya Samstha.

(3) The Government may fix the remuneration payable to the person or persons so appointed. The amount of such remuneration and other costs, if any, incurred in the management of the Zilla Granthalaya Samstha shall be payable out of the Library fund.

(13) (1) A Zilla Granthalaya Samstha. may—

(a) Provide suitable lands and buildings for public libraries and also the furniture, fittings, materials and conveniences requisite therefor;

(b) Stock such libraries with books, periodicals, newspapers, manuscripts, maps, works and specimens of art and science, lantern slides films, cinema projectors, recorders and the like:

Provided that the books that may be stocked in the libraries shall be selected from te list of books approved from time to time by the Parishad.

Provided further that the Zilla Granthalaya Samstha. shall stock also books and periodicals as may be directed, from time to time by the Parishad or by an officer authorized by the Parishad in this behalf, the aggregate value whereof shall not be less than twenty five percent of the provision made in the budget of that Samstha for the purpose of this clause;

(c) (......);

(d) With the previous sanction of the Director, shift or close any public library mentioned in sub-clause (a) of clause (9) of section2, or discontinue aid to any other public library, the payment of which is regulated by rules made under this Act;

(e) Accept any gift or endowment for any purpose connected with its activities;

Provided that no gift or endowment of an immovable property shall be accepted without the previous sanction of the Government:

(f) Provide for lecturers and the holding of classes and conduct other activities connected with public library service including social education;

(g) With the consent of the management and the previous sanction of the Parishad or an officer authorized by the Parishad in this behalf acquire any library on such conditions as may be approved by the Parishad, or an officer authorized by the Parishad in this behalf;

(h) Distribute grants for public libraries for social education purposes;

(h-1) With the previous approval of the Director, organize, or participate in, conferences for the discussion of matters relating to the development of public libraries and the library service;

(i) In general, do every thing necessary to carry out the provisions of this Act,

(2) Nothing in sub-section (i) shall apply to a library maintained by the government.

(14) (1) As soon as possible after a Zilla Granthalaya Samstha. is constituted, and thereafter as often as may be required by the Parishad, every Zilla Granthalaya Samstha. shall and whenever it considers it necessary so to do, a Zilla Granthalaya Samstha. may, prepare a scheme for establishing libraries and for spreading library service within its area in such form and manner as may be prescribed and submit it to the Parishad for sanction. The Parishad may sanction it with such alterations, if any, as it may think fit after giving the Zilla Granthalaya Samstha. an opportunity to make its representations, if any in respect of such alterations and the Zilla Granthalaya Samstha. shall thereupon give effect to the scheme so sanctioned by the Parishad.

(2) The Parishad may on application by the Zilla Granthalaya Samstha concerned, modify any scheme sanctioned under

sub-section (3) and replace it by a new scheme.

(15) (1) A Zilla Granthalaya Samstha may appoint an executive committee consisting of such of its members as it may deem fit and delegate to such committee any of its powers or functions under this Act except the power to levy library cess, to borrow money, to dispose of immovable property and to pass the budget, accounts and the audit and annual reports.

(2) A Zilla Granthalaya Samstha may also, from time to time, appoint sub-committees to enquire into and report or advise on any matters which it may refer to them.

(16) No Act of Parishad or Zilla Granthalaya Samstha shall be deemed to be invalid by reason only of the existence of any vacancy in or any defect in the constitution of that authority.

(17) (1) All property acquired or held in any area by the Zilla Granthalaya Samstha for the purpose of any public library defined in sub-clause (a) of clause (9) of section 2 shall vest in the Zilla Granthalaya Samstha of that area.

(2) Any immovable property required by the Zilla Granthalaya Samstha shall be deemed to be land needed for a public purpose within the meaning of the Land Acquisition Act, 1894 (Central Act I of 1894) and may be acquired under that Act.

(18) (1) Subject to the provisions of this Act and the rules made thereunder, a Zilla Granthalaya Samstha may make bye-laws, generally to carry out the purposes of this Act.

(2) In particular and without prejudice to the generality of the foregoing power, such bye-laws may provide for all or any of the following matters. namely:-

(a) The admission of the public to the public libraries in its area on such conditions as it may specify;

Provided that no fees shall be charged for such admission;

(b) The guarantee or security to be furnished by persons desiring to use such libraries, against injury to or misuse, destruction or loss of the property of such libraries;

(c) The manner in which the property of such libraries may be used and the protection of such property from injury, misuse, destruction or loss;

(d) The Authority to be exercised by its officers and servants in the matter of exclusion or removal from any such library, of any person who contravenes or does not comply with the provisions of this Act or the ruls or buy-laws made thereunder;

(e) The conduct of meetings of the Zilla Granthalaya Samstha and the procedure to be followed in regard to the transaction of business at such meetings and the quorum for the transaction of such business at a meeting.

Provided that a Zilla Granthalaya Samstha shall not have power to make any bye-laws affecting a public library mentioned in sub-clause (11) or sub-clause (12) of section 2.

(3) The Director may modify or cancel any bye-law, made by a Zilla Granthalaya Samstha under sub-section (2). Provided that before modifying or canceling any bye-law, the Director shall give the Zilla Granthalaya Samstha concerned a reasonable opportunity to make its representations in the matter:

(18A) (1) The Government may, by notification, remove any Chairman of the Zilla Granthalaya Samstha, who in their opinion willfully omits or refuses to carry out or disobeys the provisions of this Act, or the rules, bye-laws or lawful orders made thereunder, or abuses his position or powers vested in him.

(2) The Government shall, when they propose to remove a Chairman under sub-section (1). give the Chairman

concerned an opportunity for explanation, and the notification issued under the said sub-section shall contain a statement of the reasons of the Government for the action taken.

(3) The Government shall have power to review any order of removal published under sub-section (1) and pending such review to stay such order.

(4) Any person removed under sub-section (1) from the office of the Chairman shall not be eligible for re-election to the said office for a period of three years from the date of his removal.

(19) If, at any time, it appears to the Government that the Parishad or, as the case may be à Zilla Granthalaya Samstha has failed to perform its functions or has exceeded or abused any of the powers conferred upon it by or under this Act, the Government may communicate the particulars thereof to the Parishad or, as the case may be a Zilla Granthalaya Samstha omits to remedy such failure, excess or abuse or to give a satisfactory explanation therefore within such time as the Government may fix in this behalf the Government may suspend, dissolve or supersede the Parishad or, as the case may be a Zilla Granthalaya Samstha and cause all or any of the powers and functions of such Authority to be exercised and performed by any person or agency for such period as they may think fit or direct that it be reconstituted.

(19 A) Notwithstanding anything in this Act, the Government may, by notification constitute a Library Service for the Zilla Granthalaya Samsthas in the State and appoint to that service such category of Librarians, as may be prescribed.

CHAPTER V

Finance and Accounts

(20) (1) (a) Every Zilla Granthalaya Samstha shall levy in its area a library cess in the form of a surcharge on the property tax or house tax levied in such areas under the relevant laws providing for the levy of such property tax or house tax, at the rate of four naya paise for every rupee in the property tax or house tax so levied.

(b) A Zilla Granthalaya Samstha may, with the previous sanction of the Government and shall if so directed by them, increase the rate specified in clause (a) so as not to exceed eight naye paise for every rupee.

(2) The cess levied under sub-section (1) shall be collected:-

(a) In the twin cities of Hyderabad and Secunderanad by the Municipal Corporation of Hyderabad.

(b) In an area within the jurisdiction of a Municipal Council, by such council;

(c) In an area within the jurisdiction of a Gram Panchayat by the Gram Panchayat; and

(d) In an area in a District not included within the jurisdiction of a Municipal Council or a Gram Panchayat, by the local body having jurisdiction in such area, as if the cess were a property tax or house tax payable under the relevant laws for the time being in force in the area and all the provisions of the said laws relating to collection of property tax or house tax shall apply subject to such modifications as may be specified by the Government in the notification issued in this behalf.

(3) The cess collected under sub-section (2) shall be paid to the Zilla Granthalaya Samstha concerned in such manner as may be prescribed

(21) (1) Every Zilla Granthalaya Samstha shall maintain a fund called the "Library Fund' from which all the payments under this Act shall be met.

(2) There shall be credited to the Library Fund the following sums, namely:-

(a) The Cess collected under sub-section (2) of section 20;

(b) Contributions, gifts and income from endowments made to the Zilla Granthalaya Samstha for the benefit of public libraries;

(c) Special grants which the Government may make for any specified purpose connected with libraries and social education;

(d) Funds and other amounts collected by Zilla Granthalaya Samstha under any rules or bye-laws made under this Act;

(e) Grants released by Government from time to time.

(22) (1) An account shall be kept of the receipt and expenses of the Parishad and each Zilla Granthalaya Samstha.

(2) The accounts shall be open to inspection, shall be subject to audit, disallowance and surcharge and shall be dealt with in all other respects in such manner, as may be prescribed.

CHAPTER VI

Reports, Returns and Inspection

(23) Every Zilla Granthalaya Samstha and every person in charge of a public library shall submit such reports and returns and furnish such information to the Parishad or any person authorized by it this behalf in such a manner as the Parishad prescribes.

(24) The Parishad or any person authorized by it in this behalf may inspect any public library or any institution attached there to for the purpose of satisfying itself that the provisions of this Act and the rules and bye-laws made thereunder are duly carried out.

(24A) There shall be established by the Parishad a separate accounts, inspection, vigilance and audit cell to look after the accounts, inspection and vigilance and audit work of the Department of the Public Libraries in the manner and with such officers as may be prescribed.

On and from the date of commencement of the Andhra Pradesh Public Libraries (Amendment Act, 1989, the Chairman and Members of the State Library Committee, constituted and functioning under section 3 of the principal Act immediately before such commencement shall cease to hold office.

The Andhra Pradesh Public Libraries (Amendment) Ordinance, 1988 is hereby repealed

CHAPTER VII

Miscellaneous

(25) (1)The Government may, by notification, make rules to carry out the purpose of this Act.

(2) In particular and without prejudice to the generality if the foregoing power, such rules may provide for -

(a) The method of appointment and the nomination of members to the Parishad and the Zilla Granthalaya Samsthas.

(b) The publication of audited statements of the accounts of Zilla Granthalaya Samsthas and of the reports of the auditors;

(c) The publication of a Library Grant-in-Aid Code, regulating the grant or aid to aided libraries and the standards to be maintained by such libraries;

(d) The maintenance of State Registers of Libraries and Librarians;

(e) The employment of necessary staff for the public libraries maintained by a Zilla Granthalaya Samstha and for regulating the classification, methods of recruitment pay and allowances, discipline and conduct and other conditions of service of the staff employed in such libraries.

(f) The classification, methods of recruitment, pay and allowances, discipline and conduct and other conditions of service of the members of the Library Service constituted under section 19-A

(g) The recognition of the library associations and regulation of grants to such associations.

(3) Every rule made under this Act, shall immediately after it is made, be laid before each House of the State Legislature, if it is in session and if it is not in session in the session immediately following for a total period of fourteen days which may be comprised in one session or in two successive sessions, and if, before the expiration of the session in which it is so laid or the session immediately following; both Houses agree in making any modification in the rule or in the amendment of the rule, the rule shall thereafter have effect only in such modified form or shall stand amended as the case may be, so however that any such modification or amendment shall be without prejudice to the validity of anything previously done under that rule;

(26) (.............)

(27) (.............)

(28) (1) The Madras (Tamil Nadu) Public Libraries Act), 1948 (Madras Act XXIV of 1948) and the Hyderabad Public Libraries Act, 1955 (Hyderabad Act III of 1955) are hereby repealed

(2) Notwithstanding such repeal -

(a) The members of the .... Zilla Granthalaya Samsthas constituted under the said Acts and holding office immediately before the commencement of this Act shall be deemed to be respectively the members of the Zilla Granthalaya Samsthas constituted under this Act, and shall exercise all powers and perform all duties conferred on such committee or authorities in the respective areas in which they are functioning at such commencement until their present term expires or until a new committee or authorities are constituted under this Act, whichever is later;

(b) All rules, bye-laws and regulations made under the said Acts and in force at the commencement of this Act, shall, so far as such rules, bye-laws and regulations are not inconsistent with the provisions of this Act, continue to be in force in the respective areas in which they are in force at such commencement, and such rules shall be deemed to be rules, and such bye-laws and regulations shall be deemed to be bye-laws, made under the provisions of this Act until they are superseded or modified by rules and bye-laws made under this Act.

APPENDIX III

KARNATAKA (MYSORE) PUBLIC LIBRARIES ACT, (1965)

An Act to provide for the establishment and maintenance of Public Libraries and the organization of a comprehensive rural and urban library service in the State of Karnataka (Mysore)

Whereas it is expedient to provide for the establishment and maintenance of public libraries and the organization of a comprehensive rural and urban library service in the State of Karnataka and for matters connected therewith:-

Be it enacted by the Karnataka (Mysore) State Legislature in the Sixteenth Year of the Republic of India as follows:-

CHAPTER 1

Preliminary

(1) Short title, extent and commencement

- (1) This Act may be called the Karnataka Public Libraries Act, 1965
- (2) It extends to the whole of the State of Karnataka (Mysore)
- (3) It shall come into force as such date on the State Government may, by notification, appoint

(2) Definitions

In this Act, unless the context otherwise requires:-

- (1) Academic library means a library maintained by a university, college, school or research institution;
- (2) 'Aided library' means a library declared by the State Librarian to be eligible for aid from the Government in accordance with the rules made under this Act;

(3) 'book' includes -

(i) Every volume, part or division of a volume, and pamphlet, in any language;

(ii) Every sheet of music, map, chart or plan separately printed or lithographed;

(iii) Newspapers, periodicals and other such materials;

(4) 'Chief Librarian' means the Librarian appointed to be in charge of a City Central Library or a District Central Library and other Libraries and the Library service under the control of a City Library Authority or a District Library Authority, as the case may be;

(5) 'City Library Authority' means a Library 'Authority constituted for a city or other urban area under sections 16 and 17;

(6) 'State-owned Library' means a library maintained by a Department of the State Government, the State Legislature: the High Court or any other court or any authority of the State;

(7) 'District' means a revenue district;

(8) 'District Library Authority' means a Library Authority constituted for a district under sections 16 and 18;

(9) 'Library cess' means a cess levied under section 30,

(10) 'Local Library Authority' means a City Library Authority or a District Library Authority;

(11) 'Notification' means a notification published by the official Gazette;

(12) 'Outlier Library' means any library other than a pubic library;

(13) 'Prescribed' means prescribed by rules made under this Act;

(14) 'Public library' means:-

(a)A Library established or maintained by a Local Library Authority, including the branches and delivery stations of such library;

(b) A library established or maintained by the State Government and declared open to the public;

(c) A library established or maintained by any local authority and declared open to the public;

(d) A library declared to be eligible for aid and receiving aid from the State Government and includes, any other library notified by the State Government as a public library for the purposes of this Act;

(15) 'State Central Library' means the library declared to be the State Central Library under Chapter VI;

(16) 'State Librarian' means the State Librarian appointed under this Act;

(17) 'State Library Authority' means the Authority constituted under section 3;

(18) 'Year' means the financial year.

CHAPTER II

The Karnataka (Mysore) State Library Authority

(3) Constitution and composition of the State Library Authority

(1) As soon as may be after the commencement of this Act, the State Government shall, by notification, constitute for the purposes of this Act, an authority to be called the State Library Authority. Such authority shall be a body corporate having perpetual succession and a common seal with power, subject to the provisions of this Act, to acquire, hold and dispose or property and to contract, and may by the same name sue and be sued.

(2) The State Library Authority shall consist of:-

(a) The Minister in charge of public libraries who shall ex-officio be the President of the Authority;

(b) Four persons elected by the Karnataka (Mysore) Legislative Council from among its members;

(c) Two persons elected by the Karnataka (Mysore) Legislative Council from among its members;

(d) One person elected by the Syndicate of each of the Universities in the State from among the members of the Syndicate;

(e) One person elected by the Executive Committee of the Karnataka (Mysore) Library Association from among the members of the Association;

(f) One person elected by the City Library Authority of the City of Bangalore from among its members;

(g) One person elected by the City Library Authority of one of the cities in the State other than the City of Bangalore for which a City Library Authority is established, from among the members of such Authority; subject to the condition that such election shall be made by each City Library Authority for one term in such order of rotation as the state government may by order determine.

(h) One person elected by the District Library Authority of one of the Districts in each Revenue division of the State from among the members of such Authority subject to the condition that such election shall be made by each District Library Authority in every Revenue Division for one term in such order of rotation as the State Government may by order determine;

(i) The Secretary to the Government, Education Department;

(j) The Director of Public Instruction in Karnataka (Mysore)

(k) Three persons nominated by the State Government who in the opinion of the State Government are experts in library science:

Provided that at the first constitution of the Authority for purposes of clauses (f), (g) and (h), six persons ordinarily resident in the cities and districts of the Revenue Divisions for which the Library Authorities may be established shall be nominated by the State Government.

(3) The State Librarian shall ex-officio be the Secretary of the State Library Authority.

(4) **Functions of the State Library Authority**

The State Library Authority shall advise the Stat Government on all matters connected with the administration of this Act, shall be the managing authority for the State Central Library, and shall exercise and perform such powers and duties conferred and entrusted to the said Authority by this Act, and such other powers and duties as may be prescribed.

(5) **Nominations of Members in default of election**:

If any of the bodies referred to in sub-section (2) of section 3 does not, by such period as may be prescribed, elect a person to be a member of the State Library Authority, the State Government shall, by notification, nominate to the vacancy a person qualified for election thereto; and the person so nominated shall be deemed to be a member of the Authority as if he had duly elected by the said body.

(6) Term of Office

(1) Save as otherwise provided in this Act, the term of office of members of the State Library Authority; other than ex-officio members, shall be for a period of three years commencing from the date on which the first meting to he Authority is held after the election or nomination of the members under section 3.

(2) An outgoing member shall continue in office until the election or nomination of his successor.

(3) An outgoing member shall be eligible for re-election or re-nomination.

(7) Vacancies

In the event of a vacancy arising out of death, resignation, disability or otherwise, previous to the expiry of the term of office of any member of the State Library Authority, the vacancy shall be filled by election or nomination, as the case may be, of another person in the manner provided in sub-section (2) of section 3, shall hold office only so long as the member in whose place he is elected or nominated would have held office if the vacancy and any person elected or nominated to fill the vacancy had not occurred

(8) Disabilities for continuing as member

If any member other than an ex-officio member of the State Library Authority during the period for which he has been nominated or elected:-

(a) absents himself without excuse sufficient in the opinion of the Authority, from three consecutive meetings of the Authority or

(b) In the case of a member elected by any body referred to in sub-section (2) of section 3, ceases to be a member of the body concerned, his office in the Authority shall become vacant.

(9) Disqualifications

A person shall be disqualified for being chosen as, and for being a member of the State Library Authority, -

(a) If he has been sentenced by a criminal court for an offence involving moral turpitude and punishable with imprisonment for a term exceeding three months, such sentence not having been subsequently reversed, quashed or remitted, unless he has by order, which the State Government is hereby empowered to made in this behalf been relieved from the disqualification arising on account of such sentence;

(b) If he is an undischarged insolvent;

(c) If he is of unsound mind and stands so declared by a competent court.

(10) Meetings of the State Library Authority

(1) The State Library Authority shall meet at least twice a year on dates to be fixed by the President. One of such meetings shall be the annual meeting.

(2) The president may also, whenever he thinks fit, convene a special meeting of the Authority for the transaction of urgent business.

(3) Subject to prescribed conditions, special meetings shall be convened by the President to discuss mattes of urgent importance upon a requisition by the members of the Authority.

(4) Two-fifths of the total number of members of the Authority shall be the quorum for a meeting of the State Library Authority

(5) The President, if present, shall preside at every meeting of the Authority. In the absence of the President, the members present at the meeting shall choose one from among themselves to preside.

(11) Procedure of State Library Authority

The State Library Authority shall transact business in such manner and in accordance with such procedure as may be prescribed.

CHAPTER III

Department of Public Libraries

(12) Department of Public Libraries

For the purposes of this Act, a Department of Public Libraries shall be constituted with a State Librarian as its head and such other officers and servants as the Government may by order specify.

(13) Functions of the Department

(1) Subject to the control of the State Government, the Department of Public Libraries shall be responsible for the administration of this Act .

(2) In particular and without prejudice to the generality of the foregoing power, the Department shall—

(a) Superintend and direct all matters relating to all public libraries ;

(b) Promote the establishment of public library service so as to achieve the purposes of this Act;

(c) Supervise and direct all matters relating to libraries receiving grant from the State Government;

(d) Maintain State Registers of Libraries and of librarians;

(e) Superintend, direct, and deal with the exercise of powers and the performance of duties by Local Library Authorities under this Act;

(f) Ensure the proper utilization of the Library Funds and library man-power of the State;

(g) Perform such other functions as may be entrusted to the Department by or under the provisions of this Act.

(14) State Librarian

(1) A whole-time officer having the prescribed qualifications to practice the library profession shall be appointed by the State Government as the State Librarian;

(2) The State Librarian shall:-

(a) Function as the Librarian of the State Central Library;

(b) Superintend, direct, and deal with all matters relating to the Press and Registration of Books Act, 1867 (Central Act 25 of 1867) and to the maintenance and service of the books sent under the said Act;

(c) Control the appointments, postings and transfers of officers and servants in the State Library Service;

(d) Generally assist the State Library Authority in performing its functions;

(e) Exercise such other powers and perform such other duties as may be conferred or imposed on him by or under this Act.

(15) State Library Service

(1) Notwithstanding anything contained in any other law all posts' in the Department of Public Libraries, the State Central Library and every Lccal Library Authority shall be filled by appointment of persons belonging to the Karnataka State Library Service;

(2) The Karnataka (Mysore) State Library Service shall consist of the State Librarian, Chief Librarians of Cities and Districts, Librarians and such other classes and categories of posts as the State Government may from time to time determine. All members of the said service shall be Government servants, and their recruitment and conditions of service shall, subject to the provisions of Article 309 of the Constitution, be regulated by such rules as may be prescribed.

(3) The salary, allowances, gratuity, pension and other benefits of the members of the Karnataka (Mysore) State Library Service shall be met from the consolidated Fund of the State.

CHAPTER IV

Local Library Authorities

(16) Constitution of Local Library Authorities

(1) For the purpose of organizing and administering Public Libraries in the State there shall be constituted Local Library Authorities,—

(a) For the Cities of Bangalore, Hubli-Dharwar, Mangalore, Mysore and Belgaum, and for such other urban area having a population of more than one lakh, as the State Government may by notification specify called the City Library Authority; and

(b) For each revenue district excluding the area for which a City Library Authority is constituted called the District Library Authority;

Provided that the District Library Authority constituted for Bangalore District (Rural) shall organize and administer public libraries in Bangalore District (Rural) also, excluding the City of Bangalore.

(2) Every Local Library Authority shall by the name of the area for which it is constituted, be a body corporate having perpetual succession and a common seal with power subject to the provisions of this Act, to acquire hold and dispose of property, and to contract, and may by the same name sue and be sued.

(17) Composition of City Library Authorities

(1) Every City Library Authority shall consist of –

(a) The Mayor of the Municipal Corporation or the President of the Municipal Council or other municipal body of the City who shall ex-officio be the Chairman of the Authority;

(b) A Principal of a First Grade College in the City nominated ex-officio by the State Government who shall be the Vice-Chairman of the Authority;

(c) Two persons, elected by the Municipal Corporation, municipal council or other municipal body of the city from among its members.

(d) One person nominated by the State Government from among the members of governing bodies of aided libraries in the city;

(e) A Head Master of a High School in the city nominated ex-officio by the State Government;

(f) One person nominated by the council of the city branch, if any, of the Karnataka (Mysore) Library Association;

(g) An officer of the Department of Public instruction having jurisdiction over the city, nominated ex-officio by the state Government.

(h) Two persons nominated by the State Government from among persons ordinarily resident in the city.

(2) The Chief Librarian of the city shall ex-officio be the Secretary of the City Authority and of the Committees of the said Authority

(18) Composition of District Library Authorities

(1) Every District Library Authority shall consist of –

(a) The Deputy Commissioner of the district who shall ex-officio be the Chairman of the Authority.

(b) The Deputy Director of Public Instruction in charge of the district.

(c) Two persons elected from among its members by the District Development Council;

(d) One person elected from among its members by each municipal council council or other municipal body in the district with jurisdiction over a municipal area other than an area for which a City Library Authority is established having a population of not less than fifty thousand.

(e) Two persons nominated by the state Government from among the members of municipal councils or other municipal bodies in the district with jurisdiction over a municipal area having a population of less than fifty thousand;

(f) One person nominated by the Council of the District

Branch, if any, of the Karnataka Library Association;

(g) One person nominated by the State Government from among the members of the Taluk Development Boards in the district;

(h) Two persons nominated by the State Government from among the members of the village Panchayat and town Panchayats in the district;

(i) Two persons nominated by the State Government from among the members of the governing bodies of aided libraries in the district;

(j) A Principal of a First Grade College in the district nominated ex-officio by the State Government;

(k) A Headmaster of a High School in the district nominated ex-officio by the State Government;

(l) An officer of the Department of Public Instruction having, jurisdiction over the district or a part thereof nominated ex-officio by the State Government;

(m) Three persons nominated by the state Government from among persons ordinarily resicent in the district.

(2) The Vice-Chairman of the District Library Authority shall be elected by the members from among themselves.

(3) The Chief Librarian of the district shall ex-officio be the Secretary of the District Library Authority and of the Committees of the said Authority.

(19) Nomination of Members in default of election

If any of the bodies referred to in Section 17 or 18 does not by such period as may be prescribed elect or nominate a person to be a member of the City Library Authority or the District Library Authority as the case may be, the State Government shall by notification, nominate to the vacancy a person qualified for election thereto; and the person so nominated shall be deemed to be a member of the Authority as if he had been duly elected by the said body.

(20) Term of Office

(1) Save as otherwise provided in this Act, the term of office of members of a Local Library Authority, other than ex-officio members, shall be for a period of three years commencing from the date on which the first meeting of the Authority is held after the election or nomination, of the members under section 17,18 and 19.

(2) An outgoing member shall continue in office until the election or nomination of his successor

(3) An outgoing member shall be eligible for re-election or re-nomination.

(21) Vacancies

In the event of a vacancy arising out of death, resignation, disability or otherwise, before the expiry of the term of office of any member of a Local Library Authority, the vacancy shall be filled by election or nomination, as the case may be, of another person in the manner provided in section, 17 or section 18, as the case may be, and any person elected or nominated to fill the vacancy shall hold office only so long as the member in whose place he is elected or nominated would have held office if the vacancy had not occurred.

(22) Disabilities for continuing as member

If any member other than ex-officio member of a Local Library Authority during the period for which he has been nominated or elected,—

(a) Absents himself without excuse sufficient in the opinion of the Authority, from three consecutive meetings of the authority, or

(b) In the case of a member elected by any body referred to in section 17 or section 18 ceases to be a member of the body concerned, his office in the Authority shall become vacant.

(23) Disqualifications

A person shall be disqualified for being chosen as, and for being, a member of the Local Library Authority.

(a) if he has been sentenced by a criminal court for an offence involving moral turpitude and punishable with imprisonment for a term exceeding three months, such sentence not having been subsequently reversed, quashed or remitted, unless he has, by order, which the State Government is hereby empowered to make in this behalf, been relieved from the disqualification arising on account of such sentence;

(b) If he is an undischarged insolvent

(c) If he is of unsound mind and stands so declared by a competent court.

(24) Meetings of Local Library Authorities

(1) Every Local Library Authority shall meet at least twice a year on dates to be fixed by the Chairman. One of such meetings shall be the annual meeting.

(2) The Chairman may also, whenever he thinks fit, convene a special meeting of the Authority for the transaction of urgent business.

(3) Subject to prescribed conditions, special meetings shall be convened by the Chairman to discuss maters of urgent importance upon a requisition by the members of the Authority.

(4) A Local Library Authority shall transact business in such manner and in accordance with such procedure as may be prescribed.

(25) Powers and duties of Chairman and Vice-Chairman

(1) The Chairman of a Local Library Authority shall –

(a) Preside at the meetings of the Authority

(b) Watch over the financial and executive administration of the Authority and exercise general supervision and control.

(2) The Vice-Chairman of a Local Library Authority shall, -

(a) In the absence of the Chairman, preside at the meetings of the Authority;

(b) Exercise such powers and perform such duties of the Chairman as the Chairman may, from time to time, delegate to him.

(26) Powers and functions of Local Library Authorities

(1) It shall be the duty of every City Library Authority and every District Library Authority to provide library service to the persons residing in the area within its jurisdiction. The Library Authority shall in every City establish a City Central Library and Branch Libraries and in every district establish a District Central library and branch libraries

(2) For purposes of sub-section (1), a Local Library Authority may –

(a) Provide suitable lands and buildings for public libraries, and the furniture, fittings, equipment and other conveniences necessary for the purpose;

(b) Provide such libraries with books, periodicals, newspapers, maps, gramophone records, manuscripts works and specimens of art and science, lantern slides, films, cinema projectors, records and the like;

(c) With the previous sanction of the Government shift or close any public library;

(d) Accept any endowment or gift for any purpose connected with its activities; Provided that no gift or endowment of an immovable property shall be accepted without the previous sanction of the State Government;

(e) Provide for lectures and conduct other activities as may be conductive to the carrying out of the purposes of this Act.

(f) With the consent of the management and the previous sanction of the State Government acquire any library on such conditions as may be conductive to the furtherance of the purpose of this Act;

(g) With the sanction of the State Government do any other thing that may be conductive to the furtherance of the purpose of this Act;

(h) Exercise such other powers and perform such other duties as may be conferred or imposed by or under this Act.

(27) Library Development Plan

(1) Subject to the general or special orders of the State Government, as soon as possible after a Local Library Authority is constituted and thereafter as often as may be required by the State Librarian, every Local Library Authority shall, and whenever it considers it necessary so to do, a Local Library Authority may, prepare a plan (hereinafter referred to as the Local Library Development Plan) for establishing libraries and spreading library service withinthe jurisdiction of such authority in such form and manner and containing such particulars as may be prescribed.

(2) The salient features of every Local Library Development Plan prepared under sub-section (1) shall be published in such manner as may be prescribed along with a notice inviting objections and suggestions from all persons interested in the plan within such period as may be specified in the notice. Any objection or suggestion which may be received from any person with respect to the Local Librai, Development Plan shall be considered by the Local Library Authority and such modifications in the Plan shall be made as the Authority deems fit.

(3) The Local Library Development Plan shall thereafter be sent to the State Librarian along with a copy of the

objections and suggestions received under sub-section (2). The State Librarian shall with his comments on the Local Library Development Plan submit it to the State Government for sanction.

(4) The State Government may, if it deems fit, after ascertaining the views of the State Library Authority sanction the Local library Development Plan with such alternations as it considers necessary. The State Government may on application by the Local Library Authority concerned, modify any Local Library Development Plan sanctioned under this sub-section.

(5) (a) As soon as may be after the State Government sanctions a Local Library Development Plan under sub-section (4), the State Librarian shall in conformity with the provisions of the said Plan make an order called the Local Library order for the area, specifying the Central Library and the Branch Libraries including branches, to be located in educational institutions, prisons and hospitals and the service stations, which shall be established and maintained by the Local Library Authority, the measures to be taken by the Local Library Authority for providing adequate library service to the people in the area and the stages in which such measures shall be taken.

(b) A Local Library Order made under clause (a) may be amended in consultation with the Local Library Authority, whenever the State Librarian considers it expedient to do so.

(6) Every Local Library Authority shall give effect to the Local Library Development Plan as sanctioned by the State Government and the Local Library Order made under sub-section (5)

(28) Local Library Authority to appoint committees

(1) Every Local Library Authority shall constitute the following committees by election from among its members namely:-

(i) The Executive Committee; and

(ii) The Finance Committee,

(2) A Local Library Authority may constitute committee, and the Finance Committee.

(3) The Chairman of the Local Library Authority shall ex-officio be a member and Chairman of the Executive Committee and the Finance Committee.

(4) (a)The Executive Committee shall be responsible for the executive functions of the Local Library Authority

(b) The Finance Committee shall scrutinize proposals for increase of revenue, examine the receipts and expenditure statements, consider all new propositions affecting finance and shall generally supervise the revenue and expenditure of the Local Library Authority

(29) Advisory Library Committees

(1) For the purpose of advising on local requirements relating to library service of each branch library and each service station in a village served by traveling library service, Advisory Committee shall be constituted in accordance with the provisions of this section.

(2) Every Branch Library Committee shall consist of :-

(a) The Branch Librarian who shall ex-officio be the Chairman and convener of the Committee;

(b) One person representing the area which the Branch Library services, on the municipal council or other municipal body or the panchayat having jurisdiction over that area, elected by the body concerned.

(c) Three teachers of educational institutions in the area in which the branch library is located, nominated by the Chief Librarian of the City or the Chief Librarian of the district, as the case may be

(d) Three persons from among the registered borrowers of

the branch library nominated by the Chief Librarian of the City or the Chief Librarian of the district, as the case may be;

(3) Every Village Service Library Committee shall consist of –

(a) The Travelling Librarian visiting the service station in the village who shall ex-officio be the Chairman and convener of the Committee;

(b) Two teachers of educational institutions in the area served by the service station, nominated by the Chief Librarian of the District;

(c) Two persons from among the registered borrowers in the area served by the service station

(4) The nominated members of the Branch Library Committee and the Village Service Library Committee shall hold office for a period of three years or until their successors are nominated.

CHAPTER V

Finance and Accounts

(30) Library Cess

(1) With effect from the date of commencement of this Act:-

(a) A library cess in the form of a surcharge on –

(i) Tax on lands and buildings,

(ii) Tax on entry of goods into the local area for consumption, use or sale therein;

(iii) Tax on vehicles

(iv) Tax on professions, trades, callings and employments, shall be levied in the area within the jurisdiction of every City Library Authority under the relevant laws relating to local authorities providing for the levy of such taxes, at the rate of three paise for every rupee of the taxes so levied.

(b) A library cess in the form of a surcharge on tax on lands and buildings shall be levied in the area within the jurisdiction of every District Library Authority, under the relevant laws relating to local authorities providing for the levy of such tax at the rate of three paise for every rupee of tax so levied.

(2) A City Library Authority or District Library Authority may, with the previous sanction of the State Government, by notification, increase the rate of library cess levied on any item of tax specified in clause (a) or (b) of sub-section (1), subject to the condition that the rate shall not exceed six paise for every rupee of the tax levied.

(3) The cess levied under clause (a) or clause (b) of subsection (1) or increased under sub-section (2) shall be collected by the municipal corporation, municipal council or other municipal body, or the village panchayat or other local authority having jurisdiction over the area as if the cess were a tax referred to in the said clause payable under the relevant laws for the time being in force in the area, and all the provisions of the said laws relating to the levy and collection of the said tax shall apply subject to such modifications as may be prescribed.

"(4) Out of the cess collected by it under sub-section (3) every local authority shall be entitled to retain ten per cent of the amount collected towards the cost of collection and the balance shall be paid to the City Library Authority or the District Library Authority, as the case may be".

(31) Government grant to District Library Authority of a Portion of land revenue

(1) The State Government shall make annually a grant to every District Library Authority of an amount equal to three per cent of the land revenue collection of the district

(2) The amount granted to a District Library Authority under

sub-section (1) The State Government shall make annually a grant to every District Library Authority of an amount equal to three percent of the land revenue collection of the district

(3) Land Revenue collection of a district for the purposes of sub-section (1) shall mean -

(a) Until the revision settlement of land revenue under Chapter X of the Karnataka (Mysore) Land Revenue Act, 1964, the land revenue determined on the basis of the average land revenue collection of the district for a period of three years preceding the date of such determination;

(b) After the determination of land revenue on the basis of the aforesaid revision settlement , the land revenue collected during the year preceding the year for which the grant is made.

(32) City and District Library Funds

(1) Every City Library Authority and District Library Authority shall maintain a Fund called theCity Library Fund and the District Library Fund, as the case may be, from which all its payments under this Act shall be met.

(2) There shall be credited to the City Library Fund and the District Library Fund, as the case may be, the following sums, namely.-

(a) The amount of cess paid by the local authority under sub-section (4) of section 30,

(b) The grant under section 31,

(c) Contributions, gifts, and income from endowments, made to the Library Authority forthe benefit of public libraries.

(d) Grant which the Central Government or the State Government may make:

(e) Funds and other amounts collected by the Local Library Authority under rules or bye-laws made under his Act.

(33) State Library Fund

(1) The State Library Authority shall maintain a Fund called the State Library Fund from which all its payments under this Act shall be met.

(2) There shall be credited to the State Library Fund the following sums, namely:-

(a) The grants made by the State Government to the State Library Authority to perform the duties entrusted to it;

(b) Grants which the Central Government may make;

(c) Contributions and gifts made to the State Library Authority;

(d) Funds and other amounts collected by the State Library Authority under the rules or bye-laws made under this Act.

(34) Accounts

(1) An account shall be kept of the receipts and expenses of the State Library Authority and of each City Library Authority and district Library Authority.

(2) The accounts shall be open to inspection, and shall be subject to audit, disallowance and surcharge and shall be dealt with in all other respects in such manner as may be prescribed.

CHAPTER VI

State Central Library

(35) Vesting of Bangalore Public Library in the State Library Authority

(1) With effect from such date as the State Government may by notification appoint (hereinafter referred to in this Chapter as the appointed day), the entire management and control of the Public Library, Bangalore. now vested in the Committee of Management of the Public Library,

Bangalore, shall be vested in the State Library Authority.

(2) As from the appointed day, the Committee of Management of the Public Library, Bangalore, a society registered under the Karnataka (Mysore) Societies Registration Act, 1904, now deemed to be registered under the Karnataka (Mysore) Societies Registration Act, 1960, shall stand dissolved and all property, movable and immovable, and all rights, powers and privileges of the said society which immediately before the appointed day belonged to or vested in the said society shall vest in the State Library Authority and shall be applied for the purposes specified in this Act and such other purposes as may be prescribed.

(3) As from the appointed day, all debts and liabilities of the said society shall stand transferred to and vest in the State Library Authority.

(4) Every employee of the said society shall, as from the appointed day, become an employee of the State Government and shall hold his office under the State Government as a member of the Karnataka (Mysore) State Library Service on the same tenure, at the same remuneration, and upon the same terms and conditions, and with the same rights and privileges and to provident fund, gratuity and other matter, as he would have held the same, as an employee of the said society, and shall continue to do so unless and until his remuneration, terms and conditions are duly altered by the State Government.

(36) Karnataka State Central Library

(1) As from the appointed day, the Public Library, Bangalore, shall be the Karnataka State Central Library.

(2) (a) The Karnataka (Mysore) State Central Library shall be maintained as a reservoir of books and other materials for the proper functioning of the State Library system.

(b) In addition to a general library, the State Central Library shall consist of the following sections, namely:-

(i) A state Bureau of Copyright Collections;

(ii) A State Library for the Blind

(iii) A State Bureau of Inter-Library Loans;

(iv) A State Bibliographical Bureau;

(v) A State Bureau of Technical Service;

(vi) Such other sections as may be prescribed.

(37) Sections of State Central Library

(1) (a) One copy of each book received under the Press and Registration of Books Act, 1867 (Central Act 25 of 1867) shall be kept in the State Central Library as a Bureau of Copy right.

(b) Copies of books in the Bureau of Copyright shall not be issued by way of loan of any kind but may be made available for reference in the library premises.

(2) (a) The production and storage of books, sound record of books and kindred materials for the blind, and the issue of such books and materials for the use of the blind shall be dealt with in the section relating to the State library for the Blind.

(b) The State Central library may collaborate with other Libraries for the Blind in India and undertake such work as may be necessary for purposes of such collaboration.

(3) (a) The State Bureau of inter-library loan shall implement such schemes of inter-library loans among the public libraries and the outlier libraries in the State as may be prescribed.

(b) The State Central Library may with the approval of the State Government, collaborate in any scheme of inter-state library loans

(4) (a) The State Bibliographical Bureau shall undertake such

Bibliographical work as may be prescribed, and may for the purpose collaborate with Departments of Government and educational and other bodies in the State.

(b) The State Central Library may, with the approval of the State Government, collaborate with Bibliographical Bureaux or agencies in India and undertake such bibliographical work as may be necessary for purposes of such collaboration.

(5) (a) The State bureau of Technical Service shall be maintained for centralized technical services, such as, acquisition, classification and cataloguing of books for public libraries, academic libraries, State owned libraries, aided libraries and outlier libraries, in accordance with such schemes as may be prescribed

(b) The State Central Library may, with the approval of the State Government, collaborate with other similar of Technical Service in India and undertake such technical work as may be necessary for purposes of such collaboration:

Provided that no scheme under sub-section (3) or sub-section (5) shall be implemented in respect of any library other than a library owned or controlled by the State, except with the concurrence of the authority which owns or controls such library.

CHAPTER VII

Reports, Returns and Inspection

(38) Reports and returns

Every Local Library Authority and every person in charge of a public library shall submit such reports, and returns and furnish such information to the State Librarian or any person authorized by him in this behalf as the said librarian or authorized person may, from time to time, require.

(39) Inspection of Libraries

The State Librarian or any person authorized by him in this behalf may inspect any public library or any institution attached thereto for the purpose of satisfying himself that the provisions of this Act and the rules and bye-laws made there under are duly carried out.

(40) Annual Report

(1) The State Librarian shall, in respect of each financial year, prepare an annual report of the progress made by the Local Library Authorities during the year along with such information and particulars as may be prescribed and submit such report to the State Government before such date as the State Government may by order specify.

(2) The State Librarian shall, in respect of each financial year prepare an annual report of the activities of the State Library Authority during the year along with such information and particulars as may be prescribed and submit such report to the State Government before such date as the State Government may by order specify.

CHAPTER VIII

Miscellaneous

(41) Power to make rules

(1) The State Government may, after previous publication, by notification, make rules to carry out the purposes of this Act,

(2) In particular and without prejudice to the generality of the foregoing power, such rules may provide for -

(a) The method of election or nomination of members to the State Library Authority, the Local Library Authorities, the Branch Library Committees and the Village Service Library Committees

(b) The maintenance of a State Library Fund and the City and District Library Funds

(c) The administration, inspection and management of the State Central Library;

(d) The maintenance of accounts by the State Library Authority and the Local Library Authorities and the publication of audited statement of accounts and the reports of auditors

(e) The grants-in-aid to aided libraries and the standards to be maintained by such libraries;

(f) The maintenance of State Registers of Libraries and of Librarians;

(g) The constitution of committees by the State Library Authority and the Local Library
Authorities;

(h) The restrictions and conditions subject to which the State Library Authority or a Local
library Authority may enter into contracts, or acquire, hold or dispose of property.

(3) Every rule made under this Act shall, as soon as may be after it is made, be laid before each House of the State legislature while it is in session for a total period of thirty days which may be comprised in one session or in two or more sessions and if before the expiry of the session in which it is so laid or the sessions immediately following, both House agree in making any modification in the rule or both Houses agree that the rule should not be made, the rule shall thereafter have effect only in such modified form or be of no effect, as the case may be'; so however, that any such modification or annulment shall be without prejudice to the validity of anything previously done under that rule.

(42) Power of State Library Authority and Local Library Authorities to make bye-laws

(1) The State Library Authority and every Local library Authority may, subject to the provisions of this Act and the rules made thereunder and with the previous sanction of the State Government, by notification, make bye-laws generally to carry out the purposes of this Act.

(2) In particular and without prejudice to the generality of the foregoing power, such bye-laws may provide for all or any of the following maters, namely:-

(a) The admission of the public to the public libraries under the control of the State Library Authority or the Local Library Authority subject to such conditions as may be specified in such bye-laws; Provided that no fees shall be charged for such admission;

(b) the guarantee or security to be furnished by persons desiring to use such libraries, against injury to, or misuse, destruction or loss of the property of such libraries;

(c) The manner in which the property of such libraries may be used and the protection of such property from injury, misuse, destruction or loss.

(d) The authority to be exercised by the officers and servants of the State library Authority or the Local library Authority for the purpose of exclusion or removal from any such library of any person who contravenes or does not comply with any provisions of this Act or any rule or bye-laws made thereunder.

(43) Offences and Penalities –

Whoever –

(a) In a public library or other institution maintained under this Act acts in any manner likely to cause annoyance or disturbance to any person using such library or institution or behaves in a disorderly manner or uses violent or abusive language in any such library or institution;

(b) After due warning persists in remaining therein beyond the hours fixed for closing, shall be liable to be removed from such library or institution and shall also be punishable with the fine which may extend to rupees ten and for a second or subsequent offence with fine which may extend to rupees fifty.

(44) Control of Local Library Authorities by Government

(1) If, at any time, it appears to the State Government that a Local Library Authority has failed to perform its functions or has exceeded or abused any of the powers conferred upon it by or under this Act, the State Government may communicate the particulars thereof to the Local Library Authority and if the Local library Authority omits to remedy such failure, excess or abuse or to give an explanation which in the opinion of the State Government is satisfactory within such time as the State Government may fix in this behalf the State Government may supersede the Local Library Authority for such period as the State Government may direct.

(2) If a Local library Authority is superseded—

(a) All the powers and duties of the Authority shall during the period of supersession, be exercised and performed by such person or persons as the State Government may from time to time appoint in this behalf;

(b) All properly vested in the Local Library Authority shall during the period of supersession, vest in the State Government; and

(c) On the expiry of the period of supersesion, the Local library Authority shall be reconstituted in the manner provided in this Act.

(45) Liability of members for loss, waste or misapplication

(1) Every member of a Local library Authority shall be personally liable for the loss, waste or misapplication of any money or

other property of the Authority to which he has been a party or which has been caused or facilitated by his misconduct or neglect of his duty as a member.

(2) If after giving the member or members concerned a reasonable opportunity for showing cause to the contrary the State Librarian is satisfied that the loss waste or misapplication of any money or other property of the Local Library Authority is a direct consequence of misconduct or neglect on his or their part, the State Librarian shall by order in writing direct such member or members to pay to the Local Library Authority before a specified date, the amount required to reimburse it for such loss, waste or misapplication.

(3) If the amount is not so paid, it shall be recoverable as an arrear of land revenue.

(4) An appeal shall lie from the decision of the State Librarian to the Karnataka (Mysore) Revenue Appellate Tribunal within such period as may be prescribed and the decision of the Karnataka (Mysore) Revenue Appellate Tribunal on such appeal shall be final.

(46) Members and employees of library Authorities to be Public Servants

Every member of the State Library Authority or a Local Library Authority and every officer and servant employed under such authority shall be deemed to be a public servant within the meaning of section 21 of the Indian Penal Code.

(47) Savings of Validity of acts and proceedings

No act done, or proceedings taken under this Act shall be questioned merely on the ground –

(a) Of a vacancy or defect in the constitution of any Authority or any committee thereof; or

(b) Of any defect or irregularity in such act or proceedings not affecting the merits of the case

(48) Provisions relating to suits, etc

(1) No suit or other legal proceedings shall be instituted against the State Library Authority orLocal library Authority or any of its officers or any person acting under its direction until the expiration of two months next after notice in writing shall have been delivered or left at theoffice of the Authority or at the place or abode of such officer or person; such notice shall statethe cause of action, the relief sought, the amount of compensation, if any claimed, and the nameand place of abode of the intending plaintiff.

(2) No suit or other legal proceedings shall lie against the State Government, the StateLibrarian, the State library Authority o a Local library Authority acting under its direction, in respect of anything done or intended to have been done lawfully and in good faith under this Act or any rule, bye-law or order made thereunder.

(49) Power to remove difficulties

If any difficulty arises in giving effect to the provisions of this Act, the State Government may, by order, make such provisions as appear to it to be necessary or expedient for removing the difficulty.

(50) Transfer of certain libraries

(1) (a) With effect from such date as the State Government may by notification appoint (hereinafter referred to in this sub-section as the appointed day), the entire management and control of the Public Library , Mysore, now vested in the Committee or Management of the Public Library, Mysore, shall be vested in the Mysore City Library Authority.

(b) As from the appointed day, the Committee of Management of the Public Library, (Mysore)Karnataka a society registered under the (Mysore) Societies Registration Act, 2904 now deemed to be registered under the (Mysore) Karnataka Societies Registration Act, 1960, shall stand dissolved and all property, moveable and immoveable, and all rights, powers and privileges of the said society which immediately before the appointed by belonged to or vested in the said society shall vest in the Mysore City Library Authority and shall be applied for purposes specified in this Act and such other purposes as may be prescribed.

(c) As from the appointed day, all debts and liabilities of the said society shall stand transferred to and vest in the Mysore City Library Authority.

(d) Every employee of the said society shall, as from the appointed day, become an employee of the State Government and shall hold his office under the State Government as a Member of the Karnataka (Mysore) State Library Service on the same tenure, at the same remuneration and upon the same terms and conditions and with the same rights and privileges as to provident fund, gratuity and other matters, as he would have held the same as an employee of the said society and shall continue to do so unless and until his remuneration, terms and conditions are duly altered by the State Government.

(2) (a) The State Government may be notification transfer the Mahatma Gandhi Public Library, Mercara, to the Coorg District Library Authority, with effect from such date as may be specified in such notification.

(b) With effect from the day on which such transfer takes place all assets and liabilities appertaining to the said library shall stand transferred to and vest in the Coorg District Library Authority.

(c) With effect from the day on which such transfer takes place, every person employed by the Government in connection with the said public library shall hold his office under the State Government as a member of the

Karnataka (Mysore) State Library Service on the same tenure, at the same remuneration and upon the same terms and conditions and with the same rights and privileges as to provident fund, gratuity and other matters, as he would have held the same if the transfer had not taken place and shall continue to do so unless and until his remuneration, terms and conditions are duly altered by the State Government.

(3) (a) Notwithstanding anything contained in section 47 with effect from such date as the State Government may by notification appoint (hereafter referred to in this sub-section as the specified day), the entire management and control of Karnad Sadashiva Rao District Central Library, Mangalore shall stand transferred to the Mangalore City Library Authority.

(b) As from the specified day, the asses and liabilities of the South Kanara District Library Authority appertaining to the said District Central Library shall vest in the manglore City Library Authority, and the south Kanara District Library Authority, in such proportion and in such manner as the State Government may direct.

(c) Every Employee of South District Library Authority who was employed by the said Authority wholly or mainly in connection with the said District Central Library shall, as from the specified day, become an employee of the State Government and shall hold his office under the State Government as a member of the Mysore State Library Service on the same tenure, at the same remuneration and upon the same terms and conditions and with the same rights and privileges as to provident fund, gratuity and other matters, as he would have held the same as an employee of the South Kanara District Library Authority, and shall continue to do so unless and until his remuneration, terms and conditions are dully altered by the State Government.

(51) Amendment of the Press and Registration of Book Act. 1867 in its Application to the State of Mysore

The Press and Registration of Books Act, 1867 (Central Act XXV of 1867) shall in its application to the State of (Mysore) Karnataka be amended as follows:-

(i) In the first paragraph of section 9, for clause (a), the following clauses shall be substituted, namely:-

"(a) In any case, within one calendar month after the day on which any such book shall first be delivered out of the press, three such copies, and",

(ii) In the last paragraph of section 9, for clause (i), the following clause shall be substituted, namely:-

"(a) Any second or subsequent edition of a book in which edition no additions or alterations either in the letterpress or in the maps, block prints or other engravings belonging to the book have been made, and three copies of the first or some preceding edition of which book have been delivered under this Act or",

(iii) In section 2, for the first sentence, the following sentence shall be substituted, namely;

"Out of the three copies delivered pursuant to clause (a) of the first paragraph of section 9 of this Act, one copy shall be sent to the State Cental Library, Bangalore, referred to in the Karnataka (Mysore) Public Libraries Act, 1965, and the remaining two copies shall be disposed of in such manner as the State Government may, from time to time, determine".

(52) Repeal and Savings

(1) The Tamil Nadu (Madras) Public Libraries Act, 1948 (Madras Act XXIV of 1948) and the Hyderabad Public Libraries Act, 1955 (Hyderabad Act III of 1955) are hereby repealed.

(2) Notwithstanding such repeal —

(a) The members of the Local Library Authorities constituted under Tamil Nadu (Madras) Public Libraries Act, 1948 and holding office immediately before the commencement of this Act shall be deemed to be the members of the Local Library Authorities constituted under this Act and shall exercise all powers and perform all duties conferred on such Authorities in the respective areas in which they are functioning at such commencement until their present term expires or until new authorities are constituted under this Act, whichever is later.

(b) Anything done or any action taken (including any appointment or delegation made, fee or cess imposed notification, order, instrument or direction issued, rule, regulation, form or scheme framed) under the said Acts and in force at the commencement of this Act, shall be deemed to have been done or taken under the provisions of this Act and shall continue to be in force accordingly until they are superseded or modified by anything done or any action taken under this Act.

APPENDIX IV

MAHARASHTRA PUBLIC LIBRARIES ACT (1967)

To provide for the establishment, maintenance, organization and development of public libraries in the State of Maharashtra.

Whereas, it is expedient to provide for the establishment, maintenance, organization and development of public libraries in the State of Maharashtra and for purposes connected with the matters aforesaid; It is hereby enacted in the Eighteenth Year of the Republic of India as follows:- .

PRELIMINARY

(1) Short Title; Extent and Commencement

(1) This act may be called the Maharashtra Public Libraries Act, 1967.

(2) It extends to the whole of the State Maharashtra

(3) It shall come into force on such date as the State Government may, by notification in the Official Gazette, appoint in that behalf; and different dates may be appointed for bringing this Act into force in different areas of this State.

(2) Definitions

In this Act, unless the context otherwise requires –

(i) 'Book' includes every volume, part or division of a volume and pamphlet in any language, and every sheet of music, map, chart or plan separately printed or lithographed, newspapers, periodicals, paintings, films, slides, discs or tapes used for audio-visual information and such other materials;

(ii) 'Committee' means a Library Committee appointed under section 13;

(iii) 'Compensatory allowance' means the traveling allowance, the daily allowance or such other allowance which is paid to the members of the Council or Committee for the purpose of meeting the personal expenditure incurred by them in attending the meetings of such Council or Committee or in performing any other functions as such members for the purposes of this Act;

(iv) 'Council' means the State Library Council constituted under section 3;

(v) 'Director' means the Director of Libraries appointed under section 8;

(vi) 'District' means a revenue district;

(vii) 'Division" means a division as set out in the Schedule to this Act;

(vii) 'Municipal Corporation' means a municipal corporation constituted under the (Bombay) Mumbai Municipal Corporation Act, or the Mumbai (Bombay) provincial Municipal Corporation Act , 1949 or the City of Nagpur Corporation Act , 1948;

(ix) 'Municipality;' means a Municipal Council constituted or deemed to be constituted under the Maharashtra Municipalities Act, 1965;

(x) 'Prescribed' means prescribed by rules made under this Act;

(xi) 'Public Library' means:—

(a) A library established and maintained by the State Government for the use of the public;

(b) A library recognized by the Director for the purposes of Grant-in-aid from the Library Fund; and

(c) Any other library which the State Government by notification in the Official Gazette declares to be a pubic library for the purposes of this Act;

(xii) 'Year' means the financial year.

STATE LIBRARY COUNCIL

(3) Constitution of State Library Council

(a) As soon as may be, after the commencement of this Act, the State Government shall, by notification in the Official Gazette, constitute for the purposes of this Act, a Council to be called the State Library Council.

(b) The Council shall consist of the following members, that is to say,—

(i) The Minister for Education of the State, who shall be ex-officio President of the Council

(ii) The Deputy Minister for Education of the State, who shall be ex-officio Vice-President of the Council;

(iii) The Secretary to the Government of Maharashtra, Education and Social Welfare Department for the time being in office;

(iv) The Charity Commissioner or his nominee not below the rank of Assistant Charity Commissioner;

(v) The Director of Education, Maharashtra State for the time being in office;

(vi) Two members elected by the Maharashtra Legislative Assembly, from amongst its members;

(vii) One person elected by the Maharashtra Legislative Council, from amongst its members;

(viii) One person nominated by the State Government to represent Municipal Corporations functioning in the State of Maharashtra;

(ix) One person nominated by the State Government to represent Municipalities functioning in each of the Divisions;

(x) One member from each Division nominated by the State Government to represent the Zilla Parishads functioning in that Division;

(xi) The President of the body known as the Maharashtra Rajya Granthalaya Sangha;

(xii) One member nominated by the said Maharashtra Rajya Granthalaya Sangha from each Division to represent that Division;

(xiii) The Chairman of the body known as the Sahitya Mahamandal, a society registered under the Mumbai (Bombay) Public Trusts Act, 1950;

(xiv) Four members nominated by the State Government from amongst persons who, in its opinion, have special knowledge or interest or practical experience in matters connected with library service;

(xv) The Director of Libraries who shall also be the Secretary of the Council;

(c) A person so elected under paragraph (6) and (7) of sub-section (2) shall cease to be a member of the Council if he ceases to be a member of the Maharashtra Legislative Assembly or Maharashtra Legislative Council.

(4) Functions of Council

It shall be the function of the Council to advise the State Government on all matters connected with the administration of this Act.

(5) Term of Office of, and Allowances to Members of Council

(1) Save as otherwise provided in this Act, the members of the Council, not being members ex-officio shall hold office for a term of three years commencing on the date on which the first meeting of the Council is held after the nomination of the members under sub-section (2) of section (3).

(2) The members of the Council shall be entitled to such compensatory allowances and at such rates as may be prescribed.

(6) Casual Vacancies in Council

A vacancy in the office of a nominated or elected member of the Council occurring otherwise than be efflux of time shall be filed by nomination or election, as the case maybe, and the person nominated or elected to fill the vacancy shall hold office only for the remainder of the term for which the member whose place he takes was nominated or elected.

(7) Meetings of Council

(a) The Council shall meet not less than twice in every year, on such dates and at such hours as may be fixed by the President; and six months shall not intervene between two successive meetings.

(b) The President of the Council may, whenever he thinks fit, and shall upon the written request of not less than one-third of the total number of members of the Council, and on a date not later than thirty days after the receipt of such request, call a special meeting of the Council.

(c) One-third of the total number of members of the Council shall form the quorum;

(d) The Council shall transact business in such manner and in accordance with such procedure as may be prescribed.

DEPARTMENT OF LIBRARIES

(8) Department of Libraries

(a) For the purposes of this Act, a Department of Libraries shall be constituted by the State Government with a Director of Libraries as its head and with such other officers and servants as the State Government may think fit.

(b) The State Government shall appoint a whole-time officer having the prescribed qualifications to be the Director of Libraries.

(9) Functions of Director

(1) Subject to the superintendence, direction and control of the State Government, the Director shall be responsible for the administration of this Act.

(2) In particular, and without prejudice to the generality of the foregoing provision, the Director shall –

(a) Be responsible for the planning, maintenance, organization and development of public libraries and public library system;

(b) Superintend and direct all matters relating to public libraries;

(c) Promote the establishment of public libraries to achieve the purposes of this Act;

(d) Recognize; in accordance with the rules made under this Act, public libraries and State. Divisional and other public library associations, for the purposes of grant-in-aid from the Library Fund and sanction and disburse grants to them;

(e) Maintain accounts of the Library Fund and ensure its proper utilization;

(f) Publish annually a bibliography of all the books published in the State;

(g) Submit to the State Government every year; a report on the working of public libraries under this Act;

(h) Collect and preserve old and rare books, periodicals, manuscripts and other documents of educative value in public libraries;

(i) Organise programmes for training candidates in library

science and conduct examinations for the candidates of recognized library training courses; and

(j) Exercise such other powers and perform such other duties as may be conferred or imposed on him by rules made under this Act.

(10) State Library Service

(a) The State Government shall establish a Maharashtra State Library Service, and appoint persons thereto

(b) The Maharashtra State Library Service shall consist of such classes and categories of posts as the State Government may from time to time determine. All members of the said service shall be Government servants and their recruitment and conditions of service shall be regulated by such rules as may be made by the State Government from time to time.

(c) The salaries, allowances, gratuity, pension and other emoluments of the members of the Maharashtra State Library Service, shall be paid from the Consolidated Fund of the State.

PUBLIC LIBRARIES

(11) Establishment and Maintenance of Public Libraries

(1) The State Government may establish a State Central Library for the whole of the State, and a Divisional Library for every Division

(2) Where in any Local area, provision for library service to the public is not made to the satisfaction of the Director by any local authority, or any society registered under the Societies Registration Act, 1860 or any trust registered under the Mumbai (Bombay) Public Trust Act, 1950 or where the State Government is of the opinion that any such local authority, society or trust is not willing or is incompetent to provide library service in the public to the satisfaction of the Director

in any local area, the State Government may establish a library for the use of the public in that area.

Provided that, no such library shall be established without giving an opportunity to the local authority or society, as the case may be, the trust to show cause with the State Government should not establish a library in the said local area..

(3) All libraries established under the section shall be maintained, organized and developed by the State Government through the Department of Libraries.

(12) Functions of Public Libraries

The functions of the public libraries shall be such as may, on the advice of the Council, be prescribed.

LIBRARY COMMITTEES

(13) Constitution of Library Committees

(1) For every district, the State Government shall appoint a District Library Committee.

(2) The Committee shall consist of the following members, that is to say:-

(i) The Chairman for the time being of the Education Committee of a Zilla Parishad functioning in the district, who shall be ex-officio President of the Committee;

(ii) The President of the District Library Association of the district (if any);

(iii) One of the Chairmen of the Managing Committees of recognized public libraries functioning in each taluka of the district nominated by the State Government;

(iv) Five persons nominated by the State Government, one of whom shall be a librarian possessing the prescribed qualifications and two shall be persons representing libraries in the areas within the limits of a municipality or municipal corporation in the district;

(v) One of the Presidents of the municipalities in the district nominated by the State Government;

(vi) The Education Officer for the time being of the Zilla Parishad functioning in the district, who shall also be ex-officio Secretary of the Committee.

(3) The State Government shall also appoint a Library Committee for Greater Mumbai (Bombay) consisting of:—

(i) The Chairman for the time being of the Education Committee of the municipal corporation of Greater Mumbai (Bombay) who shall be the ex-officio President of the Committee;

(ii) Five persons nominated by the State Government one of whom shall be a librarian possessing the prescribed qualifications and two shall be persons representing libraries in Greater Mumbai (Bombay);

(iii) Education Officer for the time being of the Municipal Corporation of Greater Mumbai (Bombay);

(iv) Educational Inspector, Greater Mumbai (Bombay), who shall also be the ex-officio Secretary of the Committee;

(14) Term of Office of, and Allowances to Members of Committee

(1) Save as otherwise provided in this Act, the nominated members of the Committee shall hold office for a term of three years commencing on the date on which the first meeting of the Committee is held after their nomination.

(2) The members of the Committee shall be entitled to such compensatory allowances and at such rates as may be prescribed.

(15) Casual Vacancies in Committee

A vacancy in the office of a nominated member of the Committee occurring otherwise than by efflux of time shall be filled by nomination and the person, nominated to fill the vacancy shall hold office only for the remainder of the term for which the member whose place he takes was nominated.

(16) Functions of Committee

It shall be the function of a Committee

(i) To advise the State Government on all matters relating to development of library service in the district or, as the case may be, Greater Mumbai (Bombay) on proper lines;

(ii) To ensure that the prescribed functions of the public libraries are performed by them satisfactorily; and

(iii) To perform such other duties as may be prescribed;

(17) Manner of Transaction of Business by Committee

The Committee shall transact business in such manner, and in accordance with such procedure, as may be prescribed.

FINANCE AND ACCOUNTS

(18) Library Fund

(1) The State Government shall constitute a fund called the Library Fund.

(2) The Library Fund shall consist of:-

(a) Contribution made by the State Government under section 20;

(b) Any special grants given by the State Government under section 21;

(c) Any grants given by the Government of India to the State Government for Development of public libraries; and

(d) Any contributions of gifts made by the public for development of public libraries.

(19) Application of Library Fund

(1) The moneys in the Library Fund shall be utilized by the State Government for carrying out the purposes of this Act

(2) Without prejudice to the generality of sub-section (1), the moneys in the Library Fund may be utilized by the State Government to defray expenditure on the following:-

(a) Establishment, maintenance and development of public libraries;

(b) Compensatory allowances payable to members of the Council and of the Committee;

(c) Grants-in-Aid to public libraries and library associations recognized for the purpose by the Director of Libraries.

(20) Contribution of State Government

The State Government shall, after due appropriation made by law in this behalf, contribute to the Library Fund every year, a sum not less than twenty-five lakhs of rupees.

(21) Special Grants by State Government

The State Government may make special grants to this Library Fund.

(22) Vesting of Properties held for purpose of Government Public Libraries

All property, movable and immovable, acquired or held for the purpose of any public library maintained by the State Government shall vest in the State Government.

REPORTS AND INSPECTION

(23) Reports and Returns

Every person who is in charge of the management of a public library shall submit such reports and returns and furnish such information as the Director may from time to time require, to the Director or any person authorized by him in this behalf.

(24) Inspection of Public Libraries

The Director or any person authorized by him in this behalf shall have power to inspect a public library or any institution attached thereto for the purpose of satisfying himself that the provisions of this Act and the rules made there under are carried out.

(25) Submission of Annual Report by Director

Within six months from the end of every year, the Director shall prepare an annual report on the progress made by public libraries in those yeas and submit it to the State Government together with such information and particulars as may be prescribed.

Provided that, no such report shall be submitted to the State Government unless it is approved by the Council.

MISCELLANEOUS

(26) Rules

(1) The State Government may, by notification in the official Gazette, and subject to the condition of previous publication, make rules to carry out the purposes of this Act.

(2) In particular; and without prejudice to the generality of the foregoing power, such rules may provide for all or any of the following matters, namely:

(i) Under sub-section (2) of section 5 and sub-section (2) of section 14, the compensatory allowances payable to members of the Council and of the Committee and the rates at which such allowances shall be payable;

(ii) Under sub-section (4) of section 7 and section 17, the manner in which and the procedure in accordance with which the Council and a Committee shall transact their business;

(iii) Under sub-section (2) of section 8, the qualifications required for being appointed as the Director;

(iv) Under clause (d) of sub-section (2) of section 9, rule, in accordance with which the Director shall recognize public libraries and State, Divisional and other public library associations for the purposes of grant-in-aid from the Library Fund;

(v) Under clause (j) of sub-section (2) of section 9, the other powers and duties which the Director may exercise or perform;

(vi) Under section 12, the functions of public libraries;

(vii) Under section 13, the qualifications of a librarian to be nominated on a Committee;

(viii) Under section 25, the information and particulars to be submitted to the State Government.

(3) Every rule made under this section shall be laid as soon as may be after it is made before each House of the State legislature while it is in session for a total period of thirty days which may be comprised in one session or in two successive sessions, and if, before the expiry of the session in which it is so laid or the session immediately following both Houses agree in making any modification in the rule or both Houses agree that the rule should not be made and notify such decision in the official Gazette, the rule shall, from the

date of publication of such notification, have effect only in such modified form or be of no effect, as the case may be; so however that any such modification or annulment shall be without prejudice to the validity of anything previously done or omitted to be done under that rule.

APPENDIX V

WEST BENGAL PUBLIC LIBRARIES ACT (1979)

West Bengal Act XXXXX of 1979

(Passed by the West Bengal Legislature)

(Assent of the President was first published in the Calcutta Gazette, Extraordinary of the 7th January, 1980)

An Act to provide for the establishment of Public Libraries in the State of West Bengal and to regulate, guide, control, supervise and to grant recognition to the existing libraries in the State as also to provide for a comprehensive rural and urban library service in the State of West Bengal.

Whereas it is expedient to provide for the establishment of public libraries in the State of West Bengal and to regulate, guide, control, supervise and to grant recognition to the existing libraries in the State as also to provide for a comprehensive rural and urban library service in the State of West Bengal;

It is hereby enacted in Thirtieth Year of the Republic of India, by the Legislature of West Bengal, as follows:

CHAPTER 1

Preliminary

(1) Short title, extent and commencement

(1) This Act may be called the West Bengal Public Libraries Act, 1979.

(2) It extends to the whole of West Bengal.

(3) This section shall come into force at once and the remaining sections shall come into force on such date or dates as the

State Government may, by notification in the Official Gazette, appoint and different dates may be appointed for different sections of this Act.

(2) Definitions

In this Act, unless the context otherwise requires,

(a) 'Aided library' means a recognized library receiving aid from the Government, or from a Local library Authority;

(b) 'Central Library' mans a library declared by the State Government by notification as the Central Library;

(c) 'Director' means the Director of Public Libraries appointed under section 6;

(d) 'District' means a revenue district;

(e) 'District Library' means a library in a district established or recognized by the Government as the District Library;

(f) 'Government' means the Government of the State of West Bengal;

(g) 'Notification' means a notification published in the Official Gazette;

(h) 'Prescribed' means prescribed by rules made under this Act;

(i) 'Private library' means a library other than an aided, recognized or a public library;

(j) 'Public library' means a library established or maintained by the Government or by a Local Library Authority;

(k) 'Recognized Library' means a library recognized by the Director and declared as such for the purposes of this Act.

CHAPTER II

The State Library Council

(3) State Library Council and its Functions

(1) The Government shall constitute a State Library Council (hereinafter referred to as the Council) for the purpose of

advising the Government on the Management of the Central Library, on matters of public library system and on such other matters relating to libraries and library service as may be referred to it.

(2) The Council shall, in consultation with Local Library Authorities constituted under Chapter III, also formulate the principles governing the eligibility of private libraries to receive recognition or aid under this Act.

(3) The Council shall exercise such powers and perform such duties as may be prescribed.

(4) Composition of the Council

(1) The Council shall consist of

(a) The Minister-in-charge of Library Services who shall be the Chairman of the Council;

(b) Four persons to be elected by the members of the West Bengal Legislative Assembly from amongst themselves;

(c) Four persons to be nominated by the Government representing the interests of Universities, the West Bengal Board of Secondary Education and the West Bengal Council of Higher Secondary Education from amongst their members;

(d) Two representatives of the Bengal Library Association to be nominated by the Executive Committee of the said Association from amongst its constituted members;

(e) One representative of the employees of the libraries that will come under the purview of this Act to be elected in the manner prescribed;

(f) Two persons elected by the Local Library Authorities from amongst the members of such authorities in the manner prescribed;

(g) One District Library Officer to be nominated by the Government;

(h) One District Librarian to be nominated by the Government;

(i) The Secretary to the Government in the Education Department or his nominee;

(j) The Director of Public Instruction, West Bengal or his nominee;

(k) Four persons to be nominated by the Government who in its opinion are experts in library science and library service;

(l) The Deputy Director of Public Instruction (Social Education), West Bengal;

(m) The Director of Information and Cultural Affairs or his nominee;

(n) The Librarian, Central Library;

(o) The Librarian of the National Library, Calcutta;

(p) The Director who shall be the ex-officio Member-Secretary of the Council.

(2) The members, other than the ex-officio members, shall hold office for a period of three years:

Provided that if a nominated or an elected member ceases to hold the position by virtue of which he was so nominated or elected, he shall automatically cease to be a member of the Council

(5) Functions of the Central Library

The Central Library shall, in addition to running a library and a reading room, perform such other functions as may be entrusted to it from time to time by the Government or any other officer authorized by the Government in that behalf.

(6) Appointment and functions of Director

The Government shall appoint a Director of Libraries in accordance with the rules made under this Act and the Director shall, subject to the control of the Government, discharge the following functions:-

(a) Maintain a register of recognized Libraries;

(b) Manage the Central Library together with the branches of such library and shall superintend and direct all matters relating to the Central Library;

(c) Declare, in accordance with the rules made under this Act, by notification, the names and address of the recognized libraries in the State;

(d) Superintend and direct all matters relating to the work of all local library authorities under this Act;

(e) Submit to the Government in accordance with rules made under this Act a report on the working of all libraries under this Act;

(f) Inspect or cause to be inspected periodically through officers' authorities in this behalf all the public and recognized libraries;

(g) Take steps for removal of defects in the working of any such library as the reports on inspection of the libraries by the officers authorized under clause (f) may disclose and take measures for enforcing the rules as may be made in this behalf and in appropriate cases obtain approval of the Government for derecognizing of the library or discontinuance of financial and other assistance to such library in the event of persistent failure to abide by the rules made under this Act or otherwise which in his opinion warrants such action;

(h) Guide, control and supervise the functioning of the libraries;

(i) Take appropriate steps for prosecution of persons responsible for any loss or injury caused to any library; and

(j) Perform such other duties and exercise such other powers in accordance with this Act or the rules made there under

(7) Directorate of Libraries

(1) There shall be a 'Directorate of Libraries' to be constituted by the Government for the purposes of this Act with such

number of officers and employees as may be prescribed.

(2) The Officers and staff of the Directorate of Libraries shall be whole time Government employees and the terms and conditions of services shall be such as may be prescribed.

CHAPTER III

Local Library Authorities

(8) Constitution of Local Library Authorities

(1) For the purpose of organizing and administering public libraries in the State, there shall be constituted by the Government Local Library Authority for each district.

(2) The Local Library Authority for each district shall consist of:-

(i) The District Magistrate of the District who shall be the Chairman;

(ii) The District Library Officer, who shall function as ex-officio Member- Secretary of the Local Library Authority;

(iii) The District Social Education Officer;

(iv) Two representatives of the Association of the employees of the different public libraries to be nominated by the Government;

(v) Two members to be nominated by the Government from amongst the Commissioners of the Municipalities within the district;

(vi) Two representatives of the district branch of the Bengal Library Association to be nominated by the Executive Committee of the said Association;

(vii) One person nominated by the Sebhadhipati from amongst the members of the Zilla Parishad in the district;

(viii) Two persons nominated by the government from amongst

the members of the Panchayat Samitis in the district;

(ix) Two persons nominated by the Government of whom –

(a) One shall be a member of the Governing Bodies of recognized libraries in the district; and

(b) The other from the Advisory Committee if any, of the libraries under the District Library;

(x) A teacher of a College or Polytechnic in the district to be nominated by the Government;

(xi) A teacher of a High School or a Higher Secondary School in the district to be nominated by the Government;

(xii) A teacher of a Primary School in the district to be nominated by the Government;

(xiii) Two M.L.As of the district to be nominated by the Government;

(xiv) The Librarian/Librarians of the District Library/Libraries.

(3) The members, other than the ex-officio members, shall hold office for a period of three years;

Provided that if a nominated or an elected members ceases to hold the position by virtue of which he was so nominated or elected, he shall automatically cease to be member of the Local Library Authority.

(9) Local Library Authority shall be body Corporate

Every Local Library Authority shall be a body corporate, by the name of the area for which it is constituted, shall have perpetual succession and a common seal, and may sue or be sued in its corporate name, and shall have the right of acquiring, holding or transferring property, movable or immovable, or entering into contracts and of doing all things necessary, proper or expedient, for the purpose for which it is constituted.

(10) Power of a Local Library Authority

A Local Library Authority may –

(a) Provide suitable land and buildings for public libraries and also the furniture, fittings, materials and conveniences requisite therefore;

(b) Stock such libraries with books, periodicals, newspapers, maps, works and specimens of art and science, lantern slides, cinema reels and any other thing suitable for the purpose;

(c) Employ from time to time such officers and staff for such libraries in the manner prescribed;

(d) With the previous sanction of the Government, close or discontinue any public library organized or rum by it or change the site thereof;

(e) Recommend to the Director for withdrawal of recognition of, or discontinuance of Government grant to any public library;

(f) Accept, with the previous sanction of the Director, any gift of books, or with the previous sanction of the Government any other gift or endowment for any purpose connected with its activities;

(g) Provide for lectures and seminars on topical subjects and the holding of classes; and

(h) In general do everything necessary to carry out the purpose of this Act.

(11) Vesting of Properties in Local Library Authorities

All property, movable and immovable, acquired or held for the purpose of any public library in any area shall vest in the Local Library authority of that area.

(12) Regulations by Local Library Authorities

Subject to the provisions of this Act and the rules made

thereunder, a Local Library Authority may, with the previous approval of the Government, make regulations generally to carry out the purposes of this Act and, without prejudice to the generality of this power, such regulations may provide for—

(a) The admission of persons to public libraries in its area on such conditions and on payment of such fees as it may specify;

(b) Requiring from persons desiring to use such libraries any guarantee or security against injury to, or misuse, destruction or loss of the property of such libraries;

(c) The manner in which the property of such libraries shall be used to ensure the protection of such property from injury, misuse, destruction or loss; and

(d) Authorize it officers and employees to exclude or remove from any such library any person who contravenes or fails to comply with the provisions of this Act or the rules or regulations made there under

(13) Power of Government to Cancel or Modify regulations

(1) If at any time the Government is of pinion that any regulation made under this Act by a Local Library Authority should be cancelled or modified either wholly or in part, it shall cause the reasons for such opinion to be communicated to such Local Library Authority and shall specify a reasonable period within which such Local Library Authority may make any representation with regard therein which it may think fit.

(2) After receipt and consideration of any such representation or, if in the meantime no such representation is received after the expiry of the specified period, the Government may, at anytime by notification cancel or modify such regulation, either wholly or in part.

(3) The cancellation or modification of a regulation under sub-section (2) shall take effect from such date as the Government may in the said notification direct, or if no such date is specified

then from the date of publication of the said notification except as to anything done or suffered or omitted to be done before such date.

(14) Executive Committee

A Local Library Authority may appoint an executive committee consisting of such number of its members as it may deem fit and delegate to such committee such of its powers or duties under this Act as may be prescribed.

(15) Preparation of Scheme

(1) As son as possible after a Local Library Authority is constituted, and thereafter if required by the Director, every Local Library Authority shall prepare a scheme for establishing libraries and for spreading library service within its area and submit it to the Director for sanction, The Director may sanction it with such modifications and additions, if any, as he may think fit and the Local Library Authority shall give effect to the scheme as may be sanctioned by the Director.

(2) The Director may suo motto or on an application by the Local Library Authority concerned modify any scheme sanctioned under sub-section (1) or replace it by a new scheme.

(16) District Library Officer and District Librarian

(1) The Government shall appoint a person to be called the District Library Officer on such terms and conditions as maybe prescribed and he shall generally, subject to the control of the Director, direct, superintends and manage the affairs or the libraries in a district;

(2) (i). The Government shall, in consultation with the Local Library Authority, place a person in charge of a District Library to be called the District Librarian with such qualifications and on such terms and conditions as may be prescribed.

(ii) The District Librarian, shall, subject to the control of the Local Library Authority, manage the affairs of a District Library.

CHAPTER IV

Finance and Accounts

(17) Library Fund

(1) Every Local Library Authority shall maintain a library fund out of which payments under this Act shall be met.

(2) There shall be credited to the Library Fund the following sums:-

(a) Contributions, gifts, and income from endowments made to the Local Library Authority for the benefit of public libraries;

(b) Grants which the Government may make for the general maintenance or for any specific purpose connected with libraries or social education;

(c) Any amount collected by the Local Library Authority under any rules or regulations made under this Act.

(18) Accounts and Audit

(1) An account of all assets and liabilities of each Local Library Authority and of all contributions, gifts and income from endowments, grants made by the Government, any amount collected by the Local Library Authority under any rules made under this Act shall be maintained in the prescribed manner.

(2) The amount shall be audited annually in such manner and by such officer or authority as may be prescribed. A copy of the audit report shall be submitted to the Government in the prescribed manner.

CHAPTER V

Miscellaneous

(19) Validation of Acts

No Act of the Council or of a Local Library Authority shall be deemed to be invalid by reason only of the existence of any vacancy, initial or subsequent, of any defect, to the constitutions of the Council or the Authority.

(20) Reports and Returns

Every Local Library Authority and every person-in-charge of a public library shall submit such reports and returns and furnish such information to the Director or any person authorized by him in this behalf as the Director or the person so authorized may from time to time require.

(21) Inspection of public libraries

The Director or any person authorized by him in this behalf may inspect any public library or any institution attached therein for the purpose of satisfying himself that the provisions of this Act and the rules made thereunder are duly carried out.

(22) Penalty

(1) whoever contravenes any provisions of this Act or of any rules made there under shall, if no other penalty is provided therefore in any other Act, be punishable with fine which may extend to two hundred and fifty rupees or if having been previously convicted of such offence is again convicted of an offence under this Act, with fine which may extend to five hundred rupees.

(2) No court shall take cognizance of any offence under this Act except on a written complaint made by the Director or by any person authorized by the Director in this behalf.

(23) Power to make rules

(1) The Government may, by notification, make rules for carrying out the purposes of this Act.

(2) In particular and without prejudice to the generally of the foregoing power, such rules may provide for all or any of the matters which maybe or are required to be prescribed or made by rules.

(3) All rules made under this section shall, as soon as may be, after they are made, he laid before the House of the State Legislature for 14 days and shall be subject to such modification as the State Legislature may make during the session in which they are so laid.

(24) Amendment to the Press and Registration of Books Act, 1967

The Press and Registration of Books Act, 1867 (25 of 1867) shall, in its application to the State of West Bengal, be amended as follows:-

(1) For clause (a) of the first paragraph of section 9, the following clause shall be substituted:

"(a) In any case,, within one calendar month after the day on which any book shall first be delivered out of the press, three such copies and":

(2) In section 11, for the first paragraph, the following paragraph shall be substituted:

"Out of the three copies delivered pursuant to clause (a) of the first paragraph of section 9 of this Act, one copy shall be sent to the Central Library, and the remaining copies shall be disposed of in such manner as the Government may from time to time determine":

Appendix VI

MANIPUR PUBLIC LIBRARIES ACT, (1988)

An Act to provide for the establishment and maintenance of Public Libraries in the State of Manipur and matters connected therewith.

Be it enacted by the legislature of the State of Manipur in the Thirty-ninth Year of the Republic of India as follows:

CHAPTER I

Preliminary

1. **Short title, Extent and Commencement**

(1) This Act may be called the Manipur Public Libraries Act, 1988.

(2) It extends to the whole of the State of Manipur.

(3) It shall come into force on such date as the State Government may, by notification in the official Gazette appoint.

2. **Definitions**

In this Act, unless the context otherwise requires:—

(1) 'Aided library' means a library declared by the Director to be eligible for grant either from the State Government or from the Library Fund in accordance with the rules made under this Act;

(2) 'Committee', means the State Library Committee constituted under section 3;

(3) 'Director' means the Director of Public Libraries appointed under section 9;

(4) 'District" means the revenue district;

(5) 'State Government' means the State Government of Manipur;

(6) 'Notification' means notification published in the Manipur Gazette;

(7) 'Prescribed' means prescribed by rules made under.this Act;

(8) 'Public Library means—

(a) A library established or maintained by a District Library Authority, including the branches and delivery stations such a library

(b) A library established or maintained by the State Government and declared open to the public;

(c) A library established or maintained by any local body or co-operative society and declared open to the public;

(d) A library declared to be eligible for aid and receiving aid from the State Government or from the Library Fund; and includes any other library notified by the State Government as a public library for the purposes of this Act;

(9) 'State; means the State of Manipur.

(10) 'State Central Library' means a library established by the State Government as the State Central Library.

(11) 'District Library' means a library established by the State Government as a District Library;

(12) 'Year' means the financial year.

CHAPTER II

The State Library Committee

(3) Constitution and Composition of the State Library Committee and its functions

(1) As soon as may be after the commencement of this Act, the

State Government shall, by notification, constitute for the purpose of this Act a committee to be called the State Library Committee.

(2) The Committee shall consist of—

(a) The Minister in-charge of Education, who shall also be the Chairman of the Committee;

(b) Commissioner/Secretary to the Government in the Education Department;

(c) The Director of Public Libraries

(d) The Chief Librarian of the State Central Library;

(e) One person elected by the Syndicate of Manipur University;

(f) One person nominated by the Manipur Library Association;

(g) Two persons nominated by the State Government from among the members of the District Library Authorities;

(h) One person co-opted by the Committee;

(3) The Committee shall advise the State Government on all matters arising under this Act and shall exercise and perform such other powers and duties as may be prescribed.

(4) Terms and Office of Certain Members of the Committee

(1) Subject to the provisions of sub-section (2) of section (3) every member of the Committee other than ex-officio member shall hold office for a period of three years from the date of his election, nomination or co-option as the case may be;

Provided that such term of a member nominated or elected shall come to an end as soon as the member ceases to be a member of the body from which he was nominated or elected.

(5) Filling up causal vacancies of certain members of the Committee

Any vacancies occurring in the office of nominated, elected or co-opted member of the Committee before the expiration of his term shall be filled by nomination, election or co-option as the case may be, of another person in the manner provided in section 3 and the person so nominated, elected or co-opted in section 3 and the person so nominated, elected or co-opted shall hold office for the remaining of the term of his predecessor.

(6) Meetings of the Committee

The Committee shall meet at such time and place and shall observe such rules of procedure at its meeting as may be prescribed.

(7) Act of State Library Committee not to be invalidated by informality etc

No Act of a State Library Committee shall be deemed to be invalidated by reason only of the existence of any vacancy in or a defect in the constitution of that Committee.

(8) Control of the State Library Committee by the State Government

If, at any time, it appears to the State Government that the Committee has failed to perform its functions or has exceeded or abused any of the powers conferred upon it by or under this Act the State Government may communicate the particulars thereof to the Committee, and if the Committee omits to remedy such failure, excess or abuses or to give satisfactory explanation therefor within such time as the State Government may stipulate it may dissolve or supersede the committee and cause all or any of powers and functions of the Committee to be exercised and performed by any person or agency for such period as they may think fit or direct that it be reconstituted.

CHAPTER III

Department of Public Libraries

(9) Constitution of the Department of Public Libraries and appointment of the Director thereof and his duties

For the purposes of this Act, the State Government shall constitute a separate Department of Public Libraries and appoint a Director to be the Director of Public Libraries in-charge of the department. The Director so appointed shall subject to the control of the State Government—

(a) Supervise the State Central Library and the branches of such Library;

(b) Superintend and direct all matters relating to public libraries;

(c) Declare, in accordance with the rules made under this Act, what libraries are eligible for aid from the State Government ad supervise and direct all matters relating to such libraries;

(d) Direct and control the work of all District Library Authorities under this Act in the manner prescribed;

(e) Submit to the State Government through the State Library Committee every year, a report on the working of the libraries under this Act in the preceding year;

(f) Submit reports to the Committee on the working of libraries, whenever necessary;

(g) Perform such other duties and exercise such other powers as are imposed or conferred on him by this Act or the rules made there under

CHAPTER IV

The District Library Authorities

(10) Constitution and incorporation of District Library Authorities

(1) For the purposes of organising and administering public libraries in the State, there shall be constituted a District Library Authority for each district.

(2) Every District Library Authority shall, by the name of the area for which it is constituted, be a body corporate having

perpetual; succession and a common seal with power to acquire, hold and dispose of property, and to enter into contracts and may by the said name, sue and be sued.

(3) It shall be the duty of every District Library Authority to provide Library service in the area of its jurisdiction.

(11) Composition of District Library Authorities

(1) The District Library Authority for each district shall consist of the following members namely:

(a) Four members nominated by the State Government from among the citizens of the district who have rendered eminent service to the cause of education or public libraries or a person of social eminance.

(b) Two members elected from among themselves by the members of the governing bodies of the public libraries (other than those referred to) in sub-clause (a) and (b) of clause of section (2) in each revenue division in the district;

(c) Two members elected from among themselves by the Board of Municipalities or by the Small Town Committees in the district;

(d) Two members nominated by the district branch of the Manipur Library Association;

(e) The Librarian, District Library who shall be Secretary of the District Library Authority;

(f) The District Education officer of the district.

(2) Every District Library Authority shall elect one of its members to be its Chairman.

(12) Term of Office of members of a District Library Authority.

(1) Every member of District Library Authority other than ex-officio members, shall hold office for a period of three years from the time of his nomination or election, as the case may be.

(2) A member nominated or elected in his capacity as the holder of a particular office shall, if he ceases to be the holders of that office cease to be a member of the District Library Authority.

(13) Filling up of causal vacancies of the members of the District Library Authority

A vacancy occurring in the office of a nominated or elected member of a district Library Authority before the expiration of his term shall be filled by nomination or election, as the case maybe of another person and the person so nominated or elected shall hold office for the remaining period of the term of his predecessor.

(14) Powers and functions of District Library Authorities

A District Library Authority may –

(a) Provide suitable lands and buildings for public libraries and also the furniture, fittings materials and conveniences requisite therefor;

(b) Stock such libraries with books, periodicals, newspapers, manuscripts, maps, works and specimens of arts and science, lantern slides, films, cinema projectors, recorders and the like;

(c) Employ form time to time, such staff as it considers necessary for such libraries;

(d) With the previous sanction of the State Government, shift or close, any public library mentioned in sub-clause (a) of clause (8) of section 2, or discontinue and to any other public library, the payment of which is regulated by the prescribed Library Grant-in-aid Code;

(e) Accept any gift or endowment for any purpose connected with its activities:

Provided that no gift or endowment of an immovable property shall be accepted without the previous action of the State Government:

(f) Provide for lectures and the holding of classes and conduct other activities connected with public library service including social education;

(g) With the consent of the management ad the previous sanction of the State Government acquire any library on such conditions as may be approved by the State Government;

(h) Distribute grants for public libraries and social educational purposes;

(i) In general do everything necessary to carry out the provisions of this Act.

(15) Scheme to be submitted by District Library Authorities:

(1) As soon as possible after a District Library Authority is constituted and thereafter as often as may be required by the Director, every District Library Authority shall, ad when ever it considers it necessary so to do, a District Library Authority may prepare a scheme for establishing libraries for spreading library service within its area in such form and manner as may be prescribed, and submit it to the Director for sanction. The Director may with previous approval of State Government, sanction it with such alteration, if any, as he may think fit after giving the District Library Authority an opportunity to make its representations, if any, in respect of such alternations and the District Library Authority shall there upon give effect to the scheme so sanctioned by him.

(2) The Director may, with previous approval of State Government, on application by the District Library Authority concerned modify any schemes sanctioned under sub-section (1) or replace it by a new scheme.

(16) Executive Committee and sub-committees of District Library Authorities

(1) A District Library Authority may appoint an Executive

Committee consisting of such of its members as it may deem fit and delegate to such committee any of its powers or functions under this Act except the power to borrow money, to dispose immovable property, and to pass the budget account and the audit and annual reports.

(2) A District Library Authority may also, from time to time, appoint sub-committees to inquire into and report or advise on any matters which it may refer to them.

(17) Act of District Library Authorities not be invalidated by informality etc.

No act of a District Library Authority shall be deemed to be invalidated by reason only of the existence of any vacancy in, or any defect in the constitution of that authority.

(18) Vesting of Properties in District Library Authorities

(1) All property acquired or held in any area by the District Library Authority for the purpose of any public library defined in sub-clause (a) of clause (8) of section 2 shall vest in the District Library Authority of that area.

(2) Any immovable property required by the District Library Authority shall be deemed to be land needed for a public purpose within the meaning of the Land Acquisition Act, 1894 (No. 1 of the 1894) and may be acquired under that Act.

(19) Power of District Library Authorities to make bye-laws

(1) Subject to the provisions of this Act and the rules made there under, a District Library Authority may make bye-laws, generally to carry out the purposes of this Act.

(2) In particular and without prejudice to the generality of foregoing power, such bye-laws may provide for all or any of the following matters namely,

(a) The admission of the public to the public libraries in its area on such conditions as it may specify;

(b) The guarantee or security to be furnished by persons desiring to use such libraries, against injury to or misuse, destruction or loss of the property or such libraries;

(c) The manner in which the property of such libraries maybe used and the protection of such property from injury, misuse, destruction or loss;

(d) The authority to be exercised by its officers and servants in the matter of exclusion or removal from any such library; of any person who contravenes does not comply with the provisions of this Act or the rules or bye-laws made thereunder;

(e) The conduct of meetings of the District Library Authority and the procedure to be followed in regard to the transaction of business at a meeting;

Provided that a District Library Authority shall not have power to make any bye-laws affecting a public library mentioned in sub-clause (2) or sub-clause (12) of section 2.

(3) The Director may with previous approval of State Government modify or cancel any bye-law made by a District Library Authority under sub-section (2):

Provided that before modifying or canceling any bye-law, the Director shall give the District Library Authority concerned a reasonable opportunity to make its representations in the matter.

(20) Control of the District Library Authorities by the State Government

If, any time, it appears to the State Government that a District Library Authority has failed to perform its functions or has exceeded or abused any of the powers conferred upon it by or under this Act, the State Government may communicate the particulars thereof to the District Library Authority, and if the District Library Authority, omits to remedy such failure, excess or abuse or to give a satisfactory explanation therefore within such time as the State Government may fix in this behalf, the State Government may suspend, dissolve or supersede the District Library Authority and cause all or any of the powers and functions of such Authority to be exercised and performed by any person or agency for such period as they may think fit or direct that it be reconstituted.

CHAPTER V

Finance and Accounts

(21) Library Fund

(1) Every District Library Authority shall maintain a fund called the library fund from which all its payments under this Act shall be met.

(2) There shall be credited to the Library fund the following sums namely:

   (a) Contributions, gifts and income from endowments made to the District Library Authority for the benefit of Public Libraries.

   (b) Special grants which the State Government may make for any specified purpose connected with libraries and social education;

   (c) Fund and other amounts collected by the District Library Authority under any rules of bye-laws made under this Act

(3) The State Government shall contribute annually to the Library Fund maintained by every District Library Authority.

(22) Maintenance of Accounts

(1) An account shall be kept of the receipts and expenses of each District Library Authority.

(2) The accounts shall be opened to inspection, shall be subject to audit, and shall be dealt within all other respects in such manner, as may be prescribed.

CHAPTER VI

Reports, Returns and Inspection

(23) Reports and Returns

Every District Library Authority and every person in charge of a public library shall submit such reports and returns and furnish such information to the Director or any person authorized by him in this behalf as the Director or the person authorized may, from time, require.

(24) Inspection of Libraries

The Director or any person authorised by him in this behalf may inspect any public library or any institution attached thereto for the purpose of satisfying himself that the provisions of this Act and the rules and bye-laws made thereunder are duly carried out.

CHAPTER VII

Miscellaneous

(25) Power to make rules

(1) The State Government may, by notification make rules to carry out the purposes of this Act.

(2) In particular and without prejudice to the generality of the foregoing power, such rules may provide for –

(a) The method of appointment, nomination, co-option or election of members to the State Library Committee and District Library Authorities;

(b) The publication of audited statements of the accounts of

District Library Authorities and of the reports of the auditors;

(c) The publication of a Library Grant-in-aid Code, regulating the grant of aid to aided libraries and the standards to be maintained by such libraries;

(d) The maintenance of State Registers of Libraries and librarians.

(3) All rules made under this section shall, as soon as may be after they are made, be laid on the Table of the House of the State Legislature for fourteen days and shall be subject to such modification, whether by way of repeal or amendment, as the State Legislature may make during the session in which they are so laid.

(26) Power to remove difficulties

If any difficulty arises in giving effect to the provisions of this Act the State Government may by order make such provisions as appear to them to be necessary or expedient for removing the difficulty.

APPENDIX VII

KERALA PUBLIC LIBRARIES ACT (1989)

(Kerala Granthasala Sanghom Act, (1989)

An Act to consolidate and unify the library laws in the State and to provide for the reorganisation of the entire library system in the State of Kerala with a view to the development and maintenance of comprehensive rural and urban library service and for matters connected therewith ort incidental there to.

Preamble

Whereas the period of the notified order by which the Board of Control for the Kerala Granthasala Saghom was constituted under the Kerala Granthasala Saghom (Taking over of Management Act, 1977 expired on 21st May, 1988;

And whereas by the Kerala Granthasala Saghom (Taking over Management) Amendment Act, 1988 (20 of 1988) the period of the notified order was extended for a further period of one year;

And whereas the Public Libraries and Local Library Authority constituted under the Tamil Nadu (Madras) Public Libraries Act, 1948, in the earstwhile Malabar Disrtrict are not functioning properly;

And whereas Government consider that the taking over of the management of Kerala Granthasala Sagnhom by Government will not solve the problems confronting the libraries in the State.

And whereas Government consider that the Kerala Granthasala Sanghom which was originally registered under the Travancore Companies Act, 1114 M.E, cannot effectively function as a democratic cultural body if it continues to be a company.

And whereas the Government consider it feasible and desirable to recognize the functioning of the libraries affiliated to the Kerala Granthasala Sanghom and of the other libraries in the State;

And whereas Government have received several representations from members of the public and other bodies requesting that a comprehensive and uniform legislation for Public Libraries may be enacted, encompassing all the libraries in the State with a view to ensuring their democratic functioning and all round development and progress.

And whereas Government feel that a uniform legislation applicable to all the libraries authorities and libraries is necessary to give fillip to the library movement in the State;

Be it enacted in the Fortieth Year of the Republic of India as follows:

CHAPTER I

Preliminary

(1) Short Title, extent and commencement

(1) This Act may be called the Kerala Public Libraries (Kerala Granthasala Sanghom) Act, 1989.

(2) It extends to the whole of the State of Kerala,

(3) It shall come into force on such date as the Government, by notification in the Gazette, appoint and different dates maybe fixed for different provisions of this Act.

(2) Definitions

In this Act, unless, the context otherwise requires –

(a) "Affiliated Library' means a library affiliated to the Kerala State Library Council;

(b) "Book: includes every volume, part or division of a volume, and pamphlet in any language;

(c) "Children Library" means a library established by the State Library Council for the benefit of children:

(d) "District" means a Revenue District;

(e) "District Library Council" means a District Library Council constituted under Section 10;

(f) " Granthasala Sanghom " means the Kerala Granthasala Sanghom ;

(g) "Notification" means a notification published in the Gazette

(h) "Prescribed" means prescribed by rules made under this Act;

(i) "President of the State Library Council" means the President of the Kerala State Library Council elected by the State Executive Committee;

(j) "President of the District Library Council" means the President of the District Library Council elected by the members of the District Library Council

(k) "President of the Taluka Library Union" means the President of the Taluka Library Union elected by the members of the General Body;

(l) "Public Library" means a library established or maintained or run by the State Library Council, a District Library Council or a Taluka Library Union under this Act;

(m) "Representative of affiliated library" means a member elected by the general body of an affiliated library from among its members;

(n) "Section" means a section of this Act;

(o) "State" means the State of Kerala;

(p) "State Library Council: means the Kerala State Library Council constituted under section 3;

(q) "State Executive Committee" means the Executive Committee of the Kerala Library Council;

(r) "State Library" means a State Library established under this Act;

(s) "Taluka" means a Revenue Taluk;

(t) "Taluka Library Union" means a Taluka Library Union constituted under this Act;

(u) "Year" means the Financial year.

CHAPTER II

The Kerala State Library Council

(3) Constitution and composition of the Kerala State Library Council

(1) As soon as may be after the commencement of this Act, the Government may, by notification, constitute a Library Council for the State to be called the Kerala State Library Council which shall be a body corporate by the name aforesaid having perpetual succession and a common seal with power, subject to the provisions of this Act and the rules made thereunder, to acquire, hold and dispose of property, both movable and immovable , and to enter in to contracts and shall by the said name sue and be sued.

(2) The State Library Council shall consist of one member each from a Taluka elected by the general body of the District library Councils, and five members of whom one shall be a librarian, another person belonging to the scheduled caste or scheduled tribe and another a woman nominated by the Government.

(3) There shall be an Executive Committee for the State Library Council consisting of twenty-five members of whom fifteen shall be elected by the elected members of the State Library Council from among themselves, five non-officials nominated under sub-section (2) ad five officials, namely the Secretary to Government, Higher Education Department, the Secretary to the Government, General Education Department, the Secretary to Government, Cultural Affairs Department and the Secretary to Government, Local Administration Department and Secretary to Government, Finance.

(4) The Executive Committee shall meet at such times and at such places as the President of the State Library Council may decide and exercise such powers and functions as may be prescribed.

(5) The elected members of the Executive Committee shall elect a President, Vice-President, Secretary and Joint Secretary from among themselves to be the President, Vice-President, Secretary and Joint Secretary respectively of the State Library Council and of the Executive Committee.

(4) Term of Office

(1) Save as otherwise provided in this Act, the term of office of the members of the State Library Council, other than the ex-officio members shall be three years from the date on which the Government notifies the constitution of the State Library Council in the Gazette;

Provided that every member, other than an ex-officio member, shall continue to hold office until his successor assumes office.

(2) A member of the State Library Council shall not be eligible for re-election or re-nomination as the case maybe, for more than two terms consecutively.

(5) Vacancies

(1) A casual vacancy caused by death, resignation or disability of a member, or otherwise, in the State Library Council shall be filled as early as possible by election or nomination, as the case may be.

(2) Any person so elected or nominated to fill a casual vacancy shall hold office only so log as the members in whose place he is elected or nominated would have held office if the vacancy had not occurred.

(6) **Meeting of the State Library Council**

(1) The State Library Council shall meet at least thrice a year on dates to be fixed by the President and one of such meetings shall be the annual meeting.

(2) The president may, whenever he thinks fit, convene a special meeting of the State Library Council for the transaction of urgent business.

(3) Subject to such conditions as maybe prescribed, a special meeting shall be convened by the President to discuss matters of urgent importance upon a written requisition by not less than one-third of the total number of members of the State Library Council.

(4) One-third of the total number of the members of the State Library Council shall be the quorum for a meeting of the Council.

(5) The President or, in his absence, the Vice-President or in the absence of both, any member chosen by the members preset from among themselves shall preside over a meeting of the State Library Council,

(6) The president and the Vice-President shall exercise such other powers and perform such other duties as may be prescribed.

(7) Procedure of State Library Council

(1) The State Library Council shall transact business by resolutions passed in such manner and in accordance with such procedure as may be prescribed.

(2) Copy of every resolution shall be forwarded to the Government within fifteen days of the passing of that resolution.

(3) The Government may call for any record or information regarding any resolution from the State Library Council and the Council shall be bound to furnish such record or information.

(4) The Government may, after giving reasonable notice to the State Library Council after hearing its objections, if any, suspend or cancel or modify any resolution passed by the Council.

(8) Powers and functions of the State Library Council

(1) Subject to the other provisions of this Act and the rules made thereunder, the State Library Council may –

(a) Advise the Government on all matters connected with the administration of this Act;

(b) Advise Government on all matters connected with the overall library policy of the State;

(c) Co-ordinate the working of the District Library Councils and the Taluka Library Unions;

(d) Supervise and direct all matters relating to library service in the State;

(e) Re-organise in a phased manner the library service in the State into an integrated library system with close linkages between the several libraries as also to comprise book –banks and mutual loaning;

(f) With the prior concurrence of the Government, establish one or more State Libraries (or Children Libraries) at such place or places in the State as maybe considered necessary;

Provided further that the Thiruvananthapuram (Trivandrum) Public Library shall be deemed to be a State Library established by the State Library Council under this clause;

Provided further that the (Thiruvananthapuram) Public Library shall continue to be a Department of the Government;

(g) Organise Children's section in affiliated libraries wherever it is not in existence;

(h) Appoint and control such officers and servants as may be necessary for the efficient performance of its duties and functions under this Act and the rules made thereunder:

(i) Carry on propaganda on the importance of library development in the State by providing lectures, conferences etc, and using any media as appropriate from time to time;

(ii) Conduct such other activities as may be conducive to creating favourable atmosphere in the State for the organization of new libraries and for the better functioning of the existing libraries.

(iii) Impart training to librarians; or other library staff;

(iv) Organise activities for promoting distance education, adult education and education of libraries;

(v) Cultivate reading habit and foster book mindedness among the public;

(vi) With the prior concurrence of the Government establish and conduct schools for promoting adult education and non-formal education;

(vii Provide in the Thiruvananthapuram (Trivandrum) Public Library or in such other State Libraries, books, periodicals, newspapers, maps, radios, manuscripts, work and specimens of art and science, lantern slides, films, cinema projectors, recorders, television sets, charts, video cassette players, video cassette recorders and computer and the like;

(viii) Provide mobile Libraries to District Library Council which can give book services to each Panchayat;

(ix) Prepare project reports and seek financial assistance from the Central Government, Trusts or any charitable institutions for the implementation of the same;

(j) Do any other act that may be conductive to the furtherance of the objects of this Act with the previous sanction of the Government.

(k) Exercise such other powers and perform such other duties as are conferred on it by this Act and the rules made thereunder.

(2) The State Library Council may give to the District Library Council and the Taluka Library Unions directions in the performance of their functions under this Act and the District Library Councils and the Taluk Library Unions shall not in the discharge of their functions under this Act depart from the directions given by the said Council.

(9) Secretary of the State Library Council

(1) The Secretary of the State Library Council shall be the Chief Executive Authority of the State Library Council.

(2) It shall be the duty of the Secretary of the State Library Council to give effect to the resolutions of the said Council unless they are suspended or cancelled or modified by the government under sub-section(4) of section 7.

(3) Where a resolution passed by the State Library Council is modified by the Government under sub-section 4 of section 7, the Secretary of the State Library Council shall give effect to the resolution as so modified by the Government.

(4) The Secretary of the State Library Council shall exercise such other powers and perform such other duties as are, or maybe conferred or imposed on him by the President of the State Library Council.

(5) Suits by or against the State Library Council shall be instituted by or against the Secretary of the State Library Council.

(6) The Joint Secretary shall assist the Secretary and shall perform such other functions as may be entrusted to him by the Executive Committee.

CHAPTER III

District Library Councils

(10) Constitution of the District Library Councils

(1) For the purposes of organizing, administrating and developing library-service at the District level the Government may by notification establish District Library Councils.

(2) Every District Council shall be a body corporate, by the name of the District for which it is constituted, having perpetual succession and a common seal with power, subject to the provisions of this Act and the rules made thereunder to acquire, hold and dispose of property, both movable and immovable, to enter into contracts, and to do all things necessary, proper and expedient for the purpose for which it is constituted and shall by the said name sue and be sued.

(11) Composition of the District Library Councils

(1) Every District Library Councils shall consist of—

(a) The Presidents and Secretaries of the Taluka Library Unions in the Districts:

(b) Seven persons to be elected by the General Body of each of the Taluk library union in the District of whom one shall be a woman, and one shall be a person belonging to the scheduled castes or scheduled tribes; and

(c) The President or any other office bearer of any affiliated library in the District headquarters nominated by the Government;

(2) The elected members of very District Library Council shall elect from among themselves a District Executive Committee consisting of eleven members including a President, a Vice-President, a Secretary and a Joint Secretary.

(3) The District Executive Committee shall exercise such powers as are determined by the State Library Council and perform such functions as may be prescribed from time to time.

(12) Term of Office

(1) Save as otherwise provided in this Act the term of office of the members of a District Library Council shall be three years commencing from the date from which the Government notifies the constitution of the District Library Council in the Gazette.

Provided that every member shall continue in office until his successor assumes office.

(2) A member of a District Library Council shall be eligible for re-election to the Council.

(13) Vacancies

A casual vacancy caused by death, resignation or disability of a member or otherwise in the District Library Council shall be filled as early as possible by election of a suitable person in accordance with the provisions of Section 11 and any person so elected to fill a vacancy shall hold office only so long as the member in whose place he is elected would have held office if the vacancy had not occurred.

(14) Meetings of the District Library Council

(1) Every District Library Council shall meet at least once in every three months on dates to be fixed by the President of the Council and one of such meeting shall be the annual meeting.

(2) The President may, whenever he thinks fit, convene a special meeting of the District Library Council for the transaction of urgent business.

(3) Subject to such conditions as may be prescribed, a special

meeting shall be convened by the President, to discuss the matters or urgent importance upon a written requisition by not less than one-third of the number of members of the District Library Council.

(4) One-third of the total number of members of the District Library Council shall be the quorum for a meeting of the Council.

(5) A District Library Council shall transact business by resolutions passed in such manner and in accordance with such procedure as may be prescribed.

(6) Copy of every resolution shall be forwarded to the State Library Council within fifteen days of the passing of that resolution.

(15) Powers and duties of President and Vice-President of District Library Council

(1) The President of a District Library Council may preside over the meetings of the Councils and exercise such powers and perform such duties as may be prescribed.

(2) The Vice-President may in the absence of the President, preside over the meetings of the Council and exercise such powers and perform such duties of the President as the President may, from time to time, delegate to him.

(16) Secretary of the District Library Council

(1) The Secretary of the District Library Council shall be the chief executive authority of the District Library Council.

(2) It shall be the duty of the Secretary of District Library Council to give effect to the resolutions of the said council.

(3) The Secretary of the District Library Council shall exercise such other powers and perform such other duties as are or may be conferred or imposed on him by the President of the District Library Council.

(4) Suit by or against the District Library Council shall be instituted by or against the Secretary of the District Library Council—

(5) The Joint Secretary shall assist the Secretary and shall perform such other functions as may be entrusted to him by the Executive Committee.

(17) Powers and functions of the District Library Council

(1) Save as otherwise provided in this Act, every District Library Council shall have power:

(a) To elect members to the State Library Council to the extent of 1 for each taluk in the District;

(b) To establish new libraries within its jurisdiction with the previous sanction of the State Library Council;

(c) To supervise, co-ordinate and control the Library Service under its jurisdiction in the District and to promote co-operation between libraries and cultural and educational institutions in the country;

(d) To provide library service and mobile library service to the persons residing in the District;

(e) To provide suitable lands and building for public libraries and furniture, fittings, equipment and other conveniences necessary for the purpose;

(f) To provide such libraries with books, periodicals, newspapers, maps, radios, manuscripts, works and specimens of art and science, lantern slides, films, video films, cinema projectors, recorders, cassette, television sets, charts, tape-recorders, video cassette video players, cassette recorders and the like;

(g) To shift, recognize or close or amalgamate any public library established or maintained or rum directly by the District Library Council;

(h) To Appoint and control such officers and servants as

may be necessary for the efficient performance of its duties and functions under the Act and the rules made thereunder;

(i) To accept any endowment or gifts for any purpose connected with its activities;

(j) To provide for lectures, seminars, symposia, conferences and conduct study classes to strengthen the functioning of the libraries and conduct other activities as may be conductive to the carrying out of the purposes of this Act;

(k) With the sanction of the State Library Council to do any other thing that may be conducive to the furtherance of the purposes of this Act, and

(l) To exercise such other powers and perform such other duties as may be conferred or imposed on it by or under this Act or the rules made thereunder.

(2) The District Library Council may give to the Taluk Library Unions directions not contrary to the directions, if any, issued by the State Library Council in the Performance of their functions under this Act and the Unions shall not in the discharge of their functions under this Act depart from the directions given by the Council.

CHAPTER IV

Taluk Library Unions

(18) Constitution of Taluk Library Unions

(1) For the purpose of organising and administrating library service at the Taluk level the Government may, by notification, constitute a Taluk Library Union for each Taluk in the State.

(2) Every Taluk Library Union shall be a body corporate by the name of Taluk for which it is constituted having perpetual succession and have common seal with power subject to the provisions of this Act and the Rules made thereunder. to

acquire, hold and dispose of property, both movable and immovable to enter into contracts, and to do all things necessary, proper or expedient for the purpose for which it is constituted and shall by the said name sue and be sued.

(19) Composition of Taluk Library Unions

(1) Every Taluk Library Union shall consist of two representatives of each affiliated library in the Taluk;

(2) Every Taluk Library Union shall elect an Executive Committee of the Union consisting of nine members including a President, a Vice-President, a Secretary and a Joint Secretary.

Provided that if there is no woman or person belonging to the Scheduled Caste or Scheduled Tribe in the Taluk Library Union, then one woman and one person belonging to the Scheduled Caste or Scheduled Tribes be nominated by the Executive Committee in which case the Executive Committee shall consist of eleven members.

(3) Every Taluk Library Union shall elect seven persons as members to the District Library Councils under clause (b) of sub-section (1) of Section 2 of whom one shall be a woman and one shall be a person belonging to the Scheduled Castes or Scheduled Tribes.

(20) Terms of Office

(1) Save as otherwise provided in this act the term of office of the members of a Taluk Library Union shall be three years commencing from the date on which the Government notifies the constitution of the Taluk Library in the Gazette.

Provided that every member shall continue in office until his succcesor assumes office.

(2) A member of the Taluk Library Union shall be eligible for re-election

(21) Vacancies

A casual vacancy caused by death resignation or disability of a member or otherwise in the Taluk Library Union shall be filled as early as possible in accordance with the provisions of Section 19 and any person so taken shall hold office only so long as the member in whose place he is taken would have held office if the vacancy had not occurred.

(22) Meeting of the Taluk Library Union

(1) Every Taluk Library Union shall meet atleast once in every two months on dates to be fixed by the President of the Union and one of such meetings shall be the annual meeting.

(2) The President may whenever he thinks fit, convene a special meeting of the Taluk Libary Union for the transaction of urgent business.

(3) Subject to such conditions as may be prescribed a special meting shall be convened by the President to discuss matters of urgent importance upon a written requisition by not less than one-third of the number of members of the Taluk Library Unions.

(4) One-third of the total number of members of the Taluk Library Unions shall be the quorum for a meeting of the Union.

(5) A Taluk Library Union shall transact business by resolutions passed in such manner and in accordace with such procedure as may be prescribed.

(6) Copy of every resolution shall be forwarded to the District Library Council within 15 days of the pasing of that resolution.

(23) Powers and Duties of the President ad Vice-President of Taluk Library Unions

(1) A President of a Taluk Library Union may preside over the meetings of the Union and exercise such powers and perform such duties as may be prescribed.

(2) The Vice-President of a Taluk Library Union may, in the absence of the President, preside over the meetings of the Union and exercise such powers and perform such duties of the Presidents as the President, may, from time to time delegate to him.

(3) In the absence of both President and the Vice-President any member chosen by the members present from among themselves shall preside over a meeting of the Taluk Library Union.

(24) Secretary of the Taluk Library Union

(1) The Secretary of the Taluk Library Union shall be the Chief Executive Authority of the Taluk Library Union

(2) It shall be the duty of the Secretary of the Taluk Library Union to give effect to the resolutions of the said Union.

(3) The Secretary of the Taluk Library Union shall exercise such other powers and perform such other duties as are or may be conferred or imposed on him by the President of the Taluk Library Union.

(4) Suits by or against the Taluk Library Union shall be instituted by or against the Secretary of the Taluk Library Union

(5) The Joint Secretary shall assist the Secretary and shall perform such other functions as may be entrusted to him by the Executive Commitee.

(25) Powers and funcions of Taluk Library Union

Save as otherwise provided in this Act, every Taluk Library Union shall have powrs:-

(a) To elect members to the District library Council under subsection (3 of Section 19

(b) To supervise co-ordinate and control the library service under its jurisdicion in the Taluk and to give directions and advise to the affilited libraries in regard to their day to day functions and mangement:

(c) To provide library service including mobile library service to the persons residing in the Taluk and to establish new libraries within that areas;

(d) To provide suitable lands and buildings for affiliated libraries and furniture, fittings equipments and other conveniences necessary for the purpose;

(e) To provide such libraries with books, periodicals, newspapers, maps, manuscripts, work and specimens of art and science, lantern slides, films, cinema projectors, radio recorders, television sets, charts and video cassette players, tape recorders, video cassette recorders and the like;

(f) To provide for lectures, symposia, conferences and conduct other activities as may be conducive to the carrying out of the purposes of this Act;

(g) To accept any endowment or gift or contribute for any purposes connected with its activities;

(h) To appoint and control such officers and servants as may be necessary for the efficient performance of the duties and functions under this Act and the rules made thereunder;

(i) With the sanction of the District Library Council, to do any other thing that may be conducive to the furtherance of the purposes of this Act; and

(j) To exercise such other powers and perform such other duties as may be conferred or imposed on it by or under this Act or the Rules made thereunder.

CHAPTER V

Disqualification and Affiliation

(26) No person to be a member of more than one Council or Union

Not with standing anything contained in the foregoing

provisions, no person shall be a member of more than one District Library Council or of more than one Taluk Library Union and if a person is chosen as a member of more than one District Library Council or Taluk Library Union and he does not specify the Council/ Union of which he desires to be a member within thirty days from the date of last election or nomination, as the case may be then on the expiration of such period his membership in all the Councils and/or Unions shall cease.

(27) Disqualification of members of State Library Council, District Library Council and Taluk Library Union

A person shall be disqualified for being chosen as, or for being a member of the State Library Council, the District Library Council or the Taluk Library Union –

(a) If he absents himself without leave being granted by the State Library Council or the District Library Council or the Taluk Library Union, as the case may be, from three consecutive meetings of the Council or Union; or

(b) If he ceases to hold the office or be a member of the body or authority by virtue of which he has been elected or

(c) If he has been sentenced by a criminal court for an offence involving moral turpitude and punishable with imprisonment for a term exceeding three months, such sentence not having been subsequently reversed, quashed or remitted, or

(d) If he is of unsound mind and stands so declared by a competent court.

(28) Affiliation of Libraries

(1) Any Library other than a library established or maintained by the State Library Council or a District Library Council or a Taluk Library Union of the Taluk in which it is situated shall apply for recognition as affiliated library under this Act.

(2) The Taluk Library Union shall consider the application and if it is satisfied that the conditions prescribed for granting affiliation have been complied with recommend the application through the District Library Council to the State Library Council for affiliation and on such affiliation being granted the library shall be treated as an affiliated library;

(3) A person aggrieved by any decision of the Taluk Library Union with regard to the affiliation of library may appeal to the State Library Council in writing through the District Library Council within 30 days of such decision and the decision of the State Library Council after obtaining the opinion of the District Library Council thereon shall be final.

CHAPTER VI

Development Plans and Funds

(29) Library Development Plan

(1) Subject to the provisions of this Act and the rules made thereunder and any general or special orders of the Government, if any, in this behalf, a District Library Council may prepare a District Library Development Plan for establishing, co-ordinating and spreading library service within the entire district or part thereof, in such form and manner and containing, such particulars as may be prescribed.

(2) The District Library Development Plan shall thereafrter be forwarded to the President, of the State Library Council who shall submit it to the Government with the views of the State Library Council.

(3) The Government may, if they deem fit, sanction the District Library Development Plan with or without alterations.

(4) The Government may, on application by the District Library Council, modify any District Library Development Plan sanctioned under sub-section (3).

(5) As soon as may be after the sanctioning of the District Library Development Plan the President of the State Library Council shall, in conformity with the provisions of the said plan, make an order called the District Library Development order, specifying the extent and nature of the Library service which shall be established and maintained by the District Library Council, the measures to be taken by the District Library Council for providing adequate library service to the people in the area and the stages by which such measures shall be taken.

(6) Every District Library Council shall give effect to the District Library Development Plan as sanctioned by the Government under sub-section 3 and the District Library Development order made under sub-section 5.

(30) Government Grant to the State Library Council

(1) The government may make every year a grant to the State Library Council of a Sum which shall not be more than one per cent of the amount allotted for education in the State Budget for the year, taking into account the programmes and projects of the State Library council for that year.

(2) The amount of such grant shall be credited to the State Library Fund maintained under section 31 at such times and in such manner as may be prescribed..

(31) State Library Fund

(1) The State Library Council shall maintain a fund called the State Library Fund from which all the expenses of the State Library Council, District Library Councils and Taluk Library Unions shall be met.

(2) The following sums shall be credited to the State Library Fund.

(a) Grant which the State Government or the Central

Government may make to the State Library Council:

(b) Contributions and gifts made to the State Library Council by any other person, body or authority.

(c) Provident Fund, Superannuation Fund, Welfare Fund and other Funds of the Granthasala Sanghom transferred under sub-section 2 of Section 38.

(d) Cess collected under section 48.

(32) Distribution of funds to the District Library Councils and Taluk Library Unions

The State Library Council shall distribute from the State Library Funds such amounts as may be required for each of the District Library Councils and the Taluk Library Unions.

(33) Accounts

(1) The State Library Council and every District Library Council and Taluk Library Union shall keep complete account of their financial transactions in such form as may be prescribed.

(2) The account shall be opened to inspection and shall be subject to audit, disallowance and surcharge and shall be dealt with in all other respects in such manner as may be prescribed.

(3) The State Library Council shall with the prior consent of the Government, appoint an officer not below the rank of a Deputy Secretary in the Finance Department to be the Accounts Officer of the State Library Council who shall exercise such powers and perform such functions relating to the accounts of the State Library Council, District Library Councils and Taluk Library Unions as may be prescribed.

(4) The State Library Council shall appoint Auditors to Audit the accounts of the State Library Council and District Library Councils and Taluk Library unions.

(5) The audited annual statements of accounts shall be forwarded to the Government.

(6) The Government shall on receipt of the audited annual accounts cause the same to be laid on the table of the State legislative Assembly.

(34) Inspection of Libraries

(1) The President of the State Library Council may inspect any library under his jurisdiction for verifying whether the provisions of this Act and the rules and bye-laws made thereunder are duly observed by it.

Provided that the President of the State Library Council may delegate the power of inspection to any office bearer of the Council

(2) In all cases where such inspections are made the person conducting the inspection shall furnish a detailed report of his inspection to the State Library council and the concerned District Library Council.

(3) The concerned District Library Council may consider the report furnished under sub-section (2) and pass such resolution in regard there to as it may deem fit and the library concerned shall be bound to comply with such resolution unless it is suspended or cancelled or modified by the Government.

(4) Where a resolution referred to in sub-section (3) is modified by the government, the library shall be bound-to comply with such resolution as modified by the Government.

(5) The State Library Council may, from time to time, direct the District Library Council to prepare a gradation list of affiliated libraries functioning in the District in conformity with the principles to be laid down by the State Library Council in that behalf from time to time and forward such list to the State Library Council for approval.

(35) Grants to Affiliated Libraries

(1) Every Affiliated Library shall be entitled to receive grant

from the Taluk Library Union based on the gradation list prepared under subsection (5) of section 34 at such rates as may be prescribed.

(2) The State Library Council shall provide necessary funds to the Taluk Library Unions for the payment of the grant under subsection (1).

CHAPTER VII
Reports and Returns

(36) District Library Councils and Taluk Library Unions to submit Reports etc

Every District Library Council and Taluk Library Union shall submit such reports and returns and furnish such information to the President of the State Library Council or any person authorized by him in that behalf as the President of the State Library Council or the person so authorized may, from time to time, require.

(37) Annual Report

(1) The President of the State Library Council shall in respect of each year, prepare a report of the working of the State Library Council during that year along with such information and particulars as may be prescribed and submit such report to the Government before such date as the Government, by order, specify.

(2) The President of the State Library Council shall in respect of each Year, prepare a report of working of the District Library Council and Taluk Library Union during that year along with such information and particulars as may be prescribed and submit the report to the Government before such date as the Government may, by order, specify.

(3) The Government shall on receipt of the Annual Reports cause the same to be laid on the table of the State legislative Assembly.

CHAPTER VIII

Kerala Granthasala Sanghom

(38) Merger of the Kerala Granthasala Sanghom and transfer of its assets and liabilities

(1) Notwithstanding anything contained in the Kerala Non-Trading Companies Act, 1961 (42 of 1961) with effect on and from the date on which this section comes into force, the Kerala Granthasala Sanghom shall, by virtue of this Section, be deemed to have been merged to the Kerala State Library Council.

(2) All properties and all rights of whatever kind used, enjoyed or possessed by all interests of whatever kind owned or vested or held by the Granthasala Sanghom and all liabilities legally subsisting against the Granthasala Sanghom including the liabilities towards the dues to the employees at the commencement of the Kerala Granthasala Sanghom (Taking over or management Act, 1977 (19 of 1977), shall with effect on and from the commencement of this section and subject to such directions as may be issued by Government in this behalf, vest in the State Library Council and the State Library Council shall discharge such liabilities in the order of priority specified in the Schedule to this Act.

(3) Every Officer or other employees immediately before the commencement of the Section, in connection with the affairs of the Granthasala Sanghom shall, as from such commencement become an officer or other employee of the State Library Council and shall hold his office by the tenure, remuneration and terms and conditions of employment as may be altered as per the provisions in the Industrial Disputes Act, 1947 (Central Act 14 of 1947) and with the same rights and privileges as to pension, gratuity and other matters as he would have held under the Granthasala Sanghom if this

section had not been enacted and shall continue to do so unless and until his employment under the State Library Council is terminated or until his remuneration, terms and conditions are duly altered by the State Library Council.

Provided that if the alternation so made is not acceptable to any officer or other employee, his employment shall be terminated on payment to him by the State Library Council of an amount equivalent to three months' remuneration in the case of permanent employees and one month's remuneration in the case of other employees.

Provided further that nothing contained in this sub-section shall apply to any officer or other employee who has by notice in writing given to the State Library Council within thirty days from the commencement of this Section, intimated his intention of not becoming an officer or other employee of the said Council.

(4) Notwithstanding anything contained in the Industrial Disputes Act, 1947 (Central Act 14 of 1987), or in any other law for the time being in force, the transfer of service of any officer or other employee of the Granthasala Sanghom, to the State Library Council under sub-section 3 shall not entitle any such officer or other employee to any compensation under that Act or other Law, and no such claim shall be entertained by any Court, Tribunal or Authority.

CHAPTER IX

Transitory Provision

(39) Board of Control to remain in office for certain Period

Till the State Library Council, District Library Councils and Taluk Library Unions are constituted and the Councils and the Unions assume charge, the Board of Control, of the Kerala Granthasala Sanghom constituted by notified order made under the Kerala

Granthasala Sanghom (Taking over the Management) Act 1977, shall continue to be in charge and the Board of Control shall arrange for conducting first election to the State Library Council, District Library Councils and Taluk Library Unions in such manner and subject to such conditions as may be prescribed.

CHAPTER X

Miscellaneous

(40) Power to make Rules

(1) The Government may, after previous publication make rules, either prospectively or retrospectively to carry out the purposes of this Act.

(2) In particular and without prejudice to the generality of the foregoing powers such rules may provide for:

(a) All matters connected with election or nomination of members of the State Library Council. The District Library Councils and the Taluk Library Unions;

(b) The administration, inspection and management of State Libraries, District Libraries and Taluk Libraries;

(c) The maintenance of accounts by the State Library Council, the District Library Councils and the Taluk Library Unions and the publication of the audited statements of accounts and the reports of the Auditors.

(d) The grading of libraries, the grants to libraries and the standards to be maintained by such libraries.

(e) The Maintenance of State Registers of Libraries and of Librarians.

(f) The restriction and condition subject to which the State Library Council or a District Library Council or a Taluk Library Union may enter into a contract or hold or dispose of property;

(g) Conditions of service of the Officers and servants of the State Library Councils. The District Library Councils and the Taluk Library Unions and of the persons employed in the Libraries established or maintained by them.

(h) The powers, duties and functions of the Executive Committee of the State Library Council and the Executive Committees of the District Library Councils and Taluk Library Unions

(i) Any other matter which has to be or may be prescribed.

(3) Every rule made under this Act shall be laid as soon as may be after it is made, before the Legislative Assembly while it is in session fort a total period of fourteen days which may be comprised in one session or in two successive sessions and if before the expiry of the Session in which it is so laid or the session immediately following the Legislative Assembly makes any modifications in the rules or declares that the rules should not be made, the rules shall thereafter have effect only in such modern form or be of no effect as the case may. so however that any such modification or annulment shall be without prejudice to the validity of anything previously done under that rule.

(41) Powers of the State Library Councils to make Bye-laws

(1) The State Library Council may, subject to the provisions of this Act and the rules made thereunder and with the previous approval of the Government, by notification, make bye-laws generally to carryout the purposes of this Act.

(2) In particular and without prejudice to the generality of the foregoing powers, such bye-laws may provide for all or any of the following maters, namely:-

(b) The admission as members of the Libraries, under the control of the State Library Council or the District Library Councils or the Taluk Library Unions:

(c) The guarantee or security to be furnished by the persons desiring to use such liabilities, against injury to or misuse, destruction or loss of the property of such libraries;

(d) The manner in which the properties of such libraries may be used and the protection of such properties from injury, misuse, destruction or loss;

(e) The power to be exercised by the officers and servants of the State Library Councils and the District Library Councils or the Taluk Library Unions for the purpose of exclusion or removal from any such library of any person who contravenes any provision of this Act or any rule or bye-law made thereunder.

(3) The power to make bye-laws under this section shall be subject to the condition of previous publication of the bye-laws in the Gazette for a period of not less than forty-five days.

(42) Supersession of the State Library Council or a District Library Council or a Taluk Library Union by the Government

(1) If at any time, it appears to the Government that the State Library Council or a District Library Council or a Taluk Library Union has failed to perform any of its functions or has exceeded or abused any of the powers conferred upon it by or under this Act, the Government may communicate the particulars thereof to the State Library Council or to the District Library Council or Taluk Library Union as the case may be, and if the State Library Council or the District Library Council or the Taluk Library Union omits to remedy such failure, excess or abuse or gives an explanation which in the opinion of the Government is unsatisfactory, the Government may supersede the State Library council or the District Library Council or the Taluk Library Union as the case may be, for such period as the Government may direct.

(2) On the supersession of the State Library Council or a District Library council or a Taluk Library union under sub-section (1)

a. All the powers and duties of that Council or Union shall. during the period of supersession, be exercised and performed by such body or officer or officers of the Government, as the Government may from time to time. appoint in this behalf;

b. All properties vested in that Council or Union shall, during the period of supersession, vest in the Government and

c. On the expiry of the period of supersession, the Council or Union shall be reconstituted in the manner provided in this Act.

(43) Removal of Members

(1) Where the State Library Council or a District Library Council or a Taluk Library Union is satisfied or on a complaint or otherwise that a member of the respective Council or Union has acted in contravention of the provisions of this Act or the Rules made there under or has acted aversely against the interests of the Council or the Union, such member, by a resolution passed in such manner as may be prescribed be removed from membership

(a) By the State Library Council in the case of membership in that Council;

(b) By the District Library Council in the case of membership in that Council; and

(c) By the Taluk Library Union in the case of membership in that Union.

(2) No member shall be removed under sub-section (1) unless he has been given an opportunity of being heard.

(3) A Copy of the resolution passed under sub-section (1) shall be communicated to the member removed either in person or by registered post.

(4) A member removed under sub-section (1) shall not be eligible for re-election or renomination, until he is declared by a resolution passed by the respective Council or the Union, as the case may be, to be no longer ineligible.

(44) Validity of Acts and Proceedings

No Act done or proceedings taken under this Act, shall be questioned merely on the ground—

(a) Of any vacancy or defect in the constitution of any Council or Union or any committee thereof; or

(b) Of any defect or irregularity in such act or proceedings not affecting the merits of the case.

(45) Affiliation of existing libraries

On and from such date as the Government may fix, all the libraries affiliated to the Granthasala Sanghom and the Public Libraries established or maintained by a Local Library Authority in earstwhile Malabar Area, under the provisions of the Tamil Nadu (Madras) Public Libraries Act, 1948 (Madras Act XXIV of 1948), and the Libraries which are not affiliated to the Granthasala Sanghom but which receive grant direct from the Government as well as the State Libraries shall be deemed to be a affiliated in the State Library Council and the provisions of this Act and the rules and bye-laws made thereunder shall apply to those libraries.

(46) Transfer of Public Libraries established or maintained by a Local Library Authority under the Madras(Tamil Nadu) Public Libraries Act, 1948

(1) On and from such date as the Government may fix for each district after the constitution of District Library Council for that District all properties movable and immovable and all assets and liabilities in existence of all Local Library Authorities constituted under the Tamil Nadu (Madras) Public Libraries Act 1948 (Madras Act XXII of 1948) in the Malabar

District referred to in sub-section of section 5 of the States Reorganisation Act.156 (Central Act 37 of 1956), and all the Public Libraries in that District established or maintained by a Local Library Authority under the TamilNadu Madras Public Libraries Act 1948 (Madras Act XXIV of 1948) along with their services, delivery centers and other matters and things connected therewith shall stand transferred to, and vested in the District Library Council of that District.

(2) All properties movable or immovable and all assets and liabilities of such local Library Authority and Public Libraries in existence immediately before the date fixed under the subsection 1 for the purposes of the libraries shall vest in and be deemed to be the properties, assets and liabilities of the District Library Council of that District.

(3) All persons employed for the purposes of the libraries referred to in sub-section (1) and in service immediately before the date fixed under that sub-section shall, as from that date, stand transferred to the control and supervision of the District Library Council.

(4) The persons referred to in sub-section (3) shall be subject to the condition of service which were applicable to them immediately before the date of the transfer by that sub-section until they are altered in accordance with law.

(47) Categorizations of Libraries

The libraries eligible for grant under this Act shall be categorized as follows:-

(a) Libraries which were in existence before the commencement of this Act.

(i) Affiliated to the Kerala Granthasala Sanghom,

(ii) Established or maintained by the Local Library Authorities of the erstwhile Malabar District referred to in sub-section (2) of Section 5 of the State Re-organization Act. 1956 (Central Act 37 of 1956) and

(iii) Not affiliated to the Granthasala Sanghom or established or maintained by the Local Library Authorities of erstwhile Malabar Area, but receiving grant direct from the Government

(b) Public Libraries

(c) The State Library, and

(d) Children's Library

(48) Library Cess

(1) The State Library Council shall levy a Library Cess in the form of a surcharge on the building tax under the Kerala Panchayat's Act, 1960 (32 of 1960) or the property tax levied under the Kerala Municipalities Act, 1960 (14 of 1961) or the Kerala Municipal Corporation Act, 1961 (30 of 1961) at the rate of 5 paise for the whole rupee in the building tax or the property tax as the case may be, so levied.

(2) The cess levied under sub-section 1 shall be collected, —

(a) In an area within the jurisdiction of a Panchayat, by the Panchayat.

(b) In an area within the jurisdiction of a Municipal Council by the Municipal Council; and

(c) In an area within the jurisdiction of a Municipal Corporation by the Municipal Corporation.

as if the cess were a building tax payable under the Kerala Panchayat's Act, 1960 (32 of 1960) or a property tax payable under the Kerala Municipalities Act, 1961, (14 of 1961) or the Kerala Municipal Corporation's Act, 1961 (30 of 1961), as the case may be; and all the provisions of the said Act shall apply accordingly:

Provided that the Government may, by notification, direct that for the purposes of the collection of the Cess, the provisions of the Kerala Panchayat's Act, 1960, the Kerala Municipality Act, 1960 and the Kerala Municipal Corporations Act, 1961, as the case may be shall apply, subject to such modifications as may be specified in the notification;

(3) The cess collected under sub-section 2 shall be paid to the State Library Council by the Panchayat, Municipal Council or the Municipal Corporation as the case may be.

(49) Removal of Difficulties

(1) If any difficulty arises in giving effect, to the provisions of this Act the Government may by order, do anything not inconsistent with such provisions which appear to them to be necessary or expedient for the purpose of removing the difficulty.

Provided that no order shall be made under this section after the expiry of two years from the commencement of this Act.

(2) Every order made under the Section shall be laid, as soon as may be after it is made before the Legislative Assembly.

(50) Repeal and Saving

(1) The Madras (Tamil Nadu) Public Libraries Act, 1948 (Madras Act XXIV of 1948), as in force in the Malabar District referred to in sub-section (2) of Section 5 of the States Reorganization Act, 1956 (Central Act, 1956), and the Kerala Granthasala Sanghom (Taking over of Management) Act, 1977 (19 of 1977) are hereby repealed.

(2) Notwithstanding such repeal, the Board of Control constituted by notified order made under the Kerala Granthasala Sanghom (Taking Over of management Act, 1977 shall remain in office till the State Library Council, District Library Councils and the Taluk Library Unions are constituted by Government and those bodies assume office.

APPENDIX VIII

HARYANA PUBLIC LIBRARIES ACT, (1989)

An Act to provide for the establishment, maintenance and development of Public Libraries in the State of Haryana and for matters ancillary thereto.

Be it enacted by the Legislature of the State of Haryana in the fortieth year of the Republic of India as follows:-

(1) Short title, extent and commencement

(1) This Act may be called the Haryana Public Libraries Act, 1989.

(2) It extends to the whole of the State of Haryana

(3) It shall come into force of such date as the State Government may, by notification, in the Official Gazette appoint –

(2) Definitions

In this Act, Unless the context otherwise requires

(a) 'Authority' means the State Library Authority constituted under sub-section (1) of Section 4

(b) 'Book' includes –

(i) Every volume, part of division of a volume, be it a printed work or a manuscript or a micro-film or a video/audio cassette or a photograph.;

(ii) Every sheet of music, map, chart or plan separately printed or lithographed.

(iii) Newspaper, periodicals and other such materials;

(c) 'Book service' means reference service, lending out books to members of Public Libraries, helping groups with books, helping people to know the whereabouts of a book or books, and helping them to procure the books they need,

(d) 'Departmental Library' means a library maintained by a Department of the State Government;

(e) 'Public Library' means a library which permits members of the public to use it for reference or borrowing without charging fee or subscriptions;

(f) 'Reference service' means assistance from the library staff to the reader or user of the library to enable him to know, locate and consult books and other materials and to secure from such books and materials information relevant to his purpose;

(g) 'State' means the State of Haryana;

(h) 'Subscription Library' means a library run on the subscription of its members;

(i) 'Year' means the financial year.

(3) Establishment of Library Service

(1) The State Government shall establish, maintain and develop Library Service in the State;

(2) For carrying out the purposes of sub-section (1), the State Government may

(a) Acquire for its Public Library sufficient number of books.

(b) Offer in its Public Library an adequate book and reference service;

(c) Promote reading habit and the use of books for the people;

(d) Establish and sponsor organizations and institutions with a view to promote public interest and participation in the Public Library;

(e) Give adequate library service to all Government Departments and offices subordinate or attached to these Departments:

(f) Provide library training facilities to ensure adequately trained personnel for libraries in the State;

(g) Provide or secure suitable conditions of service for the library personnel in the State;

(h) Promote co-operation, between the Public Libraries and cultural and educational institutions

(3) The State Government shall discharge its functions and responsibilities under this section through –

(a) The State Library Authority;

(b) The State Public Library; and

(c) The Co-operating Institutions.

(4) Constitution and Establishment of Authority

(1) With effect from such date as the State Government may, by notification in this behalf, the State Government shall establish for the purpose of this Act, an Authority to be known as State Library Authority with headquarters at such places as the State Government may specify;

(2) The Authority shall consists of –

(1) The following ex-officio members—

(a) The Minister-in-charge of libraries who shall be the Chairman;

(b) The Secretary, Libraries Department;

(c) Secretary Education

(d) Secretary Finance

(e) Secretary Culture

(f) Secretary Local Bodies

(g) Secretary Social Welfare

(h) The Secretary, State Development and Panchayat Department

(i) The Director of Public Relations

(j) The Librarian of the Civil Secretariat, Haryana;

(k) The State Librarian

(l) The Vice-Chancellors of all Universities in the State;

(m) The Chairman or President, State Library Association;

(n) Director of Libraries, who shall be the Secretary

(ii) A member of the State Legislature Assembly interested in Library Development to be nominated by the State Government

(iii) Not more than four non-official members having special knowledge of libraries to be nominated by the Chairman of the Authority

(3) The Authority shall advise the State Government on all matters mentioned under section e and also in regard to promotion of library services in the State.

(4) The Authority shall meet at least once in a year.

(5) A nominated member of the Authority shall hold office during the pleasure of State Government, provided that his term of office shall not exceed four years from the date of his nomination.

(6) Whenever ay member dies, resigns, becomes incapable of acting as a member or is otherwise removed, the State Government may nominate other member for the unexpired period of such member.

(7) The Authority shall frame regulations for transacting its business and for matters in respect of which regulations are to be framed by it under this Act and may appoint committees.

(5) Standing Advisory Committee

(1) Within a month of the Constitution of the Authority an eleven member Standing Advisory Committee shall be constituted of which eight members will be nominated by the Chairman of the Authority from amongst the members of the Authority

and the Secretary, Department of Libraries , the Director, State Library Authority and the State Librarian shall be ex-officio members.

(2) The Chairman of the Authority shall nominate any members of the Standing Advisory Committee to be its Chairman and the Secretary of the Authority shall also be the Secretary of the Standing Advisory Committee.

(3) A member of the Standing Advisory Committee shall cease to hold office when he ceases to a member of the Authority.

(4) The functions of the Standing Advisory Committee shall be--

(a) To advise the State Library Directorate in all Technical matters relating to the library development and organization

(b) To make recommendations to the Authority on matters relating to the promotion and development of library service.

(6) State Library Directorate

(1) The State Government shall constitute a State Library Directorate which shall be a Department of the Government. The functions of the State Library Directorate shall be as follows:

(a) To prepare the annual as well as short or long term plans for libraries in the State in co-operation with the development and other concerned departments of the State Government and of the Central Government;

(b) To prepare and publish descriptive and statistical reports on the working of all the Public Libraries;

(c) To arrange or to secure training of various categories of library employees;

(d) To conduct inspection and render advisory service to

the District, Block and other libraries in the State;

(e) To administer the system of grant-in-aid to the subscription libraries and to undertake their inspection;

(f) To fix the boundaries of the operations of district libraries in the Districts.

(2) The Director of the Library Directorate (here in after called the Director) shall be appointed by the State Government and will have the rank of the Head of the Department.

(3) The State Library Directorate shall have staff with adequate qualifications and training

(4) The Director shall perform the following duties:

(a) He shall participate in all meetings of the Authority and the committees which may be set by the Authority;

(b) He shall be responsible for carrying our such of the recommendations of the Authority as have been approved by the State Government;

(c) He shall perform such other duties a may be prescribed in the regulations made by the Authority;

(d) Subject to any rules made by the State Government, the Director—

(i) Shall be responsible for implementing the programme of work for the year as approved by the Authority;

(ii) Shall administer the grant-in-aid to subscription libraries;

(iii) May absorb a subscription library into the Public Library of the State;

(iv) Shall decide where district and other libraries in the State are to be set up and approve the constitution and bye-laws of a Public Library

(7) **State Central Library**

The State Government shall, by an order, establish a State Central Library located in the State

(8) Book Stock of the State Central Library

(1) The Stock of books in the State Central library shall consist of books, acquired through any legislation for the time being in force providing for compulsory acquisition of books published in the State, book acquired otherwise by purchase, exchange gifts and bequests and its own publications.

(2) Materials in the State Central Library may also include films, filmstrips, tape and gramophone records, maps, charts, bulletins, photos, pictures.

(9) Mode of book acquisition

(1) The Secretary, State Legislative Assembly shall deliver to the State Librarian bound volumes of all debates and proceedings of the Legislative Assembly.

(2) The Head of a department in the State Government shall deliver to the State Central Library all books in his office no longer needed there, but which in the opinion of the State Librarian will be of use in the State Central Library.

(3) All books and other materials which have to be purchased by the State Librarians shall only be purchased on the advice of a Book Selection Committee to be constituted by the Authority.

(10) Departments of State Central Library

(1) The State Central Library shall have at least two sections viz, State Reference Library Section and the State Lending Library Section.

(2) The functions of the State Reference Library Section shall be as follows:-

(a) To maintain a representative collection of reference books and publications such as those mentioned in clause (b) of sub-section (22) of section 3,

(b) To procure and maintain in a readily available manner all books, reports, especially the reports of the Houses of Parliament and the State Legislative Assembly and Central and State Government reports together with their indexes as well as other reference materials needed for consultation.

(c) To maintain a catalogue of the important academic libraries in the State;

(d) To undertake bibliographical work, including special bibliographies for the use of scholars ad research workers and to prepare useful catalogue and bibliographies in the regional languages;

(e) To offer in co-operation with departmental and research libraries books and bibliographical service to institutions, groups and individuals and engaged in higher studies and research;

(f) To promote library service for children;

(g) To organize library conferences and book exhibitions;

(h) To provide technical assistance and information to the district and other librarians in the State;

(i) To act as the centre of the book exchange and inter-library lending within and outside of the State;

(j) To prepare and issue reports on the working of the libraries especially the public libraries in the State.

(3) The State Reference Library shall not lend books for use outside the premises of the library;

(4) The functions of the State Lending Library Section shall be as follows:-

(a) To render home-lending service

(b) To replenish from time to time the stock of District Libraries;

(c) To give book service to cultural and educational institutions and social welfare organizations;

(d) To arrange book-exhibitions and book displays on suitable occasions;

(e) To publicise its books stock

(f) To publish library report and literature;

(11) State Librarian

(1) The Officer-in-charge of the State Central Library shall be known as the State Librarian;

(2) The State Librarian shall be appointed by the State Government

(3) The State Librarian shall –

(a) Be responsible for the management of all the departments of the State Central library;

(b) Maintain the stock of books and conduct all approved activities of the State Central Libraries;

(c) Advise the Authority on all technical matters;

(d) Submit to the Director a report on the working of the library during the previous financial year, which report shall also include the detailed statements of receipts and expenditure on account of the State Central Library.

(4) The State Librarian shall be subordinate to the Director;

(5) The State Librarian shall be assisted by technical and general staff running the State Central library;

(12) The District Library

(1) There shall be a District Library in each District rendering book service to the resident of a District;

(2) In addition to the District Library under sub-section 1, there shall also be the following types of libraries namely:

(a) Municipal/city/town library;

(b) Block library

(c) Village library and

(d) Smaller book deposit centres:

(13) Functions of a District Library

The functions of the District Library shall be as follows

(a) To provide reference and bibliographical service in the District;

(b) To give special reference service to the members of the Municipal Committee/Corporation of the Town or the City in which it is situated;

(c) To give special service to the student group, study circles and other educational groups:

(d) To extend library service in the urban and rural areas by setting up branch libraries, mobile libraries and deposit centres and to extend similar service in the District through the various block libraries and other library unions;

(e) To feed block libraries with supply of suitable books;

(f) To co-operate with and help the subscription libraries in the District in accordance with the instructions of the Director;

(g) To co-operate with other institutions and groups, especially the social educational institutions and workers, in promoting library mindedness among the people;

(h) To arrange conferences, campus and seminars of librarians and other library workers in the District;

(14) District Library Committee

(1) There shall be a District Library Committee for each District Library in the State, which shall be constituted in accordance with such regulations as may be framed by the Authority;

(2) The District Library Committee shall, subject to the approval of the Authority, frame its rules of business and procedure for carrying out the functions of the District Library;

(3) The functions of the District Library Committee shall be as follows:-

(a) To supervise the work of the District Library and the various library unions;

(b) To start Branch Libraries;

(c) To take all necessary steps to develop Public Library Service in the District;

(d) To employ in accordance with the regulations framed by the Authority, staff for the District Library;

(e) To make provisions for purchase of books, films, film strips, records, furniture, equipment and book mobile for the District Library;

(f) To acquire, purchase or hire land or other properties and effects, and build, alter, repair and extend building and fit up and furnish the same with requisite furniture fittings and conveniences;

(g) To accept any endowment, bequests or gift for the purpose of promotion and development of library service as envisaged in this Act;

(h) To organize or participate in conferences and exhibitions relating to libraries and spend such sums as may be reasonable in connection with such conferences and exhibitions, and depute ay person or persons to attend any such conferences or exhibitions;

(i) To provide accommodation for lectures and other cultural and educational activities in the premises of libraries in the District Libraries;

(j) To extend library service in its area by setting up of branch library, traveling library, deposit centres and book service by mail,

(4) If any question arises whether a particular matter is or is not within the purview or power of District or any other library

committee, the decision of the Authority thereon shall be final.

(5) The District Library Committee shall meet as often as the Chairman thereof may decide to summon it, but preferably at least four times a year.

(6) The District Library Committee shall, by the name of the District for which it is constituted, be a body corporate having perpetual succession and common seal with power to acquire, hold and dispose of properties and to enter into a contract and may by the said name sue and be sued.

(15) City and Town Library Committee

(1) There shall be a City Library Committee for each City with a population of over a lakh, and a Town Library Committee for a Municipal Town with a population of not more than one lakh, constituted in accordance with such rules as may be framed by the District Library Committee concerned.

(2) The functions of a City or Town Library Committee shall, so far as maybe, the same as those of the District Library Committee within its jurisdiction.

(3) The City or Town Library Committee shall, subject to the approval of the District Library Committee concerned frame its rule of business and procedure:

(16) Block Library Committee

(1) There shall be a Block Library Committee for each Block Library and its constitution and functions shall be such as may be laid down in rules framed by the District Library Committee concerned.

(2) The Block Library Committee shall, subject to the approval of the District Library Committee concerned, frame its rules of business and procedure.

(17) Panchayat Library Committee

(1) There shall be a Panchayat Library Committee for each village library and its constitution and functions shall be such as may be laid down in rules framed by the District Library Committee concerned.

(2) The Panchayat Library Committee shall, subject to the approval of the District library Committee concerned, frame its rules of business and procedure.

(18) Employees of the Public Libraries

(1) The state government shall create cadres for public library employees similar to those of employees of Government Departments and lay down the qualifications and the other terms and conditions of service for those cadres.

(2) Within a year of its first constitution, the Authority shall frame service rules for the various categories of library employees.

(19) Public Library Fund

(1) There shall be three types of library funds in the State

(a) The State Library Fund

(b) The District Library Fund

(c) The City or Town or Block or Village Library Fund

(2) There shall be credited into the State Library Fund;

(a) The amount provided by the State Government for development, improvement and maintenance of library service in the State;

(b) The contribution received from the Central Government

(c) Any special grant that the Central or a State Government may make for any specific purposes;

(d) The amount received under the library rules of the State Central Library;

(e) Any amount received as gift, contribution or endowment for the development of public libraries in the State.

(3) There shall be credited into the District Library Fund:-

(a) The amount transferred to it from the State Library Fund, the state contribution to the District Library Fund being in no case less than the total amount of library cess collected in the District;

(b) Any special grant that the Authority may make to the District Library Committee for any specific purpose;

(c) The amount collected under the rules of the District Library;

(d) Any amount received as gift, contribution or endowment for the development of the libraries in the District;

(e) Any loan that the District Library Committee may raise.

(4) There shall be credited into a city, town, block or village library fund:-

(a) The amount raised as library cess within the limits of the City, Town, Block or Village;

(b) Any special grant that the District Library committee may make for any purpose;

(c) The amount collected under the Town or Block Library Rules;

(d) Any amount received as gift, contribution or endowment for the development of the library in the City, Town Block or Village;

(e) Any loan that a City Library Committee may raise

(20) Library Cess

Every Local Body in a District may levy in its area a Library Cess in the form of a surcharge on property tax and house tax at such rate as the Government may decide from time to time.

(21) Power of Committees to Borrow

(1) A Block, town or a Village Library Committee may borrow money on the property of its Library Fund for purchasing land, building, furniture and fixtures to be used for library purposes with the approval of the District Library Committee, who shall also approve the amount to be so borrowed which amount shall not exceed five times the amount of Library Cess accruing annually to it.

(2) A District or City Library Committee may similarly borrow money for the same purpose with the approval of the Authority who shall also approve the amount to be borrowed in any particular case within the same limit.

(22) Framing of Rules and Regulations

The Authority shall prepare model bye-laws, rules and regulations regarding the administration of library service in the state.

(23) State Library Association

The Authority shall recognize only one State Library Associations/co-operative institutions, the constitution of which shall be approved by the Authority.

(24) Power to make rules

(1) The State Government may by notification, make rules for carrying out the purposes of this Act.

(2) Every rule made under this section shall be laid as soon as may be after it is made before the house of the State Legislative Assembly while it is in session for a total period of 10 days which may be comprised in one session or in two or more successive sessions and if, before the expiry of the session in which it is so laid or the successive session aforesaid, the House agrees in making any modifications in the rules or

the House agrees that the rules shall not be made, the rules shall, thereaftrer have effect only in such modified form or be of no effect, as the case may be, so however, that any such modification or annulment shall be without prejudice to the validity of anything previously done under that rule.

APPENDIX IX

MIZORUM PUBLIC LIBRARIES ACT (1993)

(Received the assent of Governor of Mizoram on the 25th February, 1993)

An act to provide for the establishment, maintenance and development of comprehensive public libraries system in the State of Mizoram.

Be it enacted by the Legislative Assembly of the State of Mizoram in the Forty-Fourth Year of the Republic of India as follows:-

CHAPTER - 1

Preliminary

1. Short title, Extent

(1) This Act may be called the Mizoram Public Libraries Act, 1993.

(2) It shall extend to the whole of the State of Mizoram

(3) It shall come into force on such date as the Government may, by notification in the official Gazette, appoint.

(2) Definitions

In this Act, unless the context otherwise requires —]

(a) 'Council' means State Library Council

(b) 'Department' means the Department of Education and Human Resources;

(c) 'Director' means the Dissector of Public Libraries appointed as such;

(d) 'Government' means the State Government of Mizoram ;

(e) 'Notification' means a Notification published in the Mizoram Official Gazette;

(f) 'Prescribed' means prescribed by the rules made under this Act;

(g) 'Public Library' mans a library which serves the general public and includes State, District, Sub-Divisional and Village Libraries;

(h) 'Rules' means the Rules made under this Act;

(i) 'State' means the state of Mizoram;

(j) 'Year' means the Financial year.

CHAPTER II

The State Library Council

(3) Constitution of State Library Council

There shall be constituted by notification, the State Council consisting of –

(a) The following ex-officio members—

(i) The Minister of Education & Human Resources who shall be the chairman;

(ii) The Secretary of Education & Human Resources who shall be the Secretary of the council;

(iii) The Director of art & Culture;

(iv) The Director of School Education;

(v) The Director of Higher & Technical Education

(vi) The Director of Adult Education;

(vii) The Director SCERT;

(viii) The Director of Information & Public Relations;

(ix) The Station Director, AIR;

(x) The Director of Public Libraries;

(xi) The Librarian, NEHU Mizoram Campus, Aizawl; and

(xii) The State Librarian.

(b) Other members, such as –

(i) Two members of the Mizoram Legislative Assembly to be nominated by the Government;

(ii) One representative of the Mizoram Library Association;

(iii) One representative of Central YMA;

(iv) One representative of Mizo Academy of Letters and

(v) One representative of Mizoram Publication Board.

(4) Term of office of the Council

The term of office of the members of the Council shall be for a period of three years.

(5) Membership of the Council

If a member ceases to hold the position by virtue of which he was so nominated or elected, he shall automatically cease to be a member of the Council .

(6) Vacancy in the membership of the Council

A Vacancy in the office of a nominated member of the Council shall be filled by nomination and the new member shall hold office only for the remaining period of term.

(7) Meeting of the Council and the quorum

(1) The Council shall meet at least twice in a year.

(2) In the absence of the Chairman, members present at a meeting shall elect chairman for that meeting from amongst themselves.

(3) Six members shall form a quorum.

(8) Duties of the Council

(1) The Council shall advise the Government on all matters relating to libraries arising out of the provisions of this Act and also in regard to promotion and development of Library Services in the State:

(2) The Council shall take suitable steps to establish and promote a Public Library System

CHAPTER III

Department of Public Libraries

(9) Constitution of Public Libraries

(1) On the commencement of this Act, the Department of Public Libraries shall be constituted with a Director as its head;

(2) The Director shall be assisted by the Joint Director, the Deputy Director, and other necessary supporting staff.

(10) Appointment of Officers and Staff

The appointment of Officers and the supporting staff shall be made by the government in accordance with the provisions of the rules made under this Act.

(11) Conditions for absorption of existing staff

The existing Library Staff for the purpose of absorption shall have to obtain necessary qualification within a limit of time as may be prescribed.

CHAPTER IV

Categories of Public Libraries

(12) Categories of Public Libraries

The Public Libraries in the State shall be divided into four categories as follows—

(i) State Library

(ii) District Library

(iii) Sub-divisional Library; and

(iv) Village Library

(13) State Library

(1) There shall be a State library located in the Capital of the State

(2) The State Library shall consist of the following sections:-

(i) Bureau of Copy Right;

(ii) State library for the Blind;

(iii) Inter Library Loan;

(iv) State Bibliographical Bureau;

(v) Technical Services; and

(vi) Mobile Services

(14) Functions of State Library

The State Library shall function as library as well as reservoir of books.

(15) District Library

There shall be a District Library in every district headquarters of the State

(16) Sub-divisional Library

There shall be s Sub-Divisional library in each sub-divisional headquarters

(17) Village Libraries

There shall be recognized Village Libraries in such villages as may be found and considered deserving and suitable by the Government from time to time.

CHAPTER V

Financial Assistance to Recognize Village Libraries

(18) Grant-in-aid to Recognized Village Libraries

The Government may sanction Grant-in-aid to recognized

Village Libraries in accordance with the rules made under this Act.

CHAPTER VI

Miscellaneous Provisions

(19) Stat Library Association

(1) The Council may recognize any one body as the State Library Association, the constitution of which shall be approved by the Council

(2) The Director shall consult Library Association on important matters relating to the Libraries and Librarian of the State

(20) Power to make rules

(1) The Government may by notification, make rules to carry out the purpose of this Act.

(2) In particular and without prejudice to the generality of the foregoing power, such rules may provide for all or any of the following matters, namely:-

(a) The requisite qualifications for appointment as the Director, Joint Director, Deputy Director, State librarian, the District Librarian, sub-divisional Librarian and other supporting staff;

(b) The mode of payment in respect of the financial assistance and the special grant-in-aid to the recognized libraries: and

(c) Such other rules as the Government may deem necessary.

(3) Every rule made under this Act shall be laid, as soon as may be after it is made, before the Legislative Assembly of Mizoram while it is in session for a total period of seven days which may be comprised in one session or in two successive sessions and if, before the expiry of the session in which it is so laid or the session immediately following the Legislative Assembly

of Mizoram makes any modification in the rule or decides that the rule should not be made, the rule shall thereafter have effect as the case maybe , so however that any such modification or annulment shall be without prejudice to the validity of anything previously done under that rule.

Appendix X

GOA PUBLIC LIBRARIEAS ACT (1993)
(Goa Act No.14 of 1995)
(Assented to by the governor of Goa on 29.7.1995)

An Act to provide for the establishment, maintenance and development of Public Libraries in the State of Goa and for maters ancillary thereto.

Be it enacted by the Legislative Assembly of Goá in the Forty fourth year of the Republic of India as follows:

(1) Short Title, Extent and commencement

(1) This Act may be called the Goa Public Libraries Act, 1993.

(2) It extends to the whole of the State of Goa

(3) It shall come into force on such date as the State Government may, by notification, in the Official Gazette appoint.

(2) Definitions

In this Act, unless the context otherwise requires:—

(a) 'Aided Library' means a public library run by private initiative, receiving State Government assistance as per existing rules;

(b) 'Council' means the State Library Council constituted under sub-section (1) of section 4;

(c) 'Document' means embodied thought, record of work on paper or other material, fit for physical handling, transport across space, and preservation through time, and includes the following conventional and non-conventional thought embodiments; printed books, manuscripts, Braille stenographs, music in notations, ciphers (where graphice is phonetic symbols), drawing pictures, maps, microfilms, micro cards.

micro-fiche, cassettes, audio visual documents, floppy discs (non-book material)newspapers, periodicals and other serial documents.

(d) 'Book" includes—

(i) Every volume, part or division of a volume, be it a printed work or manuscript or a microfilm, or a video/audio cassette or a photograph on a compact disc;

(ii) Every sheet of music, chart or plans separately printed or lithographed.;

(iii) Newspaper, periodicals and other such materials;

(e) 'Book service' means reference service, lending out books to members of Public Libraries, helping groups with books, helping people to know the whereabouts of a book or books and helping them to procure the books they need

(f) 'Department Library' means a library maintained by a Department of Government;

(g) 'Government' weans the Government of Goa;

(h) Public Library means:—

(i) any library, established, maintained and managed by the Government and declared open to the public

(ii) Any library declared to be eligible for grant-in-aid and receiving aid from the Government or from the Library fund of the Raja Ram Mohan Roy Library Foundation

(iii) Any other library notified by the Government as a public library for the purpose of this Act.

(i) 'Reference Service' means assistance from the library staff to the reader or user of the library to enable him to know, locate and consult books and other materials and to secure from such books and materials information relevant to his purpose .

(j) 'State' means the Government of the State of Goa

(k) 'Year' means the financial year.

(3) Establishment of Library Service

(1) The Government shall establish, maintain and develop library service in the State.

(2) For carrying out the purpose of sub-section (1) the Government may,-

(a) Promote reading habit and the use of books for the benefit of the people

(b) Offer in its Public Library an adequate book, and reference service;

(c) Acquire for its Public Library sufficient number of books;

(d) Establish and sponsor organizations and institutions with a view to promote public interest and participation in the Public Library;

(e) Give adequate library service to all Government Departments and Officers subordinate or attached to these Departments;

(f) Provide library training facilities to ensure adequately trained personnel for libraries in the State;

(g) Provide or secure suitable conditions of service for the library personnel in the state;

(h) Promote co-operations between the Public Libraries and cultural and educational institutions;

(i) Promote production and publication of useful literature.

(j) Strengthen and start the libraries like prison libraries, hospital libraries for patients and home delivery libraries;

(k) Promote mobile libraries, audio libraries for blind and special libraries for hearing impaired, text book library, children library computerization, micro-filming of are documents;

(l) make special efforts to create the love for books in the masses and specially in children and the youth;

(m) promote the practice of adoption of libraries by the public undertaking sectors like Banks,

(n) make compulsory enrolment of every student in the Public Libraries on reaching standard eighth

(o) Compulsorily require to produce enrolment/membership certificate of the Public Libraries by the unemployed youth during the registration in the employment Exchange for these jobs where literacy is required

(3) The Government, shall discharge its functions and responsibilities under this section through –

(a) The State Library Council

(b) The State Library Development Cell;

(c) The Stat Public Library; and

(d) The co-operating institutions.

(4) Constitution and establishment of council

(1) With effect from such date as the Government may, by notification, specify in this behalf the Government shall establish, for the purpose of this Act, a council to be known as State Library Council, with headquarters at such place as the Government may specify;

(2) The Council shall consist of –

(1) The following ex-officio members:-

(a) The Minister in Charge of libraries who shall be the Chairman;

(b) The Secretary, Education;

(c) The Secretary, Finance;

(d) Chairman or President State Library Association;

(e) Officer who will be the member secretary of the State Library:

(f) Director, Directorate of Historical Archives and Archaeology;

(g) Librarian, Goa University;

(h) Director of School Education

(i) State Librarian

(ii) Member of the State Legislative Assembly interested in Library development to be nominated by the Government;

(iii) One member who is expert in Library Science to be nominated by the Chairman of the Council

(iv) One member of the Voluntary Organization involved in Library on Literature.

(3) The Council shall advise the Government on all matters mentioned under section 3 and also in regard to promotion and development of library service in the State.

(4) The Council shall advise the State Library Development in all technical matters relating to the Library, development organization.

(5) The Council shall meet at least twice in an year,. But not more six months shall intervene between two meetings

(6) A nominated member of the council shall hold office for the period of four years.

(7) When any member dies, resigns, becomes incapable of acting a member except member referred to in item (ii) of section (2) of section 4 or is otherwise removed, the Government may nominate any other person for the unexpired period of the term of such member.

(8) The Council shall frame regulations for transacting its business and for matters in respect of which regulations are to be framed by it under this Act & may appoint Committees.

(5) State Library Development Cell

(1) The Government shall constitute a State Library Development Cell which shall be a cell of Directorate of School Education of the Government. The functions of the State Library Development Cell shall be as follows-

(a) To prepare the annual as well as short or long term plan for libraries in the State in co-operation with the development and other concerned departments of the Government and of the Central Government;

(b) To prepare and publish descriptive and statistical reports on the working of all the Public Libraries;

(c) To arrange or to secure training of various categories of library employees;

(d) To conduct inspection of and render advisory service to the district taluka and other libraries in the State;

(e) To administer the system for grant-in-aid to the aided libraries, and undertake their inspection.

(2) The Head of the State Library Development Cell (hereinafter called the "State Library Officer") shall be a person appointed by the Government as per the recruitment rules to be notified by the government for the said post;

(3) The State library Officer shall perform the following duties-

(a) He shall participate in all meetings of the Council and the Committees which may be set up by the Council.

(b) He shall be responsible for carrying out such of the recommendations of the Council as have been approved by the government;

(c) He shall perform such other duties as may be prescribed in the regulations mad by the Council.

(d) Subject to any rules made by the government State Library Development Cell;

(i) Shall be responsible for implementing the programme of work for the year as approved by the Council.

(ii) Shall administer the grant-in-aid scheme to aided libraries.

(iii) Shall decide where district and other libraries in the State are to be set up and approve the constitution and bye-laws of a Public Library;

(iv) May absorb an aided library into the Public Library of the State.

(6) State Library

The Government shall by an order establish a State Library located in the State.

(7) Book Stock of the State Library

(1) The Stock of Books in the State Library shall consist of books obtained through any legislation for the time being in force providing for compulsory acquisition of two copies of books of every author published in the State, books acquired otherwise by purchase, exchange, gifts and bequests and its own publications.

(2) Materials in the State Library may also include films, filmstrips, slides, tape and gramophone records, maps, charts, bulletins, photos, pictures, compact disc.

(8) Certain Volumes to be delivered to State Librarians

(1) The head of department in the government shall deliver to the State Library all books in his office no longer needed there, but which in the opinion of the State Library Officer will be of use in the State Library.

(2) All books and other materials which have to be purchased by the State Library Officer shall only be purchased on the advice of a Book Selection Committee to be constituted by the Authority.

(9) Departments of State Library

(1) The State Library shall have at least two sections, viz, State Reference Library Section and the State Lending Library Section.

(2) The functions of the State Reference Library Section shall be as follows:

(a) To maintain a representative collection of reference books and publications such as those mentioned in clause (b) of sub-section (2) of section 3;

(b) To procure and maintain in a readily available manner all books, reports, especially the reports of the House of Parliament and the State Legislative Assembly and Central and State Government reports and publications together with their indices as well as other reference materials needed for consultations;

(c) To maintain a catalogue of the important academic libraries in the State;

(d) To undertake bibliographical work, including special bibliographies for the use of scholars and research workers, and to prepare useful catalogues and bibliographies in the regional languages;

(e) To offer, in co-operation with departmental and research libraries, book and bibliographical service to institutions, groups and individuals engaged in higher studies and research;

(f) To promote library service for children;

(g) To organize library conference and book exhibitions.

(h) To provide technical assistance and information to the district and other librarians in the State;

(i) To act as the centre of book exchange and inter library lending within and outside the State;

(j) To prepare and issue reports on the working of libraries, especially the public libraries in the State.

(3) The State Reference Library shall not lend books for use outside the premise of the library.

(4) The functions of the State Lending Library Section shall be as follows:

(a) To render home-lending service;

(b) To replenish from time to time the stocks of district libraries;

(c) To give book service to cultural and educational institutions and social welfare organizations;

(d) To arrange book-exhibitions and book displays on suitable occasions;

(e) To publicise its book-stocks and to arrange for extension service;

(f) To publish library reports and literature;

(10) State Library Officer

(1) "The Officer-in-charge of the State Library (here in after called the "State Librarian") shall

(a) Be responsible for the management of all the departments of the State Library;

(b) Maintain the Stock of books and conduct all approved activities of the State Library;

(c) Advise the Council on all technical matters;

(d) Submit to the Council, a report on the working of the Library during the previous financial year, which report shall also include the detailed statement of receipts and expenditure on account of the State Library.

(2) The State Library Officer shall be assisted by professional, technical and general staff running the State Library.

(3) The State Librarian shall be a person appointed by the Government as per recruitment rules to be notified by the government for the said post.

(11) The District Library

(1) There shall be a District Library in each district rendering book service to the residents of a district.

(2) In addition to the District Library under subsection 1, there shall also be the following type of libraries, namely;

(a) Municipal Library;

(b) Taluka Library;

(c) Panchayat Library;

(12) Functions of a District Library

The functions of a District Library shall be as follows:-

(a) To provide reference and bibliographical service in the district.

(b) To extend library service in the urban and rural areas by setting up taluka branch libraries, mobile libraries and deposit centres and to extend similar service in the district through the various taluka libraries and other library units;

(c) To feed taluka libraries with supply of suitable books;

(d) To co-operate with and help the aided libraries in the district in accordance with the instructions of the State Library Officer.

(e) To co-operate with other institutions and groups, especially the social educational institutions and workers, in promoting adult education and library mindedness among the people;

(f) To arrange conference, camps and seminars of librarians and other library workers in the district.

(13) District Library Committee (Repealed as per amendment)

(1) There shall be a District Library Committee for each district library in the state which shall be constituted in accordance

with such regulations as may be framed by the Council.

(2) The District Library Committee shall, subject to the approval of the Council, frame its rules of business and procedures for carrying out the functions of the District Library.

(3) The functions of a District Library Committee shall be as follows:-

(a) To supervise the work of the District Library and the various library units;

(b) To start Branch Libraries;

(c) To take all necessary steps to develop public-library service in the district;

(d) To employ in accordance with the regulations framed by the authority, staff for the District Library;

(e) To make provisions for purchase of books, films, filmstrips, records, furniture, equipment, bookmobile and other material for the District Library.

(f) To acquire, purchase or hire land or other properties and effects, and build, alter, repair and extend buildings and fit up furnish the same with requisite furniture, fittings and conveniences.

(g) To accept any endowment, bequest or gift for the purpose of promotions and development of library service as envisaged in this Act;

(h) To organize or participate in conferences and exhibitions relating to libraries and spend such sum as may be reasonable in connection with such conferences and exhibitions and depute any person or persons to attend any such conference or exhibition;

(i) To provide accommodation for lectures and other cultural and educational activities of short duration in the premises of libraries in the District Library;

(j) To arrange library timing provided that the number of

hours of daily service to the public shall not be less than the minimum laid down by the Authority;

(k) To extend library service in its area by setting up branch libraries, mobile libraries and deposit centres.

(4) If any question arises whether a particular matter is or is not within the purview of power of district or any other library committee the decision of the Authority therein shall be final.

(5) The District Library Committee shall meet as often as the Chairman thereof may decide to summon it, but preferably at least four times a year.

(14) Taluk Library Committee (Repealed in amendment)

(1) There shall be a Taluka Library Committee for each Taluka Library, and its constitution shall be such as may be laid down in rules framed by the District Library Committee concerned.

(2) The Taluka Library Committee shall, subject to the approval of the District Library Committee concerned, frame its rules of business and procedures.

(15) Village Library Committee (Repealed in amendment)

'(1) There shall be a Village Library Committee for each Village Library and its constitution shall be such as may be laid down in rules framed by the District Library Committee concerned.

(2) The Village Library Committee shall, subject to the approval of the District Library Committee concerned, frame its rules if business and procedure.

(16) Employees of the Public Library (Repealed in amendment)

(1) The Government shall create cadres for Public Library Employees similar to those of the employees of Government Departments and lay down the qualifications and the other

terms and conditions of service of those cadres,

(2) Within an year of its first constitution, the Authority shall frame rules for the various categories of library employees.

(17) Library Fund:-

(1) The Government shall constitute a fund called Library Fund.

(2) The Library Fund shall consist of –

(a) Contributions made by the Government

(b) Any grants given by the Government of India to the State Government for Development of Public Library;

(c) Any special grants given by the Government

(d) Any contribution of gifts made by the public for the development of Public Libraries.

(18) Library Cess:-

(1) The government shall levy a library cess in the form of a surcharge on the Excise Duty payable under Goa Excise Duty Act, 1964 at the rate of 0.50 (paise fifty only)per proof litre of the (I.M.F.L) Idian Made Foreign Liquor and at the rate of Rs.0.50 (paise fifty only) per bulk litre of beer.

(2) The cess levied under, sub-section

(1) Shall be collected to utilize for the purpose of implementation of this Act by the Government.

(19) Public Library Finance

(1) The Government shall frame the annual budget of Public Libraries in the State within the broad frame work of the plan and shall provide one percent of the education budget for promoting the service of public libraries in the State.

(20) Framing of Rules and Regulations

(1) The Council shall prepare model bye-laws, rules and

regulations regarding the administration of Library Service in the State

(21) State Library Association

(1) Council shall recognize only one State Library Association as co-operating institution, the constitution of which shall be approved by the Council.

(22) Powers to make rules

(1) Government may by notification make rules for carrying out the purpose of this Act.

(2) Every rule made under this section shall be laid down as soon as may be after it is made before the House of the State Legislature while it is in session for a total period of ten days which may be comprised in one session or in two or more successive sessions and if before the expiry of the session in which it is so laid or the successive sessions aforesaid, the House agrees that the rules should not be made, the rule shall thereafter have effect only in such modified form or be of no effect, as the case may be, so however, that any such modifications or amendments shall be without prejudice to the validity of anything previously done under this rule.

APPENDIX XI

GUJARAT PUBLIC LIBRARIES ACT (2001)

An Act to provide for the promotion and development of public libraries in the State of Gujarat and for that purpose to constitute State Library Development Council and for the matters connected therewith or incidental thereto.

It is hereby enacted in the Fifty-second Year of the Republic of India as follows:-

CHAPTER I : PRELIMINARY

1. Short title, extent and commencement

(1) The Act may be called the Gujarat Public Libraries Act, 2001.

(2) It extends to the whole of the State of Gujarat

(3) It shall come into force on such date as the State Government may, by notification in the Official Gazette, appoint.

2. Definitions

In this Act, unless the context otherwise requires,

(a) "Book" includes:-

(i) every volume, part or division of a volume and pamphlet in any language

(ii) manuscript in any form;

(iii) every sheet of music, map, graph, chart or plan separately printed or lithographed;

(iv) newspapers, periodicals, paintings, posters, photographs, photographic reproduction, gramophonic records, audio-video tapes, floppy, compact discs, slides, microfilms and film scripts for audio visual information and such other materials;

(v) Computer output in any form and computer programmes;

(b) "Book deposit center" means a center where books are deposited and members of the public can borrow;

(c) "Book service Centre" means a center where members of the library can borrow books through a mobile library;

(d) "Council" means the Gujarat State Library Development Council constituted under section 3;

(e) "Director" means the Director of Public Libraries;

(f) "District" means a revenue district;

(g) "Education Committee" means an Education Committee of a district panchayat constituted under clause (iii) of sub-section (I)of section 145 of the Gujarat Panchayat Act, 1993;

(h) "Extension service" means and includes the activities pertaining to preservation and promotion of cultural heritage and encouraging the intellectual, literary and scientific character of the community;

(i) "Library" means and includes collection of books, book deposit center or book service center providing library service or extension service;

(j) "Library service" means and includes providing reading facilities, lending out Books to the members of the library and assisting the readers to procure book and relevant information;

(k) "Members of the library" means registered members of the library;

(l) "Local Authority" means a municipal corporation, a municipality, a panchayat, including notified area and cantonment constituted under the relevant local authority law;

(m) "Municipal School Board" means a Municipal School Board as defined in clause (ii) of sub-section (iii) of section 2 of the Bombay Primary Education Act, 1947;

(n) "Municipality" includes the person or committee appointed under clause (c) of sub- section (1) of section 264B on the Gujarat Municipalities Act, 1963 for any notified area;

(o) "Prescribed" means prescribed by rules;

(p) "President" means the President of the Council;

(q) "Public Library means:

(i) a library within the public library system of the State

(ii) a library recognized by the Director under section 20;

(iii) any other library which the State Government may, by notification in the Official Gazette, declare to be a public library for the purposes of this Act;

(r) "Public library system" means a set up of public libraries in the State with the State Central Library at the apex and village libraries at the bottom;

(s) "Public library association" means a public library association recognized under section 21

(t) "Relevant local Authority law" means'—

(i) in relation to a municipal corporation, the Bombay Provincial Municipal Corporation Act, 1949;

(ii) in relation to a Municipality, the Gujarat Municipalities Act, 1963;

(iii) in relation to district panchayat, the Gujarat Panchayats Act, 1993;

(iv) in relation to a cantonment, the Cantonment Act, 1924;

(u) "rules" or "regulations" means the rules or regulations made under this Act;

(v) "State" means the State of Gujarat;

(w) "taluka" means the revenue taluka;

(x) "Year" means the financial year.

CHAPTER II : STATE LIBRARY DEVELOPMENT COUNCIL

3. Constitution of State Library Development Council

(1) As soon as may be after the commencement of this act, the State Government shall, by notification in the Official Gazette, constitute for the purposes of this Act, a Council to be called the Gujarat State Library Development council with effect from such date as may be specified in the notification.

(2) The Council shall consist of the following members, namely:-

(i) The Minister-in-charge of Libraries, Gujarat State, who shall be the ex-officio president of the Council;

(ii) The Secretary to the Government of Gujarat, in charge of Libraries;

(iii) Two members to be nominated by the Gujarat Legislative Assembly from amongst its members;

(iv) Two member to be nominated by the State Government from amongst the Chairpersons of all the District Education Committees;

(v) One members to be nominated by the State Government from amongst the Chairpersons of all Municipal School Boards;

(vi) One representative of public library associations to be nominated by the State Government;

(vii) Three representatives from public libraries run by voluntary agencies registered under the Societies Registration Act, 1860, or under the Bombay Public Trusts Act, 1950 or under Gujarat Co-operative Societies Act, 1961, to be elected from amongst themselves in such manner as may be presented;

(viii) Two persons from amongst renowned educationists having at least ten years experience in the filed of higher education to be nominated by the State Government;

(ix) Two persons to be nominated by the State Government, each one from amongst persons having special knowledge and experience in library services and library and information science respectively;

(x) Officer-in-charge of the State Central Library;

(xi) The Chairperson of Gujarat Sahitya Academy;

(xii) The Chairperson of Gujarati Sahitya Parishad;

(xiii) One representative to be nominated by the State Government from amongst the registered public trusts mainly carrying out the activities of the publication of books;

(xiv) One person to be co-opted by the Council;

(xv) The Director of Public Libraries who shall be the Secretary of the Council;

(3) The State Government shall appoint one of the members to be the Vice-President of the Council.

(4) The powers, duties and functions of the President of the Council shall be such as may be prescribed.

4. Head quarters of the Council

The Head quarters of the Council shall be at Gandhinagar or at such other place as the State Government may, by notification in the Official Gazette, specify.

5. Powers and functions of Council

The powers and functions of the council shall be as follows; namely:-

(i) to advise the State Government on a reference made to it or on its own motion, in regard to all matters connected with the administration of this Act and the rules;

(ii) to approve the expenditure out of the State Library Development Fund in accordance with the rules;

(iii) to direct the measures to be taken for promotion of use of books and to cultivate the reading habits among the community;

(iv) to consider the annual report on the working, administration and progress of public libraries prepared under section 24 and to make suggestions and recommendations thereon;

(v) to review from time to time, based upon the reports and inspections made under sections 22 and 23 respectively, the working and administration of all public libraries and public library associations and to suggest such ways and means to remove difficulties in becoming more useful and effective instruments of public education and library service;

(vi) to make recommendations to the State Government as regards the measures to be taken for the improvement of the administration of public libraries;

(vii) to suggest the norms and standards of performance as criteria for eligibility for the purpose of grant-in-aid or other financial assistance to public libraries and public library associations;

(viii) to suggest the formula for fixing the quantum of grant-in-aid;

(ix) to advise the State Government with regard to the objects and purposes for financial assistance other than grant-in-aid and the terms and conditions to be fulfilled for such assistance;

(x) to make suggestions and recommendations for annual development plan for libraries;

(xi) to organise and conduct library seminars, meetings and conferences;

(xii) to prepare consolidated programme in the sphere of library service in accordance with the guidelines issued by the State Government from time to time;

(xiii) to suggest for organization and promotion of efficient library service in the State

(xiv) to suggest for raising finances and for promotion of library service;

(xv) to prepare long term and short term plans for improving the library service in the State.;

(xvi) to exercise such powers, and to perform such functions, as are conferred on, or entrusted to it by or under this Act or the rules made thereunder.

6. Term of office of members

(1) Every member of the Council shall hold office during the pleasure of the State Government

(2) When a member ceases to hold the post by virtue of which he was so nominated or elected, he shall cease to be a member of the Council.

7. Filling up of vacancy

Any vacancy arises in the office of a nominated or elected member of the Council on account of death, resignation or otherwise the same shall be filled up, as soon as possible, by nomination or election, as the case may be.

8. Meetings of Council

(1) The Council shall meet on such dates, at such time and places and shall observe such rules of procedure in regard to the transaction of business at its meeting (including the quorum of such meeting) as may be provided by regulations:

Provided that the Council shall meet at least twice in a year but six months shall not intervene between two successive meetings.

(2) The President of the Council may, whenever he thinks fit call a meeting of the Council, and shall, upon written request of not less than one-third of the total numbers of members of the Council, call a special meeting of the Council on a

date not later than thirty days after the receipt of such request:

Provided that no special meeting shall be demanded within a period of two months from the date of last meeting of the Council

(3) The President or in his absence, Vice-President or in the absence of both, any member chosen by the members present from among themselves shall preside over a meeting of the Council.

9. Constitution of Committees

The Council may constitute such committees consisting of such number of members for performing such functions, as may be provided by regulations.

10. Payment of allowances to members of Council

For the performance of their duties under this Act, the members of the Council or its committee shall be paid such allowances, at such rates as may be prescribed.

CHAPTER III : DIRECTOR OF PUBLIC LIBRARIES

11. Director of Public Libraries

For the purpose of this Act, the existing Director of Public Libraries shall be the Director of Public Libraries.

12. Functions of Director

(1) Subject to superintendence, direction and control of the State Government, the Director shall be responsible for the administration of this Act,

(2) In particular and without prejudice to the generality of the provision contained in sub- section (1),.the Director shall perform the following duties and functions, namely:-

(a) supervise all matters relating to public libraries;

(b) promote the establishment and development of public libraries;

(c) be responsible for planning, maintenance, promotion and development of public libraries, organisation of public library system:

(d) recognise any institution or service conducting the training courses in library service and library and information science, and organise programmes for training of the staff of public libraries and other persons;

(e) maintain a register of recognised libraries and publish names and addresses of such libraries;

(f) administer and maintain accounts of the State Library Development Fund and ensure its proper utilisation;

(g) arrange for collecting and preserving old and rare books, manuscripts and other documents of educative value in public libraries;

(h) conduct inspection of and render advisory service to the public libraries and public library associations;

(i) to implement recommendations of the Council as have been approved by the government;

(j) administer the schemes and rules and regulations for grant-in-aid and other financial assistance to public libraries, public library associations and recognised training institutions and sanction and disburse such amount in accordance with the scheme, rules and guidelines made in this behalf from time to time.

(k) prepare and submit report as required under section 24;

(l) exercise such other powers and perform such other functions and duties, as may be conferred or imposed on him by or under this Act and the rules.

CHAPTER IV : PUBLIC LIBRARY SYSTEM

13. Public Libraries

Subject to such rules, the State Government may, by order, designate one or more library as State Central library and establish District Library for a district and Taluka Library for a taluka..

14. Establishment and management of the district and Taluka Libraries

(1) The State Government may establish and maintain a District library at the head-quarter of District and Taluka library at the head quarter or the taluka or at such other places in the taluka.

(2) Every such district Library and Taluka Library shall be managed, organized and developed by the Director.

15. Constitution of District and Taluka Library Advisory Committees

(1) The Director shall constitute for each district library a District Library Advisory Committee consisting of the following members, namely:-

(i) the Collector of the district, who shall be the ex-officio Chairman of the committee;

(ii) one representative of the public library association of the district;

(iii) one expert in library services or library ad information science;

(iv) one Principal of a college in the district;

(v) one Principal or Head-Master of a high-school or higher secondary school in the district

(vi) one Head-master of a primary school in the district

(vii) one representative of the public libraries run by voluntary agencies in the district

(viii) one lady librarian in the district;

(ix) the Assistant Director of Public Libraries in-charge of the district;

(x) The Librarian of the district library, who shall act as the secretary of the Committee;

(2) The Director shall constitute for each taluka library a Taluka Library Advisory Committee consisting of the following members, namely:-

(i) the Mamlatdar of the Taluka concerned, who shall be the ex- officio Chairman of the Committee;

(ii) one representative of the public library association of the district;

(iii) one expert in library services or library ad information science;

(iv) one Principal of a college in the taluka, if any;

(v) one Head master of high school in the taluka;

(vi) one Head master of a primary school in the taluka;

(vii) one lady librarian in the taluka, if any;

(viii) one representative of the public libraries run by voluntary agencies in the tauka;

(ix) the librarian of the taluka library, who shall act as the secretary of the committee.

16. Functions of Advisory Committees

The functions of the District Library Advisory Committees and the Taluka Library Advisory Committees shall be such as may prescribed.

CHAPTER V : FINANCE FOR PUBLIC LIBRARIES

17. Budget for public libraries

(1) The Director shall prepare, every year, the annual budget

proposal for the Directorate of Public libraries for plan and non-plan expenditure and submit it to the State Government

(2) The Director shall utilize the grant so sanctioned to defray the expenditure for the following purposes, namely:-

(a) to carry out the purposes of this Act and rules;

(b) to establish new public libraries in the State;

(c) maintenance and development of the public libraries in the State;

(d) payment of grant-in-aid and other financial assistance to the public libraries, public library associations and recognized institutions conducting training courses in library services and library and information science;

(e) such other purposes as may be prescribed.

18. State Library Development Fund

(1) There shall be a fund to be called the State library Development Fund for modernisation and development of public libraries in the State.

(2) The State Library Development Fund shall consist of –

(a) grant received from the State Government other than grant specified in sub-section (2) of section 17;

(b) any contributions or special grants from the Central Government for modernisation and development of public libraries;

(c) all money receive by way of contributions or gifts made by the public or any other agency for modernisation and development of public libraries;

(3) The money in the State Library Development Fund shall be utilised by the Director in consultation with the Council to defray the expenditure for the following purposes, namely:-

(a) modernisation and development of public libraries in the State;

(b) payment of allowances to the members of the Council under section 10;

(c) such other purposes as may be prescribed.

19. Vesting of property held for purpose of public libraries

All property movable and immovable held or acquired for the purpose of any public library established and maintained by the State shall vest in the State Government.

CHAPTER VI : RECOGNITION OF PUBLIC LIBRARIES AND PUBLIC LIBRARY ASSOCIATIONS

20. Recognition of pubic libraries

The Director may, in accordance with the rules and subject to any general or special orders of the State Government made in this behalf, recognize any library run by the voluntary agencies registered under the Societies Registration Act, 1860 or under the Bombay Public Trusts Act, 1950 or under the Gujarat Co-operative Societies Act, 1961 or any library run by local authority, open for use to the public, as a public library for the purpose of payment of grant-in-aide or other financial assistance to it.

21. Recognition of public library association

With a view to providing an incentive to library activities in the State, the Director may, in accordance with the rules, recognise any public library association in the State, registered either under the Societies Registration Act, 1860 or the Bombay Public Trusts Act, 1950 or the Gujarat Co-operative Societies Act, 1961, for the purpose of payment of grant-in-aid or other financial assistance to it.

CHAPTER VII : REPORTS AND INSPECTION

22. Reports and returns

Every person who is in charge of the management of a public library and every person who is in charge of public libraries association shall submit such reports and returns and furnish such information as the Director may, from time to time require, to the Director or any person authorized by him in this behalf.

23. Inspection of Public Libraries and Public Library Associations

The Director or an officer authorized by him in this behalf shall have powers to inspect public libraries and public libraries associations or any institution attached thereto or any institution conducting the training courses in library service and library and information science receiving financial assistance, for the purpose of satisfying himself that the provisions of this Act and the rules made thereunder are carried out.

24. Submission of Annual report

Within six months from the end of every year, the Director shall prepare an annual report. on the working and administration of and the progress made by public libraries and public libraries associations in that together with such information and particulars as may be prescribed ands submit the same to the State Government.

CHAPTER VIII : MISCELLANEOUS

25. Member of Council to be public servant

All the members of the Council while acting or purporting to act in pursuance of the provisions of this Act or any rules and regulations made thereunder, be deemed to be public servants within the meaning of section 21 of the Indian Penal Code.

26. Protection of action taken in good faith

No suit, prosecution or other legal proceeding shall be against the Council or any member and officer or servant for anything which is in good faith done or intended to be done in pursuance of the provisions of this Act or any rules and regulations made thereunder

27. Acts and proceedings of Council presumed to be valid

No act or proceeding of the Council or of any of its committees shall be invalid merely by reason of –

(a) any vacancy therein or any defect in constitution thereof, or

(b) any irregularity in its procedure not affecting the merits of the case.

28. Power to make rules

(1) The State Government may, by notification in the Official Gazette, make rules for carrying out the purposes of the Act

(2) In particular and without prejudice to the generality of the foregoing power, such rules may be made to provide for all or any of the following matters, namely:-

- (a) manner for electing representatives from public libraries under clause (vii) of sub-section (2) of section 3;
- (b) the powers, duties and function to be performed by the President under sub-section (4) of section 3;
- (c) the expenditure out of the State Library Development Fund to be approved under clause (ii) of section 5;
- (d) such other powers and functions which may be exercised and performed by the Council under clause (xvi) of section 5;
- (e) the allowances payable to members of the Council and its committee and the rates at which they shall be payable under section 10;
- (f) other powers, functions and duties to be exercised and

performed by the director under clause (1) of sub-section (2) of section 12;

(g) subject to which the State Government may designate Library as State Central Library under section 13;

(h) the functions to be performed by the District Library Advisory Committee and the Taluka Library Advisory Committee under section 16;

(i) other purposes for which the sanctioned grant may be utilized under clause (e) of sub-section (2) of section 17;

(j) other purposes for which State Library Development Fund may be utilised under clause (c) of sub-section (3) of section 18;

(k) Rules for recognizing public libraries under section 20;

(l) rules for recognizing public library associations under section 21;

(m) the information and particulars to be included in the annual report under section 24;

(n) any other matter which is to be or may be prescribed under this Act.

(3) All rules made under this section be laid for not less than thirty days before the State Legislature as soon as possible after they are made and shall be subject to rescission by the State Legislature or to such modifications as the State Legislature may make during the session in which they are so laid or the session immediately following.

(4) Any rescission or modification so made by the State Legislature shall be published in the official Gazette and shall thereupon take effect.

29. Power to make regulations

(1) The Council may make regulations not inconsistent with the provisions of this Act and the rules made thereunder

enabling it to discharge its function under this Act.

(2) In particular and without prejudice to the foregoing powers, such regulations may provide for all or any of the following matters namely:-

(a) the time, date and place at which the Council shall meet and the rules of procedure the Council shall observe in regard to transaction of its business at its meeting under sub-section (1) of section 8.

(b) other committees which council may constitute, the number of members which the committee may consist of and functions which may be performed by such committee under section 9.

APPENDIX XII

ORISSA PUBLIC LIBRARIES ACT , 2001

An act to provide for the establishment of a network of public libraries in th state of orissa and to maintain, regulate, guide, control, suervise, integrate and consolidate the libraries in the state as also to provide for a comprehensive rural and urban library service in the state and for matters connected therewith or icidental thereto.

Be it enacted by the Legislature of the State of Orissa in the Fifty-second Year of the Republic of India as follows:-

1. **Short title, extent and commencement**

(1) This Act may be called the Orissa Public Libraries Act 2001.

(2) It extends to the whole of the State of Orissa

(3) It shall come into force on such date as the State Government may, by notification, appoint

2. **Definitions**

In this Act, unless the context otherwise requires

(a) "aided library" means a library which is open to public and declared by the Director to be eligible for grant-in-aid from the Library Fund in accordance with the rules made under this Act, and includes a library which is receiving grant-in-aid from Government;

(b) "book" includes -

(i) every volume, part or division of a volume, and pamphlet, in any language

(ii) every sheet of music, map, chart or plan separately printed or lithographed; and

(iii) newspapers, periodicals, paintings, film slides paper manuscripts, palm leaf manuscripts, micro-films and discs or tapes used for audio-visual information or electronic information for the purpose of providing library services to the public;

(c) "City Library" means a public library established or declared as a City Library under sub-section (2) of section 10;

(d) "Council" means the Orissa Public Library Council constituted under section 3;

(e) "Director" means the Director of Public Libraries referred to in section 7;

(f) "Director, Culture" means Director of Culture, Government of Orissa

(g) "District Library" means a Public Library established as a District Library under sub-section (1) of section 10;

(h) "District Library Committee" means the District Library Committee constituted under section 11;

(i) "Gandhi Pathagar" means a library established by Government at Block level;

(j) "Government" means the State Government;

(k) "Library Authority" means the Orissa Public Library Authority constituted under section 4;

(l) "Library Fund" means the Orissa Public Library Fund maintained under section 12;

(m) "Library service" means the services provided to a Public Library in relation to lending of books and references, abstracts, bibliographies and indexes of books and access to information recorded by electronic media;

(n) "Prescribed" mans prescribed by rules made under this Act'

(o) "Public Library" means

(a) a library which is open to public and established or maintained by the Government;

(b) an aided library and also libraries functioning under other departments of Government open to the public and includes a Gandhi Pathagar with its branches and delivery stations, if any, and any other library which may be declared by Government, from time to time as a Public Library;

(p) "Public Library System" means an organic interlinking of all Public Libraries in the State into a network to facilitate library services in a systematic and organized manner:

(q) "Raja Ram Mohan Roy Library Foundation" means the Raja Ram Mohan Roy Library Foundation established by the Government of India for expansion of public library services in the country;

(r) "State Library" means the library established by Government at the State Capital which has been named as Hare Krishna Mahatab State Library;

(s) "Year" means the financial year.

3. Constitution of Orissa Public Library Council

(1) For the purpose of advising the Government on matters concerning the management and development of public library system and library services in the State, formulation of training policies and programmes in relation to such system and services and such other matters relating thereto as may be prescribed, the Government may, by notification, constitute a Council to be called the Orissa Public Library Council.

(2) The Council shall consist of the following members, namely:-

(a) the Minister-in-charge of the Department of Tourism and Culture (Culture), who shall be the Chairperson of the Council;

(b) Secretaries to Government in the Department of Tourism and Culture (Culture), Higher Education, School & Mass Education, Revenue, Information & Public Relations,

Panchayati Raj, Finance and Information Technology;

(c) Director, Public Libraries, who shall be the Member Secretary; and

(d) fifteen other members, to be nominated by Government as follows:-

(i) one from amongst the members of the Orissa Legislative Assembly;

(ii) one from amongst the members of Parliament representing the State of Orissa or any Constituency thereof;

(iii) one from amongst the Chairpersons of Zilla Parishads in the State;

(iv) one who, in the opinion of Government, is an expert in public library system and library services;

(v) one who is the President or Secretary of any library association in the State and has rendered valuable service for the development of library movement and education;

(vi) one from amongst the teachers of Post-graduate Teaching Department of Library and Information Science of different Universities in the State;

Provided that the members specified in sub-clauses (iii) and (vi) shall be nominated on rotation basis in the manner as may be prescribed.

(vii) three representatives of rural aided libraries from three Revenue Divisions of the State as may be nominated by concerned Revenue Divisional Commissioner;

(viii) three eminent writers, of whom two shall be women, as may be nominated by the Government;

(ix) two eminent persons from outlying Oriya speaking tracts across the State border; and

(x) one representative of the book publishers as may be nominated by the Government.

(3) The term of office of, the procedure to be followed in discharge of their functions by, and the manner of filling casual vacancies among members of the Council shall be such as may be prescribed

4. **Constitution of Public Library Authority**

(1) The Government shall, as soon as may be, after the commencement of this Act, by notification, constitute a body to be called the Orissa Public Library Authority which shall be a body corporate having perpetual succession and a common seal with power, subject to the provisions of this Act and the rules made thereunder, to acquire, hold and dispose of property and to enter into contracts and shall, by the said name, sue and be sued.

(2) The Library Authority shall consist of –

(a) the Minister-in-charge of the Department of Tourism & Culture (Culture), who shall be the Chairperson;

(b) the Secretary to Government in the Department of Tourism & Culture (Culture), who shall be the Working Chairperson; and

(c) Director, who shall be the Member-Secretary.

5. **Powers and Functions of Library Authority**

Subject to the provisions of this Act, the rules, made thereunder and the general or special direction, if any, of the Government, the Library Authority shall exercise the following powers and perform the following functions, namely:-

(a) to evolve and, subject to the approval of Government, finalize perspective plans for the development of public library system and library services in the State which shall be executed by it through the Director and to co-ordinate, and determine the standard of library services from Village level to State level;

(b) to sanction the opening of Public Libraries subject to availability of funds;

(c) to decide policy for the selection and purchase of books required by Public Libraries in the State and, for that purpose, constitute sub-committees in such manner and consisting of such persons as may be prescribed;

(d) to set up such other sub-committees as may be necessary from time to time to regulate its work;

(e) to approve and submit to Government, every year, the audited statements of accounts and utilization certificates of its funds;

(f) to accept endowments, bequests, donations, grants and transfer of any movable and immovable properties made over to the Library Authority; and

(g) to exercise such other powers and perform such other functions as may be prescribed.

6. **Powers and functions of Chairperson and Working Chairperson of Library Authority**

(1) The Chairperson shall be the head of the Library Authority and he, or his absence, the Working Chairperson shall preside over the meetings of the Library Authority

(2) The Chairperson shall supervise the implementation of policies and programmes of the Library Authority and exercise such other powers and perform such other functions as may be prescribed;

(3) The Chairperson may, in writing, delegate such of his powers and functions as he may consider necessary, to the Working Chairperson;

7. **Constitution of Directorate**

(1) The Government shall, for the purpose of carrying out the objects of this Act, constitute a separate Directorate to be called the Directorate Public Libraries, which shall be headed

by the Director of Public Libraries referred to in sub-section (2)and shall consist of such other Officers and employees as may be prescribed by way of restructuring the posts attached to the Library Section of the existing Directorate of Culture of the Government and State Library with the staff continuing against those posts in the prescribed manner.

(2) The Director, Culture shall be the Director of Public Libraries.

8. Powers and functions of Director

Subject to the control of the Government, the Director shall-

(a) be responsible to implement the plans, policies schemes and programmes of the Library Authority; and

(b) subject to the provisions of this Act, exercise such powers and perform such functions as may be prescribed

9. State Library

(1) The State Library shall be headed by the Director of Public Libraries who shall be not below the rank of a Class - I Officer;

(2) The State Library shall function as a reference library and not as a lending library in respect of the books therein, except in cases of inter-library loans.

10. District and City Libraries

(1) The Government may, by notification, establish a District Library in the headquarters of every district and, for the purpose of this section, a District Library established by Government prior to the commencement of this Act, shall be deemed to be a District Library established under this Act.

(2) Where the population of any city, town or any other urban area is two lakhs or more, the Government may, by notification, establish in that area a City Library or declare an existing library, which is established by it, to be a City Library, notwithstanding that a District Library is already existing in the concerned district:

11. Constitution of District Library Committee

(1) The Government may, by notification, constitute in the prescribed manner, a Committee in each district to be called the District Library Committee to look after the management of library services in the district.

(2) The term of office of, the procedure to be followed in discharge of its functions by, and the manner of filing casual vacancies among, members of the District Library Committee shall be such as maybe prescribed.

12. Orissa Public Library Fund

(1) The Library Authority shall have a fund called the Orissa Public Library Fund to which shall be credited –

(a) grants made by Government, Raja Ram Mohan Roy Library Foundation and other sources for the purpose of Library services in the State;

(b) contributions, donations and gifts made by any person;

(c) endowments, donations and bequests as may be made by any non- resident Indian any Corporate House; and

(d) interest on fixed deposits and receipts from any other source:

(2) All moneys credited to the Library Fund shall be deposited in such Nationalized or Scheduled Banks or invested in such manner and shall be operated in such manner, as may be prescribed.

(3) The money in the Library Fund shall be utilized for carrying out the purposes of this Act.

(4) The Director shall keep a proper account of the receipts and expenditure.

13. Accounts and Audit

(1) The Director shall keep regular accounts of receipts to and

disbursements from, the Library Fund, under the direction of the Chairperson of the Library Authority in such manner as may be prescribed.

(2) the accounts of the Library Authority and the Library Fund shall be subject to audit under the Orissa Local Fund Audit Act, 1948.

(3) The audit report shall be presented by the Director to the Chairperson and copy of the same shall be sent to the Government with a note of action taken on the report.

14. Reports and Returns

Every person who is in charge of the management of a Public Library shall submit such reports and returns and furnish such information as the Director may from time to time require, to the Director or any other officer authorized by him in this behalf.

15. Inspection of Public Libraries

The Director or any other officer authorized by him or by Government in this behalf shall have power to inspect any Public Library or any institution attached thereto, for the purpose of satisfying himself that the provisions of this Act and the rules of orders made thereunder are carried out.

16. Annual Report

The Director shall, within six months from the end of every year, prepare an annual report and the progress made by the Library Authority in providing library services in the State in that year and submit it to Government together with such information and particulars as may be prescribed which shall be laid on the Table of the Orissa Legislative Assembly.

17. Transfer of management and amalgamation of Public Libraries

On and after the commencement of this Act, the Government

may, for the purpose of proper and effective management of Public Libraries in the State, by notification,-

(a) transfer and Grandhi Pathagar to a suitable registered voluntary organization and make provision for grant-in-aid in respect thereof; and

(b) amalgamate two or more Public Libraries into a single Public Library, in accordance with the rules made under this Act.

18. Vacancies, etc, not to invalidate proceedings

No act or proceedings of the Council, Library Authority or a District Library Committee shall be invalid on the ground only of the existence of any vacancy amongst its members, or any defect in the constitution thereof..

19. Power to make rules

(1) The Government may, by notification, make rules for carrying out the provisions of this Act.

(2) In particular and without prejudice to the generality of the foregoing powers, such rules may provide for all or any of the following matters, namely:-

(a) other matters relating to public library system and library services in the State on which the Council may advise the Government under sub-section (1) of section 3;

(b) the manner of nomination on rotation basis under the proviso to clause (d) of sub-section (2) of section 3;

(c) the term of office of the Council procedure to be followed by it and the manner of filling casual vacancies therein under sub-section (3) of section 3;

(d) provisions, if any, subject to which the Library Authority shall exercise its powers and perform its functions, manner and composition of sub-committees and other powers and functions of the Library Authority under section 5;

(e) other powers and functions of the Chairperson of Library Authority under sub- section (2) of section 6;

(f) other officers and employees of the Directorate of Public Libraries, the manner of restructuring the posts and staff of the Directorate of Culture and the State Library under sub-section (1) of section 7 and the qualification and experience of other officers and employees of the Directorate;

(g) powers and functions of the Director, under clause (b) of section 8;

(h) the manner of constitution of District Library Committee, the term of office of its members, the procedure to be followed in discharge of its functions and the manner of filling causal vacancies therein under section 11;

(i) the Banks in which the moneys of the Library Fund shall be deposited, the manner in which such moneys may be invested including the manner of operation of such deposits and investments, under sub-section (2) of section 12;

(j) the manner of keeping accounts of receipts to, and disbursements from the Library Fund under sub-section (1) of section 13;

(k) the information and particulars to be-accompanied with the annual report of Library Authority under section 16;

(l) the manner of transfer of Gandhi Pathagar and amalgamation of Public Libraries under section 17;

(m) the provisions governing the grant-in-aid to aided libraries and the eligibility therefore under clause (a)of section 2 and section 17; and

(n) any other matter which is required to be, or may be, prescribed.

20. Power to remove difficulties

(1) If any difficulty arises in giving effect to the provisions of this Act, the Government may, by order published in the Gazette, make such provisions not inconsistent with the provisions of this Act, as appear to it to be necessary or expedient for removing the difficulty.

Provided that no order shall be issued under this section after the expiry of a period of two years from the date of commencement of this Act.

(2) Every order made under this section shall, as soon as may be after it is made, be laid before the Orissa Legislative Assembly.

Bibliography

1. Augustine (C.A), Library legislation: Some fundamental questions. In Kerala Library Association, National Library Week Souvenir, 1976, KLA, Trivandrum pp 99-102.
2. Barua (B.P), Library legislation and Ranganathan. In Rajagopalan, T.S (ed), Ranganathan's philosophy: assessment, impact and relevance, 1985, Vikas, New Delhi pp 659-669.
3. Bhatia (S.N), History of library legislation in India and U.K, 1963, Punjab University, Chandigrah.
4. Chatterjee (Amitave), Legal basis for public library finances: A comparative study of financial provision under the library laws and rules of five states in India. In Banerjee, S.B and Kapoor, S.K (eds), financial management of libraries and information centres, paper presented at the 12th IASLIC National Seminar, Varanasi, Dec.28-31, 1986, IASLIC, Calcutta
5. Dalal (M.J) and Limaye (C.B), A second look at library legislation, ILA Bulletin, 1981, 17 (1), pp 1-4
6. Deshpande (V.W), Library legislation in India: A critical review, ILA Bulletin, 17 (1), 1981, pp 66-71
7. Ekbate (Gopal Rao), public library system, 1987, Ekbote brothers, Hyderabad.
8. Gardner (F.M), Public library legislation: A comparative study 1971, Unesco, Paris
9. Gopalakrishnan Nair (P), Public library legislation in India: A national perspective. In Augustine C.A and Devarajan, D (Eds), Public library system in India, 1990, Ess Ess Publications, New Delhi. pp 17-29

10. Gopinath (M.A), March of library legislation in India. In Ranganathan (S.R) and Neelameghan (A), eds. Library services for all, 1966, Mysore Library Association, Bangalore

11. Gopinath (M.A), History of library legislation in India. In Ranganathan, S.R and Neelameghan A (eds). Public library systems 1972 Sarada Ranganathan Endowment in Library Science, Bangalore

12. Gopinath (M.A), Library networks and library legislation. Library science slant Doc, 18(3) 1981 pp 191-197

13. Guruswami Naidu (N), Public library finances, 1990. Ess Ess Publications, New Delhi.

14. India, Advisory Committee for Libraries, Report, 1961 Govt. of India, New Delhi

15. India, Committee on National Policy on Library and Information System. A presentation, 1986, Govt. of India, New Delhi.

16. India, Ministry of Education, Advisory Committee for Libraries. Report, 2nd ed, 1962, Manager of Publications, Delhi.

17. India, Ministry of Education, Model public libraries bill, 1963, Ministry of Education, Delhi.

18. India, Planning Commission, Working Group on Modernization of Library Services and Informatics for The Seventh Five Year Plan, 1985-90. Report, 1984, Planning Commission, New Delhi.

19. India, Planning Commission, Working Group on Libraries, Report 1965, Planning Commission, New Delhi

20. Isaac (K.A), Public library scenario in Kerala. In Isaac KA, Glimpses of Library and Information Science, 2001, Ess Ess Publications, New Delhi pp 177-192

21. Kalia (D.R), etal, Guidelines for public library system and services, Granthena, 2 (1), 1991, pp 31-84

22. Kalia (D.R) and Jain (M.K) Library legislation and development: need for a uniform pattern. Yojana, 17 (6), 1973. pp 265-268

23. Kaula (P.N), A peep into the Indian Library Law. Herald of library science, 3 (4), 1964. pp-317-321

24. Kumar (S) and Shan (Leena), (eds); Public Library Arts in India, Ess Ess Publications, Delhi

25. Mangla (P.B), Library legislation. In George K.M (ed), Indian libraries: Trends and perspectives, 1985. Orient Longman, Calcutta, pp 179-205

26. Mittal (R.L), National policy on library legislation. In Aggarwal, S.N, etal (Eds), Perspectives in Library and Information Science, 1982. Print House, Vol.2. pp 99-108.

27. Mittal (R.L), Public library law: An international survey 1971. Metropolitan Book Company, Delhi.

28. Narasimha Raju (G.V.S.L), Persistent issues of public library legislation, Granthana 3 (1), 1992 pp 29-39.

29. Nayeem (M.A), Library legislation: A proposal, ILA Bulletin, 1981, 17 (1), pp 5-10.

30. Ramiah (L.S), The state of public libraries in India: The need for alternative finance to library cess. In Raja Rammohan Roy Library Foundation, Two decades of the Foundation (1972-1992). Souvenior 1993. RRRLF, Kolkatta pp 58-66

31. Raman Nair (R), Principles for framing public library Acts. Lueknow Librarian, 24, 2; 1992. pp 118-125.

32. Raja Rammohan Roy Library Foundation, Working Group (1981). National policy on library and information system. A draft. Calcutta. 1983, RRRLF, Calcutta.

33. Ranganathan (S.R), Library development plan. Thirty year programme for India with draft library bills for the union and constituent states, 1950. Delhi University Press, Delhi.

34. Ranganathan (S.R), Library legislation and its factors. Library Herald, 64, 1959, pp 181-185.

35. Ranganathan (S.R), Library legislation and professional responsibility. Herald of Library science, 9, 1, 1970, pp 55-57.

36. Ranganathan (S.R), Modal Library Act, 1931. Madras Library Association, Madras.

37 Ranganathan (S.R), National grid of public library system based on legislation. In Kaula (P.N) (ed), National Grid of Public Library System of India based on Library Acts, 1972. The Editor, Varanasi.

38. Ranganathan (S.R) and Neelameghan (A), (Eds), Public library system in India, Srilanka, UK and USA 1972. Sarada Ranganathan Endowment for Library Science, Bangalore.

39. Rout (R.K), Library legislation in India: Problems and prospects. 1986. Reliance Publishing House, New Delhi.

40 Sadhu (S.N) and Saraf (B.N), Library legislation in India: A historical and comprehensive study 1967, Sagar Publications, New Delhi.

41. Satyanarayana (K.B). Law of Public Libraries in India, 1962. Allahabad Law Book Co., Allahabad.

42. Sharma (Pande S.K), Public Libraries in India, 1905. Ess Ess Publications, Delhi.

43. Srirsestava (S.N), Library legislation in India. International Library Review, 1972, 4, (8).

44. Thomas (V.K), Public Libraries in India – Development and Finance 1997. Vikas Publishing House, New Delhi.

45. Trehan (G.L), A second look at library legislation in India. I.L.A Bulletin, 17 (1), 1981, 11-15.

46. Ujlamkar (K.M), Salient features of Maharashtra Public Libraries Act 1967, 1986. Padmashri S.R.Ranganathan Smaraka Samithi, Puna.

47. Venkatappaiah (V), Indian library legislation 2 vol, 1990 Daya Publishing House, Delhi

48. Venkatappaiah (V), Model library Acts – a comparative study. Granthana, 4, 1-2, 1993, pp 19-28.

49. Venkatappaiah (V), Model public libraries act, 1989. Indian Library Association, Delhi

50. Venkatappaiah (V), Public library acts in the States: A study ILA Bulletin 1991, 26 (4), pp 187-197.

INDEX